D0893451

Library of the Chathams
Chatham, New Jersey

Presented by

The Friends of
The Library

This book purchased
with funds raised at
the annual Book Sale

ZOOLAND

THE CULTURAL LIVES OF LAW

Edited by Austin Sarat

IRUS BRAVERMAN

Zooland

The Institution of Captivity

STANFORD LAW BOOKS

An Imprint of Stanford University Press
Stanford, California

Stanford University Press
Stanford, California

Printed in the United States of America on acid-free, archival-quality
paper

Library of Congress Cataloging-in-Publication Data

Braverman, Irus, 1970– author.
    Zooland : the institution of captivity / Irus Braverman.
        pages cm. — (The cultural lives of law)
    Includes bibliographical references and index.
    ISBN 978-0-8047-8357-6 (cloth : alk. paper) —
ISBN 978-0-8047-8358-3 (pbk. : alk. paper)
        1. Zoos—North America—Management.   2. Zoo animals—
North America.   3. Human-animal relationships—North America.
I. Title.   II. Series: Cultural lives of law.
    QL76.5.N7B73 2012
    590.73—dc23
                                                            2012019749

Typeset by Westchester Publishing Services

To Ariel, my little Lion of God

Table of Contents

Acknowledgments

I live close to the Buffalo Zoo. Only a few hundred yards away, in fact. I can practically hear the distinct lion roars as I sit in my study and write these words. On clear days, my daughter and I see the giraffes munching hay as we sit on the curb, waiting for her school bus to arrive. Indeed, the zoo has been entangled with my family's everyday life since we moved to this house. For my little one, Tamar, not a day goes by without seeing her best friend, the lion (for some reason, "Toot"); my older, Ariel, is enamored with the gorillas and has been closely following the social dramas that span their lives, deaths, and births.

Besides the pleasure of writing about something that has come to mean so much for my girls, this research has also witnessed a good deal of turbulence. The world, as I was soon to find out, is in fact divided into two opposing camps: zoo lovers and zoo haters. "And where are you?" everyone wanted to know. After agonizing about this question for over three years, I have finally come to terms with the tensions as well as the unique perspectives gained by sitting on the fence. This is not exactly as exciting as being an animal rights activist, I admit, and for certain zoo people my position was suspect. But for the most part, zoo personnel respected me for this approach. "We can't expect her to be a grant writer for the zoo association," Dr. Donna Fernandes told her staff at the Buffalo Zoo when they had returned upset from the law school after my presentation about zoos and surveillance. Donna, too, was "quite upset" at times. I would like to take this opportunity to deeply thank her for her dedication and for her support of this project for the last three years.

I would also like to sincerely thank Kristen Lukas—Gorilla SSP coordinator and curator of conservation and science at Cleveland Metroparks Zoo—whose openness and generosity touched my heart during the most frustrating phases of this project. My gratitude also extends to all the interviewees, who have patiently described their work to me amid their immensely busy schedules. I would like to especially thank Judith Block, emeritus of the Smithsonian's National Zoo, Jim Breheny of the Bronx Zoo, zoo designer Jon Coe, William Conway of the Wildlife Conservation Society, Lee Ehmke of the Minnesota Zoo, Roby Elsner of Zoo Miami, Elaine Huddleston of the Louisville Zoo, Rob Laidlaw of Zoocheck Canada, Sarah Long of the Population Management Committee at the Saint Louis Zoo, Randi Meyerson of the Toledo Zoo, Jean Miller of the Buffalo Zoo, William Rapley of the Toronto Zoo, Rachél Watkins Rogers of Zoo Miami, and Tara Stoinski of Zoo Atlanta, as well as Dan Wharton, formerly of the Central Park Zoo, and Robert Wiese of the San Diego Zoo, for showing me into their world. Very special thanks are also due to those who have provided helpful comments on the manuscript: Donna Fernandes, for commenting on the entire manuscript; Kristen Lukas, for commenting on the introduction, Chapter 7, and the conclusion; Jon Coe, for his comments on the introduction and Chapters 1 and 3, Jean Miller, for comments on Chapter 5; Kris Vehrs of the Association of Zoos and Aquariums, architect Gwen Howard, and Chris Draper and Tracy Copolla of the Born Free Foundation for their comments on Chapter 6; and Sara Hallager for her comments on Chapter 7.

From the many colleagues who have helped me in various stages of this project, I would especially like to thank David Delaney, who provided invaluable insights on the manuscript in various stages; Guyora Binder, who has always encouraged me to find a balance between empirical research and theory; David Murakami Wood, who kindly led me through the rocky frontiers of zooveillance; Jack Schlegel, who diligently read and commented on every single draft, and always with great humor; and Errol Meidinger, whose feel for politics assisted me through the difficulties of writing an ethnography of an institution that does not readily open its doors to strangers. Many thanks also to Jody Emel, David Engel, Ariel Handel, Randy Malamud, Lynda Schneekloth, and Winnifred Sullivan for their advice on various aspects of this book in different phases. Editor Kate Wahl of Stanford University Press was an enthusiastic supporter of this project from the day it was submitted to her press. Her comprehensive comments were instrumental in making this a much more readable book than it could have ever been otherwise. I am especially indebted to the many research assistants who have helped me fine-tune this work. My research assistant Joseph

Holler deserves a very special acknowledgment here, as someone whose curiosity and engagement have made even the dreariest of moments in the editing process into a worthwhile intellectual experience.

I feel blessed to have had the support of each one of the special people I acknowledged, and so many others whom I may have inadvertently neglected. Although this book would not have existed without them, I am solely responsible for its contents.

Finally, many thanks to my family for their love and support. To my life partner, Gregor Harvey, who read through numerous drafts and listened patiently to my complaints, debates, and revelations, and to my two daughters, Tamar and Ariel, who were (almost) always excited to visit yet another zoo. I would like to dedicate this book to my precious Ariel—in Hebrew, Lion of God: may you always be open to the wonders of life, *neshama sheli*, my soul.

* * *

Portions of this book have been adapted from previously published articles and chapters with permission: "Looking at Zoos," in *Cultural Studies*; "States of Exemption: The Legal and Animal Geographies of American Zoos," in *Environment and Planning A*; "Zoo Registrars: A Bewildering Bureaucracy," in *Duke Environmental Law & Policy Forum*; "Zooveillance: Explorations in Captive Animal Management," in *Surveillance & Society*; and "Zootopia: Utopia and Dystopia in the Zoological Garden," in *Earth Perfect? Utopia, Nature, and the Garden*, edited by Annette Giesecke and Naomi Jacobs (Kentucky: Black Dog Press, 2012).

Abbreviations

APHIS	Animal and Plant Health Inspection Service
ARKS	Animal Records Keeping System
AWA	Animal Welfare Act
AZA	Association of Zoos and Aquariums
CBW	Captive-Bred Wildlife
CDC	Centers for Disease Control
CITES	Convention on International Trade in Endangered Species of Wild Fauna and Flora
EAZA	European Association of Zoos and Aquaria
ESA	Endangered Species Act
FDA	Food and Drug Administration
FWS	Fish and Wildlife Service
IATA	International Air Transport Association
ICZN	International Commission on Zoological Nomenclature
IDA	In Defense of Animals
IR	Institutional Representative
ISIS	International Species Information System
IUCN	International Union for Conservation of Nature
MedARKS	Medical Animal Records Keeping System
OSHA	Occupational Safety and Health Administration
PETA	People for the Ethical Treatment of Animals
PMC	Population Management Center
PMP	Population Management Plan
RCP	Regional Collection Plan

RFID	Radio Frequency Identification
SPARKS	Single Population Animal Records Keeping System
SSP	Species Survival Plan
TAG	Taxon Advisory Group
USDA	United States Department of Agriculture
WAZA	World Association of Zoos and Aquariums
WCC	Wildlife Contraception Center
WCMC	Wildlife Conservation and Management Committee
ZIMS	Zoological Information Management System

Introduction

Timmy the gorilla was born in Cameroon in 1959. He was captured in 1960, barely a year old, by gorilla hunter Dr. Deets Pickett.[1] The *New York Times* interviewed Pickett about his transfer of eight more baby gorillas to the United States that same year. He described the journey as a harrowing ordeal, with the infant gorillas arriving "half-dead from cold, respiratory ailments and lack of motherly love."[2] Pickett continues: "I got eight baby gorillas in Yaoundé, Cameroon. . . . The youngest were grieving for their mothers, who had been killed by the natives. At Douala on the seacoast . . . all collapsed with heatstroke and one died. At Paris, where it was cold, two more died of pneumonia. When we arrived in New York, five were unconscious, Hibou nearly dead."[3] For the next flight from New York to St. Louis, "two of the baby gorillas rode with Dr. Pickett in the cabin . . . the other two, moaning and grumbling, were carried, crated, in the cargo hold."[4] Fortunate to survive capture and transfer to the United States, Timmy was sold to the Memphis Zoo for approximately five thousand dollars.[5] Six years later, Timmy was sold and transferred from Memphis to Cleveland Metroparks Zoo.[6]

Timmy had very little social experience and was quite awkward around other gorillas, spending most of his time in a solitary enclosure. Over the years, he showed little interest in females, despite two introductions arranged by zookeepers. By 1990, the zoo decided to provide Timmy with an experienced companion, and female gorilla Kribe-Kate was transferred from the Kansas City Zoo. Kate was chosen specifically because she was "very savvy in gorilla social behavior. She knew exactly how to approach him."[7]

Soon, Timmy's love for gorilla Kate became the talk of Cleveland.[8] But despite their "robust sexual activities,"[9] the pair could not produce offspring.[10] The Association of Zoos and Aquariums (AZA) stepped in and suggested that, given Timmy's newfound sexual interest and Kate's lack of fecundity, Timmy should be transferred to the Bronx Zoo in New York City.[11] There he would have access to four females and hopefully produce the offspring that would help ensure the continued existence of his species.[12] Les Fisher, then chairman of the Gorilla Species Survival Plan® (SSP), justified the move: "We have to be careful to keep the breeding stock healthy. . . . If we're not careful, we'll end up with father gorillas breeding with daughters, and that would hurt the breed. That's why we were happy when we learned that Timmy, a handsome specimen born in the wild, could be used to breed."[13]

The decision to move Timmy sparked a strong reaction by Cleveland residents. Many picketed outside the zoo, carrying signs saying "Keep Timmy Here,"[14] and more than 1,500 people signed a petition to keep Timmy in Cleveland.[15] A letter, purportedly written by Timmy, was published in the local newspaper. In the letter, Timmy professed his love for Kate and his fear at being moved to the Bronx.[16] Animal rights groups concerned with Timmy's emotional welfare took their protests to court, suing Cleveland Metroparks Zoo and seeking a restraining order to keep Timmy in Cleveland with Kate.[17] The suit failed. The federal judge found that the concern over humane treatment in transit was adequately addressed by the zoo's compliance with the law.

One hour after the court decided in favor of the zoo, Timmy left for the Bronx, accompanied by two veterinarians, two keepers, and the zoo director.[18] This move was significantly smoother than the transfer from Cameroon. Cleveland Zoo spokeswoman Sue Allen was quoted, "He had a good trip. He ate some grapes, drank some Gatorade and was awake most of the time. When he was moved, he seemed curious about his environment, but seemed to be doing well."[19]

Upon his arrival at the Bronx Zoo, Timmy underwent a gradual protocol of quarantine and introduction to females. Dan Wharton, then Bronx Zoo curator and Gorilla SSP coordinator, explained the art of gorilla matchmaking: "We will slowly introduce him to a female by letting them see one another, though they will be separated. When he is ready to touch her, we will proceed

Figure 1. Timmy the Gorilla at age thirty-three, Bronx Zoo, 1992. His keeper says, "I particularly like this sitting pose, where Timmy occupies one of the older Bronx Zoo yards. It shows him outside, how he'd typically sit at the doorway and watch over the gorillas in his group" (Roby Elsner, Miami Zoo manager of primates, formerly supervisor of gorillas, Louisville Zoo). Photo courtesy of Tom and Jan Parkes.

to that. It will go as slow or as fast as Timmy wishes. We have no intention of rushing him along."[20]

Less than two years following his arrival at the Bronx Zoo, Timmy produced his first offspring. Over the next several years, Timmy bred prolifically.[21] His twelve surviving offspring, including a set of twins, were all born at the Bronx Zoo. They currently reside in the Bronx, Boston, Omaha, and Detroit zoos. Two of Timmy's grandchildren, M'Domo and Sia, are still in the Bronx, while a third, Zola, has been moved to Calgary.[22]

As a result of Timmy's robust reproduction, he soon "went from being a totally unrepresented founder into one that was slightly overrepresented."[23] Dan Wharton explained that "keeping him in a reproductive group, from a genetic management point of view, did not make sense."[24] Additionally, Timmy's large troop at the Bronx had begun to overwhelm him in his old age. The Gorilla SSP

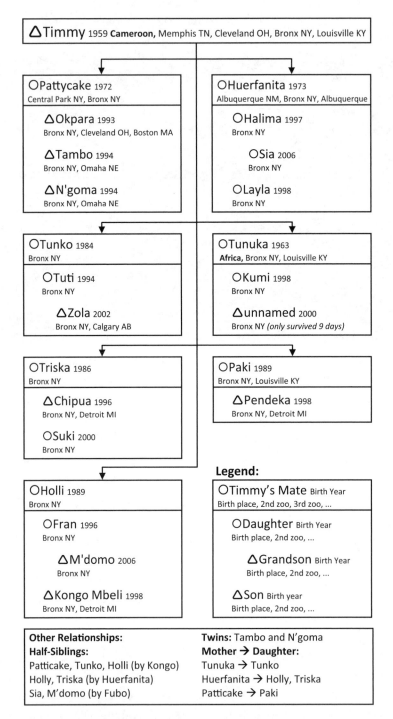

Figure 2. Timmy's family tree. Illustration by author; compiled from data in Thomas Wilms and Undine Bender, *International Studbook for the Western Lowland Gorilla.*

program thus recommended another transfer for Timmy—this time to an institution with nonreproducing females. Wharton suggested, "This time from a health point of view, it made sense to have Timmy in a group with older females."[25] Therefore, Timmy was moved to Louisville Zoo's Gorilla Forest in 2004, along with two females from his social group, Paki and Tunuka.[26] At the Gorilla Forest, Timmy led a group of three females: Paki, Mia Moja, and Kweli. Timmy was "laid-back and well-liked by females"[27] and, in his old age, helped the three females form a strong bond. The females would need this strong bond before joining Mshindi, a rambunctious male silverback that the AZA hoped to breed with Mia Moja.[28]

When he celebrated his fiftieth birthday in 2009, Timmy was the oldest male gorilla in North America.[29] As a birthday gift, the Louisville Zoo offered five-dollar discounts to families that donated old cell phones for recycling. Cell phone production requires the mining of coltan, which threatens gorilla habitat in Congo.[30] Also in observance of Timmy's birthday, Louisville's mayor officially declared January 17 as "Timmy the Gorilla Day."[31]

* * *

Timmy's story parallels the dramatic transformations undertaken by North American zoos and aquariums over the last several decades.[32] While early zoos and menageries were dedicated largely to entertaining the public, modern zoos emphasize conservation and education as their central institutional missions. Zoo animals, once displayed in concrete and metal cages, are now presented in exhibits designed to resemble their natural habitats. Zoogoers are also meant to feel immersed in the zoo's naturalistic environment, thereby forgetting that they are still in the midst of what some of the interviewees have described as "the dust and grime" of the city.[33] Moreover, the human stance of domination and control toward animals has been redefined as one of care and stewardship.

This new emphasis on conservation and care has ushered in a paradigmatic shift in management. Whereas animals used to be managed by individual zoos with no relation to each other, the project of governing zoo animals is becoming increasingly cooperative, collective, and global. Advancements in monitoring and database management systems enable new configurations of information about animals and new possibilities for collaborative networks between distant zoos. The AZA, the zoo industry's central organization, claims that "today's accredited zoos and aquariums are not the institutions of even two decades ago. Not only do they connect people with animals, they've transcended into leaders in conservation, education, and science."[34]

Timmy is a primate, and in this sense his story blurs the divide between humans and other animals.[35] At the same time, Timmy's story is also the story of all zoo animals, and, as such, it illuminates several aspects of how North American zoos govern captive animals. First, it demonstrates how zoos naturalize their spaces, classify their animals, and produce an experience of seeing for their human visitors. Second, Timmy's story highlights the everyday processes by which zoo animals are named, identified, and recorded within the zoo world and registered in global databases and networks. Third, Timmy's story exemplifies how animals are translated into law, and how law manifests itself in the material world of animal spaces and bodies. Finally, it calls attention to the uniqueness of the zoo's collective form of management and especially to the importance of captive reproduction for this management.[36] Throughout, Timmy's story illuminates the purported role of zoos as the animals' exclusive caregivers.

Naturalizing, Classifying, and Seeing Timmy

Timmy's story illuminates not only *why* zoo animals are transferred between zoos and *how* zoos reach such decisions to transfer their animals, but also the deeper assumptions that weigh into these decisions. The most crucial assumption underlying the entire institution of captivity is the classification of zoo animals as wild and therefore as representatives of their unconfined conspecifics. Take this assumption away, and you take away the raison d'être of the zoo. According to zoo personnel, there are two reasons to hold Timmy in captivity and to work so hard toward maintaining a viable captive population of his species. First, Timmy is of interest to zoo visitors precisely because of his perceived wildness, here displayed under captive and controlled conditions; and second, keeping Timmy and his wildness in captivity contributes to the conservation of gorillas and their habitats in nature.

Throughout his captive life, Timmy has lived at the heart of American cities. Yet over the years, his exhibit spaces looked more and more like oases of nature. Carefully designed to immerse zoogoers in nature, zoos increasingly provide an escape for their visitors by transplanting them from the urban space in which they live into a completely different geographical space that is natural and wild.[37] "Our guests come here to get that respite from the urban environment," says Susan Chin, vice president of planning and design and chief architect of the Bronx Zoo.[38] "You have places to go where you can see trees and squirrels and ducks and muskrats. It's an oasis. It's Eden. It's a place where you can get away from the dust, the dirt, the grime, the buildings."

Immersion is currently the *bon ton* of zoo design. Through immersing their visitors in nature, zoos attempt to instruct them to care for all of nature.[39] The Congo exhibit at the Bronx Zoo—Timmy's home from 1991 to 2004—illustrates how the zoo's education of the public toward conservation is made into a participatory experience. Pat Thomas, general curator of the Bronx Zoo, describes an additional admission fee collected from each visitor for conservation: "The visitor could essentially pick whatever project he wants and that's where his money would go."[40] In the Congo exhibit, "there is also a little drop box, [and] if people wanted to put in extra money they could. You wouldn't expect that there would be a whole lot of money in that drop box. But after visitors see our gorillas, literally inches away from them, I was impressed [by] how much money people would put in that drop box. So, at least in the short term, those animals are inspiring people to care, to throw in an extra dollar or two."[41]

The award-winning Gorilla Forest exhibit at the Louisville Zoo[42]—Timmy's home from 2004—was similarly designed to immerse zoogoers in an experience of the Congo rainforest and to connect that experience with knowledge of habitat destruction. According to the zoo's website, "This multi-faceted exhibit immerses you, the visitor, into the world of gorillas . . . [where] you are in the gorilla's realm."[43] Unique design features use illusions to bridge the audio and tactile barriers between zoogoers and zoo animals. Visitors enter a two-story atrium constructed of glass walls for unobstructed viewing of the gorillas. The gorillas can press a button to broadcast gorilla sounds into the public atrium. As a result, "the public becomes part of the troop, being surrounded by the gorillas in a space that is detailed in a similar manner as the exhibit space."[44] Exhibit designer Jon Coe explains: "The ropes inside the gorilla rooms actually extend out above the public space where they support a cargo net filled with straw, like a nest. So when the gorillas move the rope network, sometimes straw shakes down on the public. But the big idea is to try to make the gorilla areas and public areas indistinguishable from each other, all one family."[45] Both the role of zoo design to immerse the public in nature and this design's contribution to the project of governing animals are discussed in Chapter 1.

Zoos not only naturalize their spaces; they also naturalize their animals through classifying them as wild. In Timmy's case, his classification as a wild animal and the resulting perceptions about his gorilla nature were used to justify his movements through American zoos. Because he was born in the wild, his genotype was deemed desirable for breeding captive gorillas. In the wild, he would naturally lead and breed with a troop of several females. Since this was impossible in Cleveland, he was moved to the Bronx. In the words of longtime gorilla keeper Roby Elsner, "So we knew that if the animal himself had a say in the situation he would vote for being moved to a group that had multiple females because that's really the normal social group for these animals."[46] While on the one hand, Timmy the gorilla is imagined here as voting for his own move as if he were human, on the other hand he maintains his natural identity as a gorilla that is supposed to live in a multi-female group rather than alone or in a pair. The state of this animal in the wild is thereby invoked to justify the administrative decision to move its conspecific from one zoo to another. The process of naturalizing the captive animal—namely, of perceiving this animal as wild— conflates the notions of "wild" and "captive" to the point that the second becomes a subset of the first. Charismatic animals like Timmy are naturalized into becoming ambassadors for their species, encouraging zoogoers to care about what are portrayed as their counterparts in the wild. The methods and implications of classifying zoo animals as both wild and captive are explored in Chapter 2.

Zoo professionals strongly believe that by seeing zoo animals like Timmy in a naturalistic setting, zoogoers will alter not only their beliefs about the importance of nature but also their everyday consumer choices. They believe that through looking at animals, the human public will be taught to care about these animals and, by extension, about the animals' body doubles in the wild and therefore about nature at large. Chapter 3 further explores how zoos craft the experience of seeing animals so as to transform the beliefs and behaviors of zoogoers. Yet alongside its visible aspects, the zoo also contains numerous invisible spaces, such as holding areas and veterinary facilities, which constitute the zoo's backstage. Away from the public eye, these spaces are carefully designed to enable routine care for the animals, including quarantine, veterinary examination, food preparation, effective cleaning, and video monitoring.

Naming, Recording, and Registering Timmy

Alongside naturalizing, classifying, and seeing zoos and their animals, various technologies of naming and identification function in the project of governing captive animals. The name that the public affiliates with this animal is "Timmy," or his official studbook name: Tiny Tim. Lately, the practice of assigning gorillas with common human Western names, such as Timmy or Helen, the oldest male and female gorillas in captivity, has gone out of fashion. Timmy's younger cohabitants at Louisville have African-sounding names to associate them with wild habitat, even though most of them have been born and raised in American cities. In Swahili, a lingua franca in Africa, Mshindi means champion, Kweli means truth, and Mia Moja means one hundred.[47]

In addition to his common name—or, in zoo terminology, his "house" name—Timmy has been assigned several institutional number sequences. Timmy's number in both the North American Studbook for the Western Lowland Gorilla and the International Studbook for the Western Lowland Gorilla is 282. Timmy also has an institutional identity number from each zoo: his Cleveland Zoo number is 661201, his Bronx Zoo number is 911329, and his Louisville Zoo number is 102476.[48] These numbers are only used for in-house record keeping at each facility. Another form of identification, this time a global accession number that can be accessed by all accredited zoos worldwide, was also configured for Timmy as part of the newly introduced database: the Zoological Information Management System (ZIMS). Additionally, a warehouse-assigned number that can be read by a hand-held Radio Frequency Identification device (RFID) was inscribed onto a microchip and inserted under Timmy's skin. This last naming mechanism has been used to ensure that a correct link is made between Timmy's name and his body.

Finally, Timmy also has a scientific name: *Gorilla gorilla gorilla* (incidentally, *gorilla* in ancient Carthaginian means "hairy person"). This clarifies that Timmy belongs to the subspecies of Western lowland gorilla. Furthermore, it distinguishes Timmy from three other gorilla subspecies and associates him with the wild population of approximately 110,500 Western lowland gorillas, almost 80 percent of which are in the Republic of the Congo and Gabon.[49]

In addition to his name, birth, and location, an array of information about Timmy is continuously recorded and entered into institutional and central database systems. Each captive animal has its own institutional record, referred to in the zoo world as a specimen report. The individual zoos that have held Timmy manage files that contain all of Timmy's information, as routinely documented by his zookeepers. Here, for example, is a sample of Timmy's specimen report from his first day in Louisville:

> 25 May 2004 Behavior note
>
> 0715   Timmy, Tunuka, and Paki okay upon initial check.
>
> 0830   Jane fed citrus and mush to 1.2. Timmy ate in 1, Tunuka ate in 2 and Paki ate in 3. Timmy and Tunuka both left then returned to the stalls in front of their food bowls. Timmy did not eat his mush cones.
>
> 0915   Gave Tunuka her birth control pill in part of a banana and each of the 1.2 received a banana for allowing the shift doors to close to stalls 2 & 3 for cleaning. The stalls were very wet and there was normal looking poopoos in normal amounts. The uncooked asparagus, leafeater biscuits and uncooked yellow squash were left untouched. Half of the HiPro biscuits were left. Most of the cooked asparagus had been eaten as well as all of the cooked squash, kale, escarole, iceberg and rice cakes.
>
> 1330   Roby attempted to hand feed individuals cooked carrots.... Toward the end of hand feeding, Timmy stood up and stiff stanced at Roby with diverted eye glances. He soon calmed, however.[50]

Another important source of information about Timmy—and almost every other captive animal, for that matter—is his MedARKS (Medical Animal Records Keeping System) report. Timmy's medical life fills over seven hundred report pages written in overwhelming detail. Here, for example, is a small sample of Timmy's medical report, again from his first days at the Louisville Zoo:

> 10.Jun.2004
>
> Problem: quarantine;
>
> anthelmintic treatment; blood collection; blood pressure measurement (indirect); cornea neovascularization—left eye (Confirmed); corneal opacity—left eye (Confirmed); culture—rectum; caries—right lower molar (Confirmed); dental extraction—right lower premolar; dental scaling—ultrasonic; ECG; endodontic procedure—right lower canine; enlargement/hypertrophy—left ventricle
>
> (Confirmed);OPHTHALMIC EXAM; QUARANTINE EXAMINATION; phthisis bulbi—left eye (Confirmed); radiograph; hyperferremi (Confirmed); increased chemistry result—iron saturation (Confirmed); tuberculin testing—left eyelid; URINE COLLECTION; vaccination—measles; vaccination—Ipol; TRACHEAL WASH[51]

Timmy's specimen and MedARKS reports both reflect the copious amount of data that zoos produce about captive animals through their lifetime.

Alongside Timmy's individual institutional and medical reports, zoos also manage databases about the other captive members of his species. However, this type of information management is relevant only to those animals that are managed collectively by zoos, which are the minority of captive animals.[52] The North American Studbook for the Western Lowland Gorilla consists of the following specific data field entries for all managed gorillas in North America: "Stud #, Sex, Birth Date, Sire, Dam, Location, Date, Local ID, Event, Rearing, Name."[53] As the most global list of captive gorillas, the International Studbook for the Western Lowland Gorilla includes all the gorillas of the North American Studbook, as well as gorillas managed by participating zoos in Australia, Asia, Africa, Europe, the Middle East, and South and Central America. In 2010, for example, 856 living captive gorillas were recorded in the studbook, including 351 in North American zoos and 408 in European zoos.[54]

The project of naming, recording, and documenting captive animals is further explored in Chapters 4 and 5. Whereas Chapter 4 depicts the various actions that establish zoo records—naming, listing, identifying, recording, and tracking zoo animals—Chapter 5 focuses on the central bureaucrat who executes the informational and legal routines practiced by zoos: the zoo registrar.

Regulating Timmy

Timmy's story demonstrates both the complexity and the centrality of law to the everyday operations of contemporary zoos—and by law, I mean everything from federal statutes and case law through departmental regulations, city ordinances, and industry standards as well as routines and practices that are not codified into written rules and standards. Each of Timmy's transfers from zoo to zoo was prescribed by numerous legal maneuvers. First, the relevant zoos had to sign a loan agreement. The initial two-way loan between Timmy's owner, Cleveland Metroparks Zoo, and the Bronx Zoo later became a three-way loan agreement between Cleveland, Bronx, and Louisville. This agreement determined the division of responsibilities between the three zoos, as well as the ownership of any offspring: "Owner of the female will be the owner of the 3rd, 6th, 9th, and so on viable offspring; Owner of the male will be the owner of the 2nd, 5th, 8th, and so on viable offspring; [and] Receiving institution will be the owner of the 1st, 4th, 7th, and so on viable offspring."[55] Although the notion of ownership is said to be much less relevant under today's collective management system, it is still the dominant language of formal communications between zoos.

Timmy's physical transfers between zoos were also subject to heavy regulation by a range of official bodies, including the International Air Transport Association (IATA) and AZA, among many others. IATA's Live Animal Regulations specify every inch of the container used for shipping gorillas, including its sides, floor, roof, door, ventilation, and food and water containers. The front of the container, to quote one example,

> must consist of strong iron bars, spaced in such a manner that the animal cannot push its arms through the bars. The bars must have a sheet of welded mesh fixed at a distance of 7.5 cm in front of them. A wooden shutter with slots or holes for ventilation must cover the whole front in order to reduce the amount of light inside the container as well as to reduce the disturbance to the animal and to protect the handling personnel.[56]

AZA's Standardized Animal Care Guidelines for Gorillas establish an additional set of requirements for gorilla transfers. For example, the guidelines establish a requirement of pre-shipment physical exam and post-shipment quarantine of thirty to sixty days, maintaining that "before clearance, gorillas need 2 negative tuberculin tests, 3 negative fecal examinations [and] updated vaccinations."[57]

Despite the Cleveland and Bronx Zoos' careful compliance with all the above requirements, zoo critics framed Timmy's move as a form of "bad management" performed by a coldhearted and overly scientific zoo community. They appealed to the federal court system to prevent the move. "It was 6 A.M. on Halloween of 1991, and all of us were in the federal court with our attorneys," Cleveland Metroparks Zoo director Steve Taylor described in an interview.[58] Dan Wharton, the Bronx Zoo's curator at the time, explained that the U.S. District Court judge for the Northern District of Ohio saw "no point of relief under the law." This, Wharton said, was "because all laws were being followed in this move, which is of course how the zoo profession always operates. So the case was dismissed and the animal moved the next morning, and that was that."[59] This judicial decision "set a precedent that zoos can send animals from institution to institution," thereby affirming and legitimizing the collective work of North American zoos for years to come.[60]

These snapshots from Timmy's legal life are illustrative of the materiality and immediacy of law beyond the books. Indeed, as much as they are two-dimensional inscriptions, laws are also embodied in the materiality of containers, in the realities of tuberculin tests, in the possibilities of animal transfers between zoos, and—most essentially, perhaps—in the viability of Timmy's offspring. The detailed project of zoo laws is the focus of Chapter 6.

The Species Survival Plan: Collectively Reproducing Timmy

A Species Survival Plan, or SSP, dictated Timmy's various moves and reproduction throughout his life. The SSP and its recommendations are at the heart of a sophisticated AZA administration that was created in the early 1980s to better manage selected zoo animal populations. The Gorilla SSP was one of the first of what are now over five hundred SSPs, each managing the breeding and transfers of a species "to maintain a healthy and self-sustaining population that is both genetically diverse and demographically stable."[61] Every SSP maintains a studbook and a breeding and transfer plan—both under the guidance of one of forty-six Taxon Advisory Groups (TAGs). The Ape TAG, for example, oversees the Gorilla SSP along with SSPs for bonobos, chimpanzees, gibbons, and orangutans. AZA's Wildlife Conservation and Management Committee and its Population Management Center oversee the operations of the various animal programs, effectively administering what zoo professionals often refer to as the science of small population management.

Gorillas were a feature of public display in North American zoos as early as 1897, but did not successfully breed in captivity until 1956. With the first captive-born baby gorilla at the Columbus (Ohio) Zoo, the North American regional population of gorillas took its first step toward the sustainable population that it is today.[62] In 2011, the managed gorilla population numbered 342 individuals (165 males, 177 females), distributed among fifty-two AZA zoos.[63] Although these zoos are dispersed throughout the country, they have been collaborating for several decades to produce a detailed life plan for each and every captive gorilla in North America. In 2011, the AZA classified the Gorilla SSP as a "green" program. This means that the population is sustainable demographically for one hundred years or more with a high amount of gene diversity, defined as the measure of genetic variation retained in a specific captive animal population relative to the wild-born population that started the studbook.[64] Green, yellow, and red programs are the codes through which AZA-accredited zoos today evaluate and prioritize their animal species. Under this system, genetics, demography, and space translate into careful recommendations about the animal's life and death.

Dan Wharton clarifies that although the SSP formulates plans for every captive gorilla, not all gorillas receive recommendations to move or breed. In fact, such recommendations refer only to a small subset of the total captive gorilla population "where an improvement can be made." In Wharton's words, "Ideally, you're always looking to make improvements that you know have some element of a positive outcome on all fronts. That is, it's good for the animal, it's good for the institutions involved, it's good for the program, [and] it's good for the species. You know, on all levels."[65] As Timmy's story suggests, deciding on improvements for a particular animal species requires juggling multiple and often conflicting interests: those of the individual animal and its species both in zoos and in the wild, those of individual institutions, and, finally, those of AZA's animal programs. Wharton offers a historical perspective on the changes that have occurred in gorilla management:

> Keep in mind [that] until the 1960s, very few gorillas had come into captivity, and in the earliest days, none of them had lived a long time. So . . . everybody was working in a major vacuum at that point. . . . But as we get into the 1990s and the 2000s, a lot of the animals from the '60s were now old animals, and so we had more of a representational age distribution in the population. So there were a lot of things about managing gorillas in zoos that were becoming more and more evident now that the population in zoos had gradually become larger because of the reproduction that had happened.[66]

Wharton also points out that the changes he describes are the result of the gradual transformation of zoos into conservation institutions. This transformation, he explains, was a reaction to both public opinion and to the dramatic legal developments that occurred at the time, as well as a result of differences in the educational background of zoo professionals themselves.[67]

Indeed, until the 1960s, zoos had very little experience either with older gorillas (gorillas usually did not survive to old age in captivity, and typically lived only until their mid-thirties in the wild) or with gorilla reproduction (when needed, zoos would take gorillas from the wild). Starting in the 1970s, several key legal restrictions on animal purchases came into effect. Most prominently, the protection of gorillas under the Endangered Species Act of 1973 prohibited zoos from obtaining "new blood" from the wild to invigorate their populations. To maximize genetic diversity, then, they needed to figure out a way to make the most of the "living founders" that were already in captivity. Since that time, zoos have been reliant on captive breeding as the primary source of recruitment to their collectively managed populations.[68]

The controversial recommendation to transfer Timmy from Cleveland to the Bronx was thus informed by a relatively experienced SSP team with specialized knowledge about the captive management of gorillas. In light of this experience, the recommendation was "pretty straightforward," at least to the zoo professionals involved. Wharton explains that "the Timmy case came out of our interest at that point in the history of the program," which was "to be sure not to lose the opportunity to get genetic representation from all the animals that were in the populations that were living founders."[69] A "living founder" is an animal brought from the wild into a zoo and that thereby increases genetic diversity in the zoo's captive population. Timmy was one of 102 breeding gorilla founders in North America and, as such, the SSP deemed his genes more valuable than those of captive-born gorillas. Even so, after Timmy had sired thirteen offspring, the SSP decided that there were more than enough living representations of his genes and recommended to cease his reproductive endeavors by shifting him to a nonbreeding group in a different zoo.[70]

Every year, the Gorilla SSP generates new breeding and transfer recommendations with a two-year projection goal. According to the 2011 North American Breeding and Transfer Plan for Gorillas, "The SSP is recommending 48 breeding pairs in this management plan with the goal of maintaining 360 gorillas in the population. The SSP has planned 27 transfer recommendations: 8 males and 19 females will move between institutions to permit breeding, fulfill institutional requests, build bachelor groups, approximate composition of species-typical mixed-sex groups, and/or socialize individuals."[71] The system that zoos have developed over the years to collectively manage selected zoo animals is the apex of zoo management, and the focus of Chapter 7.

Caring About Timmy: Zoos and Conservation

The incredible amount of work that zoos undertake to govern captive animals brings up the unavoidable question: Why? The interviewees' almost unanimous response has been, in one word, *care*.[72] Notions of care, in the way that zoo personnel interpret this term, also underlie Timmy's story and the project of governing captive animals in North American zoos at large. Steve Wing, curator at Louisville Zoo, observed that Timmy had seen great improvements in gorilla care in his lifetime. "Society has changed, and zoos changed right along with it. Gorillas used to be kept in exhibits with concrete. Now we have . . . exhibits full of mulch for them to live on, natural wood and ropes."[73] From isolation in individual cells, gorillas are now kept in "species-typical harem groupings and/or all-male groups."[74] Monumental change can also be seen between the dangerous manner in which Timmy was transferred to the United States in 1960 and the elaborate care given in his transfers to the Bronx and Louisville zoos.

Caring for a gorilla, especially one of Timmy's old age, entails a range of everyday practices. According to Wharton, the increasing number of gorillas reaching old age in captivity is ample evidence of the many changes that zoo care has undergone in the last few decades. Zoos now collaborate to share best practices in care, including routine physicals, flu vaccines, weight, urine, and other biological sample submissions. Geriatric gorillas receive specialized training, enrichment, and even a modified diet that includes fruit smoothies and, at the Louisville Zoo, a special mush recipe made from Mazuri Primate Browse biscuits, peeled and mashed bananas, Gerber baby cereal, and hot water.[75]

But care for Timmy means more than care for him as an individual animal. It also implies care for the sustainability of his species in zoos, what is often referred to as *ex situ* conservation. *Ex situ* conservation manifests in laws, regulations, and standards that attend to the welfare and well-being of wild animals under a range of administrative processes orchestrated by the AZA. For instance, the AZA offers animal care manuals for ten species—and a dozen additional manuals are currently in progress.[76] These manuals assemble "basic requirements, best practices, and animal care recommendations to maximize capacity for excellence in animal care and welfare."[77] The draft of the gorilla care manual, to take one example, includes 102 pages of comprehensive instructions for gorilla keeping, including the required temperature, humidity, and illumination of gorilla spaces; the behavioral aspects of typical repertoire, social groups, and training of gorilla groups; and prenatal and neonatal care.[78]

Finally, zoos maintain that through care for Timmy and his species in captivity, they also care for gorillas and their habitats in the wild, what is often referred to as *in situ* conservation. *In situ* conservation programs are required of any institution seeking accreditation by the AZA and are becoming standard practice for North American zoos.[79] Accordingly, the AZA boasts of generating $130 million in support of conservation projects every year.[80] Zoogoers are also encouraged to participate in conservation. For example, visitors of the Gorilla Forest in Louisville "may donate money to Kentucky's Blanton Forest, the Dian Fossey Gorilla Fund International, or the Bushmeat Crisis Task Force. Contributions exceeded $5,500 within the first year. Donations have helped fund tracker salaries, training, and equipment for the Tayna Reserve, a community based reserve in the Democratic Republic of the Congo."[81]

Conservation and care are deeply intertwined in the agenda of contemporary zoos. Indeed, to promote care under the current constraints, zoos must become conservation centers. But at the same time, to become conservation centers, zoos must foster care. In the language of two prominent zoo professionals, "We believe that it is essential for us to foster caring concerns and caring behaviors for animals and nature if we are to stay in business, and if we are to carry out the world conservation strategy of *Caring for the Earth*."[82] Increasingly, zoos have come to realize that their own survival depends on their ability to forge a stronger link between care and conservation. In the words of the two zoo professionals:

> The dilemma for us is obvious; the exotic, the distant, the distinctively different plant and animal species draw people to our institutions, but caring behaviour is most readily expressed for those creatures close at hand and familiar, that might be considered part of the family and certainly part of the neighbourhood. If our institutions are to achieve maximal impact in the conservation of biological diversity globally, we have to help extend the close caring relationships of people and understand the challenges inherent in moving people across what are emotional as well as intellectual bridges to larger and more distant entities.[83]

Evidently, conservation is a murky and contentious term, even among zoo professionals. Does conservation only refer to *in situ* animal populations, or does it also refer to the state of animals in zoos? The AZA repeatedly emphasizes that its mission is not limited to the conservation of *ex situ* populations but that it aims to conserve *in situ* populations as well. Indeed, the title of AZA's central initiative for breeding zoo animals—Species Survival Plan— already implies a connection between the project of breeding zoo animals and that of saving wildlife. Along these lines, the mission of SSPs is to "oversee the population management of select species within AZA member institutions . . . and to enhance conservation of [these] species in the wild."[84] With this dual conservation goal in mind, accredited North American zoos see themselves as both virtual and actual mini-ecosystems within which selected animals are collectively managed and cared for.

However, many zoo professionals espouse a narrower definition of conservation. Gorilla SSP coordinator Kristen Lukas is not alone in her belief that "conservation is the protection of wild animals or habitat in the wild, period."[85] For

Lukas, managing captive animal populations falls under "a population sustainability issue," which is not and cannot be considered conservation. The conflicts in the zoo world regarding the use of the term conservation—whether it refers to *in situ*, *ex situ*, or both—illuminate the changes that zoos are currently undergoing and the challenges they face today. Conservation, in this respect, refers not only to *in situ* or *ex situ* animal populations, but also to the everyday dilemmas that contemporary zoos face and to their conservation as viable institutions.

The conservation narrative of zoos is also contested by organizations that question the very authority of zoos as exclusive caregivers for captive animals and that criticize zoos' contribution to the conservation of wild animals. Certain animal protection organizations and individuals have even argued that there is no place for zoos in modern society, that zoos do nothing to address the primary causes of global biodiversity loss, and that most captive-bred animals are not endangered and could not survive in the wild.[86] Who cares more for the zoo animal: pro-zoo or anti-zoo people? Zookeepers or AZA's animal program coordinators? And how does the zoo care for its captive animals? For animals in the wild?

This battle of care has played out quite clearly in Timmy's story. To prove their superior care, zoo personnel and animal protectionists both claimed to be the authentic and exclusive spokespersons for Timmy. On the one hand, animal protectionists publicized a letter ostensibly written by Timmy, claiming to know his feelings for Kate; they also hired a lawyer to represent Timmy's interests. In an interview at Cleveland Metroparks Zoo, this lawyer vowed to see that Timmy received "what is best for him." "Just look at Timmy," the lawyer said. "If he is so depressed now, what will happen to him when he is shipped to the Bronx Zoo for the rest of his life?"[87] On the other hand, zoo professionals also claimed to know how Timmy felt about this move. Wharton suggested in this context that "an animal doesn't know the difference between Cleveland and the Bronx. The animal knows that he went in a truck and the truck vibrated and there were keepers sitting next to him while he was being transported, giving him treats.... The concept of being transported approximately 750 miles is not going to be a burden to the animal from an emotional point of view."[88] Zoo people and animal protectionists alike thus portrayed Timmy as lacking agency, which in turn enabled them to step in as the "expert authorities"[89] over Timmy's emotional and physical state, in post-Foucauldian terms, or as his exclusive "spokespersons," in the language of science and technology studies.[90]

Conceptualizing Zoos

This book neither supports nor condemns zoos. Rather, it provides a detailed account of how zoos work. A multitude of interrelated governance technologies operate in the process of institutionalizing captivity:[91] naturalizing, classifying, seeing, naming, registering, regulating, and—the most intense expression of zoo governance—collectively reproducing and contracepting zoo animals. Together, these seven technologies of governance institute a power of care for captive zoo animals. Although not necessarily exhaustive or mutually exclusive, these technologies are presented here in a purposeful order.

This book's explorations of animal governance as practiced by contemporary zoos draw on French historian and philosopher Michel Foucault's studies of the panopticon and of pastoral power.[92] The rich literature that has developed around these concepts focuses its critique on the project of governing human populations. I posit that these conceptualizations of governance as a topic for human subjects do not suffice to reflect the inherently fused nature of governing humans and nonhumans. This book thus extends the scope of Foucault's humanistic orientation to nonhumans, compares and contrasts human and nonhuman modalities, and attempts to expose their surprising interconnections. Considering that categories of human and nonhuman are fluid across cultures and through history, an expansion of existing notions of governance to include the governance of nonhuman populations contributes to an understanding of what it means to be human.

In *Discipline and Punish*, Michel Foucault compares modern society with Jeremy Bentham's panopticon design for prisons.[93] This design comprises a stadium-like circular structure with an inspection house at its center, from which inspectors are able to watch the inmates, who are stationed around the perimeter. The cells and tower are designed so that the guard can see the prisoners but the prisoners cannot see the guard, giving each individual prisoner the feeling of always being watched. The concept of this design is to allow a guard to observe all the inmates of a prison without the inmates being able to know when they are being watched.

In society, the panopticon functions through systems of inspection: the restaurant chef never knows when health inspectors will come, and the driver never knows when traffic police have set a checkpoint; so the chef keeps the kitchen clean and the driver keeps to the speed limit. Advancements in architectural design also enable enhanced visibility. It is through this visibility, Foucault writes, that modern society exercises its controlling systems of power and knowledge. "Inspection functions ceaselessly. The gaze is alert everywhere."[94]

Foucault's focus is on how the panoptic gaze disciplines its human subjects.[95] This book, by contrast, demonstrates the relevance and importance of applying the panoptic scheme to nonhuman animal subjects. Although the subject of the gaze at the zoo is the nonhuman rather than the human animal, that subject may still be disciplined: its body and actions can be trained to fit ideas about correct reproduction and proper behavior, for example training gorillas to allow blood collection, receive an ultrasound, or hold an infant properly.[96]

No less importantly, this book illustrates the effects of the gaze on the humans who are doing the gazing. Through the zoo's design of the spectacular event,[97] it sets to discipline its human public to care about the individual zoo animal and, by extension, also about the animal's body doubles in the wild and even about nature at large. This interpretation of the panopticon resonates with Jeremy Bentham's original articulation of the term,[98] as illustrated by Jacques-Alain Miller: "The house of calculations, the whole of the vast, efficient system, was designed to be a school for mankind. The public was welcome to view the spectacle."[99] More broadly even, aside from their use in the project of governing zoo animals, the naturalization, classification, naming, identification, recording, registration, legalization, and reproduction of zoo animals are also various technologies for disciplining *humans* into proper human-nature relations.

Although the terms panopticon and surveillance have negative connotations and evoke an image of authoritarian control, I should clarify at the outset that my application of these terms is fundamentally different. In fact, this book's second conceptual focus on pastoral power broadens the scope of the panoptic to include the zoo's governance of animal populations in the name of conservation, stewardship, and care. Taking advantage of this framing of captive animal management as a form of care, and of care as an exercise of power, this book sheds new light on an understudied property of panoptic surveillance: surveillance as an instance of the power of care.

Care and power may seem mutually exclusive.[100] However, this book attempts to rethink both in such a way that reveals their interdependency. From the perspective of zoos, the extensive power to govern zoo animals is driven by a desire to care for and save animals, both in zoos and in the wild. AZA senior vice president Paul Boyle highlights this point by stating: "Zoo people care about animals; they care about the places where these animals come from."[101]

The intertwined nature of care and power is emphasized in Foucault's notion of pastoral power. It is precisely this intertwined nature that has drawn me to Foucault's analysis in the first place, rather than utilizing the myriad explorations of care in other disciplines, especially feminist studies, which are beyond the scope of this book.[102] Pastoral power—Foucault's least-quoted technology of power—was developed in his recently translated lectures *Security, Territory, Population*.[103] There, he traces the genealogy of pastoral power as beginning with Hebraic or Eastern traditions, then adopted by the Church, and finally applied in forms of Western state-based governmentality of the early modern period.[104] Although most of Foucault's analysis of pastoral power is quite specific to the institution of the European Church, he expands the concept to include numerous secular examples, including the captain's power of care over the ship and crew, the shepherd's power of care over the flock of sheep, and even the baker's power of care for customers.

Whereas zoos have existed for centuries in almost all societies, their modern Western manifestations as institutions for conservation—namely, as institutions that practice control through care—are uniquely grounded in the Western pastoral tradition that Foucault explores. This book selectively draws on three defining characteristics of Foucault's pastoral power to illuminate the working of contemporary institutions of captivity. First, Foucault asserts that pastoral power is fundamentally a beneficent power: a power of care. The pastor, or shepherd, "looks after the flock, it looks after the individuals of the flock, it sees to it that the sheep do not suffer."[105] Moreover, the shepherd must assure food, must cure those ill or injured, and must arrange for his sheep's mating in order to produce the best lambs.[106] This duty of care for animals, both *in* and *ex situ*, is also at the heart of contemporary North American zoo operations. The zoo industry's animal care manuals describe such functions in great detail. More broadly, a sophisticated administration orchestrated by the AZA is dedicated to calculating optimal breeding options so as to ensure both the survival of zoo and wild animals as well as the survival of the zoo institution itself.

The shepherd's power manifests itself, therefore, in routine duties and tasks and in its "zeal, devotion, and endless application."[107] The shepherd "is not someone whose strength strikes men's eyes," but rather "someone who keeps watch."[108] In this context, zoos care about their animals by using sight and observation as key features in the process of knowing the zoo animal and extracting information about its genetic, demographic, and behavioral nature. In addition to how zoo personnel see their animals, zoos also prescribe a very particular way of seeing animals to their public. Enabling the human public to see zoo animals in certain situations but not in others institutes the proper public stance toward animal-human relations. From the perspective of zoos, their duty is not only to care for their animals but also to educate humans in how to care for wildlife and nature. In fulfilling this mission, zoo officials believe, they may help to save both humans and nature.[109]

Second, pastoral power is exercised over a flock and thus over a multiplicity of movement.[110] Not only are zoo animals dislocated from their territorial habitats, but even within zooland, they are constantly on the move between institutions. The AZA's governance of these animals is thus aterritorial. Indeed, much like a gigantic Noah's Ark, animals are constantly in motion—here, transferred from zoo to zoo—to conserve their population according to reproductive needs. While zoos claim to advance conservation in the wild through the mobilization of zoo animals, these animals are at the same time confined within the borders of zooland, rendering the project of governing zoo animals also highly territorial in complex ways.

Third and finally, pastoral power is an individualizing power. "The shepherd counts the sheep; he counts them in the evening to see that they are all there, and he looks after each of them individually. He does everything for the totality of his flock, but he does everything also for each sheep of the flock."[111] At the zoo, the project of caring is both global and quite particular. As zoo biologist Sara Hallager clarifies, "Caring for a flamingo is very different from caring for a parrot."[112] Here we arrive at the essential paradox of pastoral power, which is highly relevant to zoos as institutions of captivity. This pastoral paradox manifests in the various everyday conflicts between the zoo's concerns for the individual captive animal vis-à-vis its concerns for the collective animal population. Although this paradox exists in the background of all zoo operations, it seems that zoos more readily sacrifice the individual animal for the benefit of the flock, rather than the other way around. Animal activists, however, offer a different balancing scheme, based on the assumption that the individual animal should not be sacrificed in the name of its species. Foucault frames this contention between various groups—each claiming to be the exclusive caregiver for the animal and its only shepherd—the "great battle of pastorship."[113]

In the case of Timmy the gorilla, care for the individual might have pre-scribed that he stay with barren Kate at Cleveland Metroparks Zoo, which is precisely what animal activists demanded.[114] But concern for the collective zoo gorilla population dictated and justified the zoo's decision to move Timmy to the Bronx Zoo, with its fertile female gorillas.[115] Such empirical manifestations of the essential paradox of pastoral power—translated here into a war between pro- and anti-zoo people—shed new light on the charged relationship between the individual and the flock. This war can be boiled down to the questions: Who cares more, and more properly, about animals? Who is the better pastor?

How I Wrote this Book

My initial interest in zoos was sparked by my daughter Ariel. She was only two years old when she first dragged me to visit the zoo around the corner from our house. Waiting in the long line at the zoo's entrance, I found myself wondering: What is all this about? I decided that I would take my next seminar to explore this site in more depth. Fortunately, Buffalo Zoo director Donna Fernandes was happy to show my students around. Even more fortunately, Fernandes expanded the tour to show us where zoo animals spend their time when they are not on exhibit. She also mentioned in passing that many animals are transferred between zoos as part of their collective management. After the tour I asked Fernandes if she would be willing to tell me more about this collective endeavor. I have been trying to un-derstand the intricacies of the zoo's project of governing captive animals ever since.

At the end of our first interview, Fernandes referred me to some of her staff and to other zoo directors. From that point on, interviewees were selected based on a snowball method.[116] Between May 2009 and March 2012, I conducted over seventy semi-structured, in-depth interviews with various zoo administrators, mainly directors, curators, and registrars, as well as with several animal protec-tion activists. Interviews evolved into ongoing relationships, and these contin-ued interactions afforded me the opportunity to pursue new questions and sources throughout the writing process. Much of the discourse that developed with the different professionals is recorded in the footnotes, which serve as a discussion board between conflicting perspectives. In addition to the inter-views, I attended AZA member meetings and visited several different zoos, re-turning to the Buffalo Zoo dozens of times. Finally, I extended my observations by analyzing various legal documents: codes, regulations, treaties, congressional hearings, court cases, and AZA's accreditation and animal program, plans, and manuals.[117]

My extensive use of interviews and my focus on the perspective of zoo professionals, who make the everyday decisions about what zoos look like and what zoogoers see, distinguish the analysis presented here from most scholarly examinations of zoos.[118] Keeping a grounded perspective through researching such a highly politicized subject proved to be a challenge. As one of my interviewees explained, "There are many people out there that would do anything to discredit zoos." Although she herself is critical of certain aspects of zoo operations, she clarified, she would not want her criticisms to be manipulated into an overall attack on zoos as such. At times, the interviewees' suspicion was implicit. I learned, for example, that many of my prospective interviewees made sure to check in with people whose names I had casually dropped to see that I could indeed be trusted. Other interviewees asked me directly whether I was an animal rights activist. Criticism toward zoos was legitimate, apparently, so long as it did not come from the animal rights front.

Although an analysis of the animosity between pro-zoo and anti-zoo people could fill up an entire book, this is not my purpose here. In fact, having just finished a book on the political struggles over the natural landscape in Israel/ Palestine,[119] I had had my fill of war stories and adamantly refused to engage in what, in certain respects, seemed to be more of the same. Although this book begins with an animal—Timmy the gorilla—it is not one that focuses on animals or animal rights; it is also not an AZA manifesto. This book focuses on the human practices of managing animals through care. I deliberately refrain from taking a position for or against the legitimacy of zoos as institutions of captivity. What I am interested in, rather, is exploring this highly complex institution— the institution of captivity—that sheds new light on so many of our assumptions as humans.

CHAPTER ONE

Naturalizing Zoo Animals

> We urgently need urban-based institutions that will carry not just the
> images but also fervent messages about the unnecessary and massive loss
> of wildlife habitats around the world, which is unsustainable and is an
> evil thing.
>
> David Hancocks, *A Different Nature* [1]

One would expect that an ancient institution such as the zoo would have long
exhausted popular appeal, particularly in comparison with high-tech attractions
like amusement parks. But the zoo continues to attract the masses. As of September 2011, there were 214 accredited zoos and aquariums and over 800 nonaccredited zoos in the United States[2]—more than twice the number of zoos than in any
other country in the world.[3] Every year, 175 million people visit AZA's accredited
zoos to see 751,931 individual animals.[4] Alongside churches, museums, theaters,
shopping malls, and theme parks, zoos occupy a central place in the culture of
North America.

What is it that makes zoos so attractive in today's society of spectacles? Although one could come up with many sophisticated answers, mine can be summarized in one word: nature. In this chapter, I explore the history of the zoo and
the particular kinds of nature presented there, from the zoo's ancient origins as a
menagerie—an aristocratic exhibition of exotic animals—to its manifestation as
a twenty-first-century conservation park. A great deal of human work must be
invested to create nature amidst an urban landscape—and even more work must
be invested to make such human work invisible. I refer to the zoo's dual work of
producing nature and obscuring its production as naturalization.

American Zoos: A Brief History

Contemporary North American zoos are products of a long process of institutional evolution. Historians trace the institution of the zoo back to exotic animal collections owned by the royalty of ancient civilizations, including King Wen Wang of China and King Nebuchadnezzar of Babylon.[5] Most of the Greek city-states also had zoos and Roman emperors kept private collections of animals for amusement or for use in the arena. These royal menageries, which exhibited the power and wealth of the ruler, mostly lacked any scientific or educational agendas.[6]

The next major phase in the zoo's institutional evolution was the zoological garden, distinguished from its predecessor by its taxonomic classification of animals. The science of classification was a primary concern at this stage of the zoo's evolution, and animals were exhibited in cages that were organized taxonomically.[7] Zoological gardens were then designed as living museums, intended for the promotion of scientific agendas and for educating the general public. The earliest zoological gardens open to the public were founded with animals from private royal menageries. For example, the oldest existing zoo, the Vienna Zoo in Austria, evolved from the imperial menagerie at the Schönbrunn Palace in Vienna and was opened to the public in 1765. In 1795, the Jardin des Plantes was founded in Paris with animals from the royal menagerie in Versailles; its primary mission was scientific research and education.

The twentieth century saw a move on the part of many zoos toward ideologies of interconnection and unity within biological diversity, manifest in new designs that removed physical bars and walls between animals and the public.[8] Carl Hagenbeck, often considered the founder of modern zoos, made the first steps in this direction when he opened the first bar-less zoo in the world in 1907. Whereas in traditional zoos the means of achieving separation and enclosure were highly visible, Hagenbeck contrived to make them invisible. Specifically, he attempted to make all apparatuses and attempts at classification—indeed, any trace of human intervention—vanish in favor of seeing the animals themselves.[9] Hagenbeck's paradigm-changing design at Hamburg-Stellingen zoo is described by the *Zoo and Aquarium Visitor* journal: "In [Hagenbeck's] zoo of the future, nothing more than unseen ditches were to separate wild animals from members of the public."[10]

In America, zoos came into existence during the transition from a rural and agricultural nation to an urban and industrial one.[11] In 1860, Central Park Zoo, arguably the first public zoo in the United States, opened in New York. Influenced by the English garden style of informal landscape, the legendary founder of American landscape design, Frederick Law Olmsted, believed that nature could offer psychological recreation to tired city workers. Nature, under Olmsted's interpretation, was to be represented by winding paths and wide vistas to picturesque pastoral spots, with the least visible artifice possible.[12] Zoos added a variation to this theme by placing animals in the pastoral landscape.[13] American zoos were also products of the movement to create public parks on the outskirts of cities, a trend tied to late nineteenth-century anxiety about urban moral and social decay.[14] As such, many American zoos were founded as divisions of public parks departments.

Although European zoos served as both model and inspiration for building zoos in the United States, American zoo planners conceived of their parks as distinct from the formal urban gardens that were European zoos.[15] Having more land to work with and guided by a Puritan aesthetic, American zoos portrayed themselves as places of moral recreation, often making reference to scripture. Moreover, American architects have increasingly departed from Europe's colonial-style architecture in favor of more exotic and natural forms of design that are meant to enhance the visitor's experience of nature. Claiming the mantle of scientific truth, zoological parks encouraged popular natural history studies, using their landscape layout to advance this mission. Like public parks, they provided a retreat for city dwellers and a balance of nature and culture where a middle-class ethos could be enforced.[16]

The emergence of the discipline of ecology and its associated environmental movement in the 1970s has brought about the most recent stage in the zoo's institutional evolution: the zoo as a biopark or conservation society.[17] Today, the industry organization of accredited North American zoos, the AZA, prioritizes conservation and education in the mission of zoos. Founded in 1924, the AZA (originally the American Association of Zoological Parks and Aquariums) is a nonprofit 501c(3) organization "dedicated to the advancement of zoos and aquariums in the areas of conservation, education, science, and recreation."[18]

The various stages of the zoo's evolution are more than relics of the past. The myriad expressions of these different institutional phases are also inscribed onto the current landscapes of North American zoos, where traces of their convoluted histories can still be observed. Zoos contain physical evidence of the cage phase, and the bar-less design of Hagenbeck's zoological parks is still prevalent in contemporary exhibit design. At the same time, zoos have drastically shifted their focus from emphasizing public entertainment through spectacular animal exhibits to becoming vehicles for the preservation of species and the conservation of ecosystems.[19] In this last phase, zoos have taken upon themselves (and have been publicly entrusted with) the responsibility of caring for animals and of educating the public to care.

Nature at the Urban Zoo

Since the late nineteenth century, cities have come to be read as monuments to progress and order. It is from these monuments that the movements for conservation have emerged. Roderick Nash notes that "appreciation of wilderness began in the cities."[20] During this time, zoos have developed as urban institutions[21]—as places where nature can be introduced to the metropolis and converted into a domesticated spectacle. Modern zoos have thus come to represent the ultimate triumph of man over nature, of city over country, of reason over wildness and chaos.[22] This process has been accompanied by nostalgia for lost nature[23] and for the animals that have been progressively removed from the everyday life of the urban dweller.[24] Zoos tell us something, then, about the construction of metropolitan cultures and identities, of what it was, and is, to be a modern city dweller.[25]

Eric Baratay and Elizabeth Hardouin-Fugier suggest, furthermore, that if the city is a human zoo, the zoo is a reproduction of the modern city.[26] Desmond Morris adds that North American zoos are a product and symbol of the alienation of urban life: overcrowding, anxiety, aggression, and nervous disorders characterizing both.[27] Finally, Thomas Birch claims that Western urban spaces are centers of imperial power and that wilderness areas function as prisons. In his words,

> Urban centers of Western civilization are the centers of imperial power and global domination and oppression. Whatever comes from them, including classic liberalism, is therefore likely to be tainted by the values, ideology, and practices of imperialism, as the mainstream white man (and his emulators) seeks to discharge (impose) his "white man's burden," the burden of his "enlightenment," on all the others, of all sorts, on this planet.[28]

According to Birch, Western cities are centers of imperialist ideas about nature.[29] To be allowed into civilization, he argues, wildness must be confined and regulated.[30] And if the wildness of distant wilderness must be confined, then it is even more urgent to confine and control the wildness at the heart of the city. The city is therefore precisely where nature, wildness, and animals *should* be—safe under the constant regulatory gaze of zoo staff and the public. Within the city, exotic wild animals may only be experienced in the spatial confines and under the regulatory constraints of the modern zoo. This perspective highlights that caring for these animals is inevitably an expression of power over them: at the urban zoo and, increasingly so, also in the wild, captive animals depend completely upon human care for their survival. In the words of president and CEO of the Phoenix Zoo Bert Castro: "I'm a firm believer that animals have to be managed wherever they are because of all of the encroachment [and] the burdens that are put upon them. I believe that if you don't have people looking out, managing, and caring for them, animals will disappear and go extinct. That's the bottom line. We've seen it happen."[31]

Such ideas about the human domination of nature and the city's alienation from this nature reinforce the bifurcated relationship between nature and culture. Within this relationship, nature connotes a sphere of authenticity and purity,[32] of an ultimate other.[33] Neil Smith frames this approach as "first nature"—defined as a primary, pristine, and abundant external nature untouched by human activity. In contrast, "second nature" is defined as those forms of nature that have been transformed by human activity.[34] Like many conservation institutions, zoos are founded upon the traditional separation between humans and animals and between culture and nature that exists under the "first nature" paradigm. Thus, zoos ironically reinforce the ideals behind the alienation of nature and its destruction—the very ideals that they arguably fight against as conservation institutions.

The nature-culture divide is indeed quite prevalent in the operations and design of contemporary North American zoos. As part of its location in the metropolis, the zoo offers an affordable escape from urban life into what some of the interviewees here have referred to as an "illusion of nature." Jim Breheny, Bronx Zoo director, elaborates in an interview: "My job is to instill in these people that have absolutely no connection whatsoever to nature anymore the appropriate sense of awe, respect, and appreciation for animals."[35] The escape that the zoo provides for its visitors is their transplantation from the urban space in which they live into a completely different space that is natural and wild. "Our guests come here to get that respite from the urban environment," says Susan Chin, vice president of planning and design and chief architect at the Bronx Zoo. "You have places to go where you can see trees and squirrels and ducks and muskrats," she adds, referring to these places as oases, even as Eden.[36] Paul Harpley, manager of interpretation, culture, and design at the Toronto Zoo, observes, "Without the city, there would also not be a zoo in the way we think about zoos, because we wouldn't need to bring the other to the urban."[37] The dual existence of the zoo in between the natural and the urban makes it into what Leo Marx refers to as a "middle landscape"—a "machine in the garden" or, even more relevant, a "garden within a machine."[38] The intensely focused, close, and clear sight of nature produced at the zoo speaks not only to the beauty of nature but also to the technical ability to reconstruct that beauty and make it even more perfect than nature.[39]

Zoogeography: Globalizing the City

It's my desire to try to expose people to habitats around the world.
Donna Fernandes, president and CEO, Buffalo Zoo[40]

The zoo appeals to the public by associating itself with nature. But instead of introducing city people to the nature in their own backyards, zoos usually provide a vicarious journey into a distant and exotic nature in a faraway land.[41] "Who can afford to go to Africa right now?" asks the Bronx Zoo's Susan Chin. Visiting the zoo "is like a family vacation," she adds.[42] Like other vehicles of mass communication, including the *National Geographic* magazine and nature programs shown on television,[43] the zoo provides its visitors with a highly visualized local experience of a disappearing global nature.[44] Yet unlike televised presentations, the zoo's representation of nature promises an authentic experience of that nature. In line with this goal, nature at the zoo is typically organized according to geographical zones. For the most part, this organization is based on mappings of the world into continents, such as Africa and Eurasia. Zoo professionals refer to this geographical emphasis as "zoogeography."

Zoogeography is the study of the distribution patterns of animals in nature and of the processes that regulate these distributions.[45] It is a specific interpretation of nature in which pockets of nature are identified by their geography (for instance, Africa, the Americas), rather than their habitat (desert, rainforest) or taxonomy (primates, reptiles). This approach translates into a continent-based

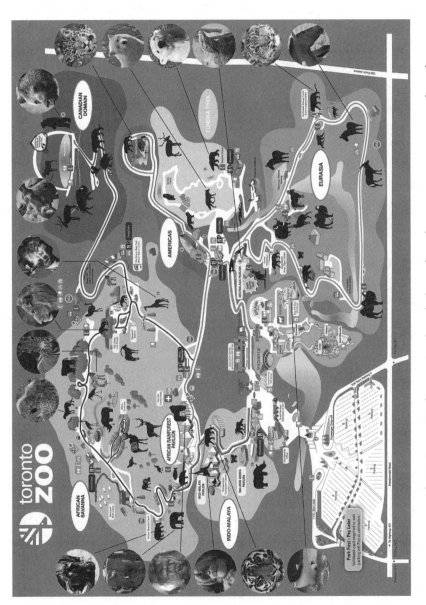

Figure 3. Zoogeography in Toronto Zoo's map. Traveling clockwise from the entrance, zoogoers pass through Indo-Malaya, African Rainforest and Savannah, the Canadian Domain, Americas and Tundra, Eurasia, and finally the Australasia Pavilion. Courtesy of the Toronto Zoo.

organization of the zoo. The Toronto Zoo was the first to introduce zoogeography design on a large scale.[46] The zoo's vision of nature is encoded and provided to zoogoers in its map, with exhibits organized within color-coded geographic regions traversed by walking paths. Paul Harpley of the Toronto Zoo is proud that his zoo "practically has the whole world represented."[47] This encyclopedic wholeness echoes the zoo's utopian aspiration to create another world, in effect helping to define real nature as that which can be found only in exotic places.[48]

The ambition to render the entire world, as represented in assemblages of animals and habitats, subordinate to the controlling vision of the spectator is not new. It was already present for the Great Exhibition of 1851 in London, in the form of Wyld's Great Globe, a brick rotunda into which the visitor entered to see plaster casts of the world's continents and oceans. The spectacular power of such world representations stems from their design to afford a vantage point over a micro-world that claims to be representative of a larger totality.

Within the walls of the average contemporary zoo, enormous distances of both space and time shrink, and the most profound variations in climate and landscape collapse. Penguins from the Antarctic swim a few yards away from Kenyan lions, while giraffes roam near polar bears. Zoogoers move through the species and landscapes in whatever pattern and at whatever pace they choose.[49] At the same time, this movement is also very much planned and geared toward producing a particular nature experience.[50] Among its other characteristics, this experience must be instantaneous. According to Rick Brusca of the Arizona-Sonora Desert Museum: "I think Americans are just too lazy. They want instant gratification and they don't want to have to spend all day driving around looking for zebras. They want to go to a zoo and see one in a cage. It's terrible, but if you are an American with a different point of view then you go visit Africa and visit the big game parks . . . And it's a wonderful experience—a million times better than a zoo."[51]

Notwithstanding, most zoos require a great deal of walking, something that many Americans at the dawn of the twenty-first century find hard to do. At the Buffalo Zoo, for example, the zoogoer who desires to see the gorillas, lions, and giraffes must first traverse most of the zoo; and it can take visitors four to six hours to tour the North Carolina Zoo, with over five miles of trails.[52] Aside from hinting toward nature hikes and connecting zoogoers with their own physical body, the walk is also necessary for establishing an authentic sense of difference between the geographic regions represented in the zoo's space.[53]

Immersion Design: Naturalizing the City

Whatever exhibit you dream to create, COST artisans deliver stunning realism and authenticity combined with durable, weather resistant, animal-safe construction methodologies. These exhibits will immerse your visitors in environments that are interactive, sensory stimulating and truly authentic.

COST advertisement[54]

In addition to zoogeography, the illusion of nature in the midst of the modern zoo's urban space is also created through what is commonly referred to as "immersion design." As designer Chin explains, "By immersion I mean that you're really designing a space that people feel like they are part of the habitat."[55] Jon Coe, the exhibit designer who first coined this term in 1975, explains that immersion design is not only the idea of showing animals in the context of nature rather than in the context of architecture; it is also the soliciting of experiences that make people feel part of, rather than external observers of, this nature.[56] He recounts the evolution of this concept:

Immersion means what it means in the dictionary: deeply and fully involved. Now, that got off to a slow start because most of us [designers] said that it would never work: the gorillas will kill all the trees or they will fall out of the trees and kill themselves. . . . The immersion concept was not just about the visitor. From the beginning, it was equally about animal welfare. . . . Up until that time, the paradigm of animal care was "we know what is best for the animal and we are going to do this and this." . . . [By contrast,] I developed the idea that immersion is a biocentric view, especially for the animals. In other words, we do not know what the animals need. . . . So the closer you can recreate the environment in which they evolved, the more apt you are to meet needs which you did not even know existed.

Initially at least, naturalistic design was the central component of immersion; it was also what distinguished this form of design from earlier zoo designs, and even from Hagenbeck's "zoos of the future." Coe explains:

Hagenbeck . . . created an emotional landscape, but it was not a natural landscape. And it was very broad, huge rockwork things, [but] it . . . was not at all specific and people usually were not immersed in it. Usually, people went along park paths with flowers, looking at that grand panorama and at one point they would climb up to it. But I don't believe he had the idea of trying to create nature and a romantic image of

Figure 4. Watani Grasslands Reserve, North Carolina Zoo. North Carolina was the first American zoo designed from its inception around the "natural habitat" philosophy, presenting animals and plants in exhibits that closely resemble their habitats in the wild. Courtesy of Tom Gillespie / North Carolina Zoo.

nature. [Also,] he did not do anything specific to say, "this is what it is like to be in a thornbush in Africa." They were all very generic images.[57]

However, even the founders of immersion design soon realized the problems with adhering to strictly naturalistic exhibits. According to Coe, "We soon moved away from this idea that if we create these diverse natural habitats we will really solve the animals' needs and it will be great [because] we saw that we didn't. Even these really nice diverse exhibits are still a fraction of what [animals] have in the wild and they are still bored out of their skins most of the time. So then we realized that you have to have enrichment and training." A debate ensued: should zoo exhibits be more naturalistic or more realistic? "Naturalistic meant . . . soft architecture rather than hard, climbing structures with poles as compared to concrete," Coe explains. "But realistic means that the animal does not care what it looks like as long as it can *function* naturally . . . In practical terms, we can give them a whole lot more that's artificial in an indoor environment. . . . And if I can use very high tech Wi-Fi things to give the animals control over the gates, absolutely!"[58] The zoo exhibit is thus designed to be a place of "stunning realism and authenticity," with naturalistic scenes to immerse the zoogoer and realistic functions to enrich the animal.[59]

During our shared walk through the Congo Gorilla Forest exhibit at the Bronx Zoo, Director Jim Breheny points out that immersion design requires paying close attention to the minute details of exhibit space:

> It drives me crazy: you go to certain zoos and you'll see a fence or you'll see a stainless steel food pan. You're going to spend sixteen million dollars on this exhibit to make people think that you're transporting them to the Congo Basin, and then they're going to go there and see a gorilla picking sliced carrots out of a stainless steel food pan? [That] doesn't make any sense to me. That's the kind of attention we give to detail. . . . At no point do you see the apartment that's three hundred feet away. You don't see that because that would make you forget that you are in the Congo.[60]

Although much less prominent than sight, another important sense evoked at the immersion-designed zoo is sound. Most immersion exhibits are designed to buffer animals from the stress invoked by the sound of visitors. At the same time, these exhibits also re-create and intensify animal sounds for the visitors to be immersed in. The Saint Louis Zoo's website asks, for example,

> Have you ever noticed that in almost every habitat you hear an amazing variety of insect drones and chirps, bird calls and frog choruses? The Zoo has recreated these sounds of nature in its exhibits, thanks to a state-of-the-art audio system installed along the visitor pathways. Keep your ears open for the chatter of macaque monkeys in the trees, the high-pitched squeaks of bats in the cave and the sudden rattle of a Missouri rattlesnake coming from the undergrowth.[61]

Breheny similarly points to the recorded bird chirping at the Congo exhibit, explaining that zoos use these artificial elements because they are much easier to manage and maintain than many natural elements. He also tells me that most of the trees and rocks in this exhibit are artificial. The artificial has been disguised so well that Breheny must point it out to me. When I inquire whether zoogoers, too, are instructed as to which materials in the exhibit are artificial, Breheny replies: "Why would we want to do that? For 90 percent of the people who come here, this is as close as they are going to get to a field experience."[62] Bronx Zoo designer Susan Chin further alludes to what she calls the "blurring of lines" between the authentic and the artificial, explaining that

> [this is] our whole point: we don't want you to know where that line is. We want to blur the line so you feel like you're in nature. We don't want you to feel like you're in a

contrived space, though sometimes it's going to be pretty obvious, like in [the] Madagascar [exhibit]. But even then, as you walk through Madagascar because you're in a building, you might forget for a little while that you're in a building in the Bronx Zoo. When you're looking at those lemurs and they are leaping about and they're doing their thing, you might actually forget.[63]

The production of nature at the zoo thus entails a great deal of human work. Buffalo Zoo's architect Gwen Howard illustrates the amount of work and the level of detail that goes into producing an "authentic fake" through exhibit design: "The fake is very prescribed. You're going to build me one tree; it's going to be this diameter, this kind of species; it's going to have six primary branches, and . . . each of those would have a minimum of three to five secondary branches."[64]

At the zoo exhibit, the eye alone cannot be trusted to distinguish the authentic from the artificial.[65] By making visitors feel as though they are part of nature, the exhibit thus erodes the boundaries between nature and artifact. This way, zoos not only take on the role of representing nature, but they also make people believe that the zoo's representation of nature *is* nature, or, better yet, an improved version of this nature.

At the same time, the zoo's nature is distinguished from wild nature. Zoo design must include elements that promote a safe and sanitized environment for both zoogoers and zoo animals, including moats, glass windows, air pipes, exit signs, and water sprinklers. Other distinctions between the zoo's nature and wild nature also exist. For example, most predatory relationships are eliminated from zoo exhibits. Unlike in the wild, "here you don't see animals killing animals," says Breheny. "Our visitors could never see that," he adds. "They make no connection between a piece of hamburger on a Styrofoam plate and a cow."[66] Cindy Lee, curator of fishes at the Toronto Zoo, explains similarly that "you wouldn't want that seal to do what it does in the wild, which is balance a fish or a penguin on its head and rip it up into pieces while throwing it into the air. You wouldn't want your child to see a lion tear up a goat—it's inhumane. They do eat animals here, but these animals are killed humanely."[67]

In effect, the zoo's immersion exhibit displays much more than wild animals. It displays *humanized* animals—animals that, in a variety of ways, must comply with the human expectations of their improved, humane nature. In effect, such animals are displays of the human power to modify and improve upon the unruly elements of nature. Scholar Paul Shepard frames this notion particularly well when stating that "the extension of the human idea to the wild . . . will see in the behaviours and interrelationships among animals infinite cruelties and will seek to prevent them. . . . Humane action will try to prevent dogs from eating cats and men from eating dogs."[68]

Yet not all animal relations are humanized by the zoo to fit ideals of courteous behavior. Lee Ehmke, Minnesota Zoo director and president of the World Association of Zoos and Aquariums Council, tells me that "fish are murdered on a daily basis in front of the public."[69] "The further down the food chain they are," he explains, "the less people are concerned about these animals." Some businesses even specialize in producing animals to be consumed as food for zoo carnivores. For example, RodentPro.com® is a company that specializes in the production and distribution of frozen mice, rats, rabbits, guinea pigs, chicks, and quail, providing "premium quality feeder animals to the reptile, birds of prey, aquatic and carnivore communities since 1993."[70] The company's "hot deals" (accompanied by an image of a small rodent in a cooking fire) include "weaned rats on sale while supplies last for only \$.74 each" and an eight-week special for quail "for only \$1.29 each." Another company, Layne Laboratories Inc., states in an advertisement for food animal products that "all animals are raised . . . in . . . a low stress environment, fully automated to control temperature, humidity, light cycles, and water availability . . . [and] cleaned and inspected daily. The result is a healthier animal, high in nutritional value, exactly what birds and reptiles want for dinner. So don't make them wait while you hunt for food. Order in tonight."[71]

Although captive animals are permitted to eat certain animals, internal zoo regulations dictate that, except for rare occasions, they can neither hunt for prey, nor can they be fed with live animals, even when they are tucked away from the public eye in the confines of the zoo's holding areas. Moreover, when zoo animals are fed dead animals, this is typically done discreetly. The event that comes closest to hunting in most North American zoos is the feeding of snakes with whole prey. This event, too, is usually confined to holding areas rather than exhibit spaces so as not to offend the public.[72] In the words of Rick Brusca, former director of the Arizona-Sonora Desert Museum:

It's one of the ironies of zoos: that they keep large hunting predators in captivity, but don't let them hunt because of "visitor perceptions." Not only is this preventing the public from obtaining a nuanced and accurate understanding the role of these animals in natural ecosystems, but it prevents the animals themselves from experiencing one of their most fundamental behaviors. . . . But, of course, the same prey animals are raised in "factory farms" and killed by humans before they are fed to the zoo animals, in some cases in huge commercial operations, so the irony is multileveled.[73]

To maintain the zoogoer's immersion in a pleasant image of nature, even nonviolent natural events such as sickness, aging, and death are rendered invisible at the zoo. Breheny explains:

> We have animals here that get old. Sometimes they don't move as well or their coats aren't as shiny and they may be blind in one eye. They're not attractive to look at. You'd be surprised that we get letters [complaining] about that. So which is it? Do you want us to kill everything when it's in its prime and breed more so that everything is bright-eyed and bushy-tailed, or is it OK for us to exhibit older animals or animals with handicaps?[74]

Breheny's frustration expresses one of the daily dilemmas of zoo directors, who struggle to strike a balance between the display of animals for public entertainment, public education, and animal conservation—while also providing animals with what they view as the best possible care.

Zoo directors thus constantly negotiate the image of nature reproduced at the zoo. This nature must be harmonious, pleasant, and manicured so as to elicit compassion and awe on the part of the zoogoer, rather than alienation and fear. Additionally, this nature should not distract zoogoers from the zoo's central mission: conservation.[75] Designing a zoo nature that is accessible to the human zoogoer yet devoid of signs of human presence contributes to the objectification of wild nature and thus to its alienation. In other words, the zoo's sanitized and human-free depiction of nature makes wild nature remarkably inaccessible, thereby further reinforcing the human-nature divide.

Even as zoo exhibits are meticulously designed to simulate an immersion in nature, the very opposite effect is created right outside their space. Gift shops, food vendors, animal shows, themed rides, and petting zoos produce distinctly urban commercial spaces that inevitably bleed into the spaces of exhibits.[76] "Has anyone really been immersed in a zoo exhibit and forgotten that they were in a zoo in the middle of the city?" asks journalist Vicki Croke. "Most of us never go under the spell—we can see the exit sign, and we detect the very un-junglelike smells of hotdogs and popcorn."[77] Why would zoos invest millions of dollars to export their visitors to the Congo, only to interrupt the experience with the realities of a hot dog stand just outside the exhibit? I return to this question later in the chapter.

The Zoo's Human Nature

At the modern zoo, the role of humans is carved out carefully. On the one hand, humans are physically absent from the zoo's natural exhibits. By designing such physical divides between human and nonhuman animals, the zoo systematically reiterates the relational divide between them. On the other hand, humans are indirectly implicated as the prime cause for nature's destruction and as having the exclusive power to save this nature. Such a portrayal of humans as omnipotent agents who can destroy and redeem nature enables the emergence of zoo professionals as the animals' exclusive caregivers, effectively instituting their power of care.

Humans are made invisible at the zoo in at least three ways. First, although masses of people frequent zoos at any given time, actual human artifacts are typically not displayed as part of the zoo exhibit. For instance, Lee Ehmke of Minnesota Zoo tells me that he strongly opposes any inclusion of humans in zoo exhibits.[78] "At the Vienna Zoo," he explains, "human artifacts are injected into natural themes to try to tell a story about the relationship [between] people and animals. However, I think it can be very confusing for people to have the human element mixed with the animal."[79] As I discuss in Chapter 3, such sensitivity in the display of humans is very much a result of the controversial history of human exhibits in zoos.

Second, any human work that has gone into the exhibit's construction must be made invisible. For example, the Jungle World exhibit at the Bronx Zoo depends on the continued labor of "architects, zoologists, botanists, graphic designers, construction workers, welders, carpenters, painters, electricians, plumbers, audio specialists, gardeners, cabinet-makers, and glaziers."[80] Along with all other human labor, this labor is naturalized to transparency. Under this reconstruction of the exhibit space as natural, it is especially important to ensure the invisibility of buildings. "The most dangerous animal in the zoo is the architect," former Bronx Zoo director William Conway was quoted saying,[81] illustrating the suspicious attitude of many zoo personnel toward what they conceive as quintessentially unnatural things, such as buildings and their human designers.

Third, zoo exhibits are designed so that zoogoers do not encounter too many other zoogoers.[82] Exhibit designer Jon Coe explains: "The problem is [that] people are inherently so social that 'cross viewing' and 'overcrowded viewing' areas distract from the focus on the animals and their 'natural' context."[83] Again, the idea behind such invisibility is that anything human will unavoidably taint the purity

Figure 5. Constructing nature. Design technicians build artificial rocks at an animal exhibit. Courtesy of Tom Gillespie / North Carolina Zoo.

of the natural experience. The zoo thus reinforces an image of a first nature[84]— observed and, through this process, objectified by man.[85]

Conserving Nature, Caring for Nature

The Association of Zoos and Aquariums envisions a world where, as a result of the work of accredited zoos and aquariums, all people respect, value and conserve wildlife and wild places.

AZA's Five-Year Strategic Plan: 2011–2015[86]

The zoo teaches [that] animals play an important role in our lives and also that [we] care about the ethics of how they are managed.

Donna Fernandes, president and CEO, Buffalo Zoo[87]

Since the 1970s, North American zoos have increasingly stressed their role in saving endangered animals and natural habitats. This relatively new orientation of zoos toward nature conservation has called into serious question the practice of live animal trade, previously a major source of zoo animals.[88] Over the same period, many wild animals were reclassified as endangered, both by the American Endangered Species Act (ESA) of 1973 and by the Convention on International Trade in Endangered Species of Wild Fauna and Flora (CITES), enacted through the ESA in 1975. Accredited North American zoos have therefore defined self-sustaining populations as a new priority, maintaining that captive animal populations can be sustained over many generations by breeding alone, without taking animals from the wild.[89] In addition, populations of zoo animals can potentially serve as a reserve for the species' dwindling populations in the wild.[90]

Beyond the role of conservation in prescribing alternative paths of conduct to the public, the zoo's focus on conservation has also been essential for its own institutional survival. Holding animals in captivity for the sole purpose of spectatorship is no longer justifiable in many circles. Instead, zoogoers and zoo professionals alike want to be convinced that captivity is also good for animals—if not the captive animals then at least their counterparts in the wild. To survive as a public institution, the zoo must convince its public of the sincerity and authenticity of its conservation agenda.

In the words of Minnesota Zoo's Lee Ehmke, "I think part of [the zoo's conservation mission] is that we want [the public] to appreciate the animals as something greater than just something brought here to perform . . . to understand them as part of a greater whole."[91] "Animals are just the hook," proclaims Jim Breheny of the Bronx Zoo along the same lines.[92] Through the exposure of zoogoers to these animals, he says, a detailed educational project can take place that emphasizes the role of humans in conservation. Carmi Penny, curator at the San Diego Zoo and the Peccary and Hippo Taxon Advisory Group (TAG) chair, suggests that to better reflect the current mission of zoos, the term "conservation" must be replaced with "stewardship." In his words, "Stewardship in this context is taking care of the resources and the planet that we live on. And, frankly, it goes back to . . . the Old Testament: stewardship is what we were supposed to do with the Earth."[93] The term stewardship, Penny believes, also reconciles the tensions between the zoo's *in situ* and *ex situ* missions. "The term stewardship applies to both sides of the coin. You know, we support stewardship in northern Kenya. We also support stewardship in San Diego, by teaching people how to be better citizens of the planet. And that's really what it comes down to: teaching people to be better citizens of the planet." Penny believes, in other words, that the term stewardship is better suited than that of conservation to reflect the ethics of care that fuel conservation projects by zoos in both Kenya and San Diego.

A dictionary definition of "care" regards it as "the provision of what is necessary for the health, welfare, maintenance, and protection of someone or something."[94] Care could be considered at different levels of engagement: thinking or caring *that*, feeling or caring *about*, and acting in caring *for*.[95] Although "caring *that*" may or may not lead to "caring *about*," and "caring *that*" or "caring *about*" may or may not lead to "caring *for*," zoo professionals argue that routine acts of caring for animals can lead to caring deeply about their welfare and future.[96] Either way, the various manifestations of care are inseparable from power: to exercise care, one must necessarily exercise a certain degree of power over the subject of care.[97]

The dynamics between care and power also inform the practices of other animal-related industries besides zoos. Vicky Singleton explores notions of control and care in the context of cattle raising in Britain,[98] contrasting the control enabled by the new Cattle Tracing System with the care of more traditional farming practices. The result, according to Singleton, is the collision between the control dream of the regulatory system and the responsive, flexible, and unpredictable care practices of the farmers.[99] Christopher Gad and Peter Lauritsen provide another account of the relations between power and care, this time from the perspective of Danish inspection boats. The authors suggest that inspectors of fishing boats, while at once controlling these boats, also care deeply about both fish and fishermen. This ethic of care, they suggest, also manifests in the quality of their inspection work. They explain, "Some inspectors argue that what is really at stake in inspection work is the well-being of fish and fish stocks, and that they are employed by the state, which has a responsibility to care about the environment."[100] Whereas in the context of cattle practices in Britain, control is juxtaposed with care, both in the Danish fisheries and in zoos control and care are so tightly interwoven that it makes no sense to speak about one without the other. Indeed, conservation is a central goal of captive management by zoos. From this goal flows a series of care ethics toward zoo animals and toward nature more generally. And if care flows from the notion of conservation, the reverse is also true: conservation in zoos has evolved as a result of the establishment of institutional care toward captive animals.

Zoos justify the animals' state of captivity by establishing a broad call for action to the public to both care and conserve. "If you want to save polar bears as species," Randi Meyerson, the Toledo Zoo veterinarian and Polar Bear SSP coordinator, tells me, "you've got to get people to change their habits at home. . . . If people don't see something, they don't care as much. So it puts a face on something that's going on so far away."[101] Buffalo Zoo's Donna Fernandes comments along these lines that "unless you can re-create how wonderful those habitats are with a good horticultural program and the appropriate animals displayed in those habitats, you don't get people to care about it. . . . Unless you see what's at risk, how are you going to get people to change their behavior and be more responsible as citizens?"[102] The zoo's institution of care, in other words, is not limited to "zooland"; it also instructs zoogoers how to conduct their daily lives elsewhere. It attempts to do so by fostering a link between the object of care at the zoo and objects of care in distant spaces. Indeed, the zoo's agenda encompasses human interactions with animals wherever they may be.

Moreover, Regional Collection Plans (RCPs) drafted by various TAGs will often include position statements that are directed toward all humans, not just zoo visitors. For example, the 2010 Bear TAG's RCP states: "The TAG opposes the keeping of bears in conditions that diminish their physical or psychological well-being, portray them as human caricatures, exploit misperceptions of bear natural history, or endanger the lives and well-being of bears or humans.[103] Meyerson explains: "In India there was a large problem with sloth bears being stolen from their moms. And they would teach them to dance in the streets, and that's how they would raise money." When I ask her why dancing bears in India posed a problem to zoos in the United States, she replies, "The way they did it is not humane. They put a ring in their nose and [put them] on a chain in the street—just not where a wild animal should be. . . . I mean, it's just so unnatural to do what they do. . . . Bears—they're not domesticated at all; plus, they get taken from their moms as little babies and then pretty much they are in a type of servitude, and then they are made to do these things."[104]

Similarly, the Ape RCP includes statements concerning "things that we feel strongly about."[105] Tara Stoinski, manager of conservation partnerships in Zoo Atlanta and Ape TAG chair, notes, for example, that "we have a policy in place that very much encourages mother rearing of apes, and [which says] that the only situations where . . . babies should be removed from their moms is if their life is in danger or their mother dies." Furthermore,

> We want people to have the correct opinions about apes. We want people to know that apes are endangered. We want people to know that an entertainment ape that you see on television was probably taken away from its mother when it was a baby, that it has

a very limited "shelf life." . . . So issues that we feel are very important for apes, whether it be within zoos or within the larger societal context . . . we include in the RCP.[106]

Care by zoos, then, is not limited to the animals held in their facilities; it also extends to the animals' body doubles in other locations—whether in the wild, on the streets of India, or on television. In fact, it is precisely through care that the connections between near and far spaces, peoples, and animals can be asserted. Zoogoers (and then humans at large) are guided toward caring for the animal and, metonymically, for the species that the particular animal represents and, again metonymically, also for the entire natural habitat of this species. Through caring for the zoo animal, humans are instructed to take responsibility for their impact on its conspecifics and their habitat in nature. In other words, by teaching other humans how to act humanely to animals, humans from zoos impose their own ideas about what is human, what is animal, and the important distinctions between the two. Underlying the heightened focus of zoos on conservation, stewardship, and care is the assumption that along with their capacity to destroy nature, humans are also capable of saving this nature.

"Buying Time for Wildlife": Consuming to Conserve

"It is [now] up to zoos . . . to buy time for wildlife," says William Conway,[107] Bronx Zoo director between 1966 and 1999 and a tireless advocate of transforming zoos into conservation institutions. Conway implies a responsibility and, with it, an assumption that humans are actually capable of "buying" such time. But why buy time? What kind of wildlife or nature is imagined in the act of buying time? And is the use of consumer language (to *buy*) coincidental, or does it relay a consumerist vision of conservation? These questions bring me to consider how nature is consumed at the zoo—and the nature of the consumption that is practiced there.

To be able to save animals, zoos must first survive in a world of competing recreational sites and increasingly limited public budgets. They must generate revenue. "If you want to fulfill your mission at all," says Donna Fernandes, "step one is to stay solvent."[108] Zoos have more or less figured out how to reproduce animals. Beyond being a more ecologically sustainable conservation policy, this ability of zoos eliminates a major zoo expenditure: buying and trading wild animals. Yet the relatively limited number of animal sales does not necessarily mean that zoo animals are no longer evaluated in dollar figures. Although Jim Breheny assures me that his animals are never price tagged, he notes that in exceptional cases, even the most charismatic animals are bought and sold.[109] He explains:

> We [the Bronx Zoo] have a written policy that is very structured and specific about how we can . . . get rid of animals or send animals out. . . . For example, we couldn't give an animal to you. We try to give them to AZA accredited [institutions]. We do give some animals to private facilities, but . . . we don't give animals to people like shooting ranches that are going to kill them or animal auctions where we don't know what the final disposition of the animal is. [In any case,] we don't put a monetary value on animals. We will buy animals from other institutions, but we won't sell them. If we said we wouldn't buy animals from other institutions, we'd never get any animals, because 95 percent of the zoos aren't in the situation that we are in. . . . Unfortunately, they have to sell animals because they rely on that income. . . . Animals that are not in the SSP, zoos sell them.[110]

According to Breheny, then, under certain circumstances animals are indeed valued in dollar figures, and even bought and sold. Fernandes clarifies:

> We generally only charge for shipping costs for any animal we send to another zoo, even if it is not an endangered species. I suspect that is true for most other AZA zoos, but certainly not the case for nonaccredited zoos, which often do need to buy and sell their animals to other non-AZA zoos since they are ineligible to receive specimens from AZA-accredited zoos if the animals are part of a managed population (SSP).[111]

In addition to the cost of the animals themselves, the project of producing nature in the midst of an urban landscape is expensive.[112] At the very least, the zoo must make a profit that would cover such expenses.

Gift shops are the zoo's most conspicuous sites of consumption.[113] They are strategically situated at the zoo's entrances and exits and are often also scattered throughout the grounds. In contrast to the traditional zoo exhibit, in most of the gift shops I visited little attention is paid to how the relationship between animals and humans is displayed. Conservation-themed puzzles are positioned alongside hunting gadgets, and *Curious George* books—deemed misguided by many zoo people[114]—are sold alongside the politically correct *Panda Bear Panda Bear, What Do You See?* Fernandes confirms that there are no set guidelines for determining which products to sell at her zoo's gift shop.[115]

Invitations to consume are also scattered throughout the zoo. At the Buffalo Zoo, for instance, signs invite visitors to buy crackers for a dollar each to feed the elephants. Additionally, large signs are placed in central locations throughout the zoo to announce various exhibit sponsorships: the Buffalo Exterminators sponsor the otter exhibit, and Time Warner Cable sponsors the two Amur tigers—named, accordingly, Thyme and Warner. At another area of the zoo, one sea lion kiss sells for twenty dollars. "We just recently had a guy propose to his girlfriend here. . . . He had come out for a kiss, and then after she got her kiss, he kneeled down with the ring. Of course, the sea lion kept trying to kiss him as he's trying to pull out the ring and propose."[116] Finally, the Buffalo Zoo even organizes an annual art show, "Art Gone Wild," where art produced by animals, mostly paintings by gorillas and elephants, is exhibited and sold to the public. As Susan Davis observes in the context of San Diego's Sea World,[117] a virtual maze of advertising, public relations, and entertainment renders the zoo an exhaustively commercial space. The zoo is a site of controlled sales of goods (foods and souvenirs) and experiences (rides and performances), all themed to fit the zoogoer's consumer profile.[118]

Earlier, I mentioned how Timmy the gorilla's birthday celebration was tied to a ticket-discount promotion that encouraged zoogoers to bring their old cell phones for recycling, both generating profits for the Louisville Zoo and relieving pressure on gorilla habitats in the Democratic Republic of the Congo. Other zoos are increasingly committing themselves to similar conservation projects. In an article from January 2012 titled "Zoo Boise's New Mission," Steve Burnes, the zoo's director, describes the recent changes undertaken by his zoo in its mission to become "a new kind of wildlife foundation that generates ten percent interest for the conservation of animals." "In addition to the conservation fee," Burnes writes,

> Zoo Boise implemented a series of new revenue generating activities for visitors, including feeding goats and sheep in the new zoo farm, creating a giraffe feeding station, and opening a solar powered boat ride to see a monkey exhibit and end up at our new African Plains Exhibit. All of these activities cost the visitor between $0.25 and $3.00. *In the past, Zoo Boise had hoped that visitors would be inspired to take action to save animals once they left the Zoo. Now, we have turned the act of visiting the zoo into the conservation action.* Visitors only need to show up, participate in activities they or their children would enjoy, and by the end of their stay they will have contributed on average $3.00–$10.00 per family to wildlife conservation.[119]

This, arguably, is zoo conservation at its best, creating a place where individual and collective, *ex situ* and *in situ* conservation messages can mutually exist through consumption. According to the AZA, $130 million is spent by accredited zoos in support of conservation projects every year.[120]

The language of consumption is also prescribed to zoos through various legal norms. For example, the Endangered Species Act of 1973 maintains that any commerce of an endangered species requires the initiation of an "enhancement program"—namely, a contribution to the welfare of the same species in the wild.[121] "Generally, zoo animals do very little to benefit their species in the wild," senior biologist Mike Carpenter of the U.S. Fish and Wildlife Service tells me in an interview. To fix this imbalance, he says, "we discount [or compromise] this animal entirely to benefit the animals in the wild."[122] For example, zoos that borrowed panda bears from China were required to pay up to $1,000,000 per panda per year to the Chinese government. In turn, China was mandated to invest at least half of this sum into protecting panda bears in the wild. By sacrificing their freedom, zoo animals thus not only raise money for the zoo but are also financial ambassadors of their collective kind.

Consuming at the zoo, however, is different from shopping at the mall.[123] Most importantly, it is different because of the unique product offered at the zoo: nature. In modern Western culture, "nature" connotes a sphere of authenticity and purity that stands in stark contrast to today's consumer society.[124] It follows that, as a place of nature, the zoo represents the noncommercial world outside the marketplace. The zoo must therefore bridge the gap between its function as place of recreational consumption, on the one hand, and its role in presenting and preserving an inherently anticommercial nature, on the other hand. More than simply selling a product, the zoo sells an ideal: "Buy a (small plush) panda bear, save a (big wild) panda bear," is the zoo's implicit conservation-through-consumption message.[125] By suggesting that profits from a toy panda contribute to conservation of wild pandas, the zoo transforms the consumer's purchase into an act of care. The message often lacks subtlety, as the zoo employee behind the counter at Buffalo Zoo's gift shop instructs zoogoers: "Whatever you spend goes into saving animals."[126] From a slightly different angle, Jennifer Price argues that shopping for nature commodities at the mall is a safe way to express environmental concerns within the familiar satisfactions of consumerism, even while this activity may dampen awareness of the environmentally exploitive aspects of mass consumption itself.[127]

The zoo frames its conservation call to zoogoers as a call to consume in more ecologically responsible ways, even outside the zoo's gates. Well-placed signs direct and control zoogoers' vision, instructing them how to consume properly. A sign posted at Buffalo Zoo's polar bear exhibit provides an apt example. It reads: "Ten ways to consume wisely: Plant a tree . . . Turn your lights off . . . Use reusable cloth bags for shopping," and so on. Similar notions are expressed at the zoo's Rainforest Falls exhibit: "Be a Rainforest Protector! Doing our part to save rainforests," reads the sign at the entrance. "Buy baskets, jewelry and clothing made by native groups living in and around rainforests. By earning money this way they can stop cutting down the rainforest for fuel or crops. . . . Refuse to buy anything made from old-growth rainforest woods. . . . Cross off foods made with palm oil." Fernandes explains her zoo's signage:

> We're trying to present this wonderful experience for people, but also educate them about what's happening out there, and even small steps that they can take . . . like, you know, use low-energy lightbulbs, and turn my heat down, and let my hair dry naturally, always shop with the reusable shopping bags, and always bring a mug to the coffee shop, rather than getting a cup.

At the zoo, then, ecologically mindful consumption is perceived not only as an external constraint to mainstream consumption but also as the very means by which contemporary humans can conserve.

As one might expect, many have contested the zoo's conservation-through-consumption message. Rob Laidlaw is the founder and director of Zoocheck Canada, a national animal protection charity established to protect wildlife in captivity and in the wild. Laidlaw suggests that although conservation is in fact a central component of "zoo business," it is a mere "cover-up" for the zoos' real, self-sustaining motivations. Laidlaw believes, in other words, that instead of consuming to conserve, zoos are in fact conserving to consume. He quotes a series of figures to prove his point:

> On average, it costs about $16,800 a year to maintain one black rhino in a zoo, and . . . about $1,000 to maintain that one black rhino in the wild. . . . [Furthermore,] it was about $269,000 a year to maintain [all sixteen] black rhinos in captivity. . . . What do you get if you put that $269,000 into Garamba National Park? You get thirty-one rhinos because there's thirty-one rhinos in the park. Now that might be enough to convince anyone that we've almost doubled our investment. If we can actually keep these thirty-one in the wild instead of these sixteen in captivity, then we're ahead. But you get more than that when you protect the wild, because in this particular study they found you also get four thousand elephants; you get thirty thousand buffalo; you get

the entire giraffe population of Zaire; you get fourteen ungulate species, sixteen carnivore species, ten primate species. You get ninety-three small mammal species. You get 492,000 hectares of land. You support all the villages around the park because there's an economy based on the park.[128]

Zoo people would probably argue in response that Laidlaw's account overlooks the emotional need that zoos fulfill for most urban Americans, as well as the potential impact of zoos in educating for conservation. Without zoos, they would say, many urbanites would not have direct access to nature and would not learn to care for it, however constructed and constricted the zoo's version of this nature may be. Another argument against Laidlaw's statement is that donations to *in situ* and *ex situ* conservation are not necessarily interchangeable:

> In most cases money for zoo exhibits and operations come from different sources than international conservation money and are not, realistically, interchangeable. For example, a city may provide some funding for its popular zoo, but absent the zoo, [the city] would not send money to support a national park in far-off Congo; Ford Motor Company gave large donations to Zoo Atlanta for their gorilla exhibits because the families that go to the zoo also buy Ford station wagons; Ford would not send this money to Congo; and finally, many concerned citizens know Congo is a generally corrupt and politically unstable country unable to protect its wildlife, while the zoo is well managed and audited, so they give their donations to the zoo."[129]

Conclusion

Situated at the heart of the modern North American city, contemporary North American zoos are where the general public is exposed to nature, educated about its meaning, and disciplined into the proper human relationship to it. At the zoo, nature is presented as geographically situated in exotic lands, harmonious and sanitized, devoid of human presence, and juxtaposed to modern urban life. Such an interpretation of nature, designed to immerse the zoogoer in the exhibit, assumes nature as a preexisting entity—a "first nature," if you will—thus reinforcing an understanding of humans and nature as separate and alien.

Although less obviously so, the plush animals at the zoo's gift shop and the wooden or plastic horses of the zoo's carousel are also part of the zoo's representation of animals and nature. At the gift shop and along zoo paths, zoo animals are not only displayed and seen, but are also visibly and explicitly commodified.

However, unlike shopping at the mall, the aim of consumption at the zoo is, arguably, the conservation of nature, thus entangling conservation and consumption in sophisticated ways. Zoo, wild, and stuffed animals are conflated here into one marketable entity, consumed in various ways by humans who act within the zoo's pastoral framework of care and control. Alongside their naturalization of zoo space, zoos also naturalize their animals. This form of naturalization translates into the project of classifying zoo animals as wild, the topic of the next chapter.

CHAPTER TWO

Classifying Zoo Animals

Animals are divided into: (a) belonging to the Emperor, (b) embalmed, (c) tame, (d) suckling pigs, (e) sirens, (f) fabulous, (g) stray dogs, (h) included in the present classification, (i) frenzied, (j) innumerable, (k) drawn with a very fine camelhair brush, (l) *et cetera*, (m) having just broken the water pitcher, (n) that from a long way off look like flies.

The Celestial Emporium of Benevolent Knowledge's Taxonomy, described in Jorge Luis Borges, "The Analytical Language of John Wilkins"[1]

STRANGER: You remember how that part of the art of knowledge which was concerned with command, had to do with the rearing of living creatures—I mean, with animals in herds?

YOUNG SOCRATES: Yes.

STRANGER: In that case, there was already implied a division of all animals into tame and wild; those whose nature can be tamed are called tame, and those which cannot be tamed are called wild.

Plato, *Statesman*[2]

Humans have long classified, measured, and standardized themselves and just about everything around them—human races, books, taxes, jobs, diseases, etc.[3] In the eighteenth century, the founder of modern biological classification, Carl Linnaeus, created a taxonomic system through which he carefully and methodically classified plants and then animals. A system well familiar still today to young science students, Linnaean taxonomy originally divided all life forms into kingdoms, and from there into class, order, genus, and species.[4] Linnaeus is especially noted for placing human beings with other animals in his taxonomic ordering of nature, thereby taking a large step away from the Christian assumptions of his time. Indeed, in the tenth edition of *Systema Naturae* of 1758, Linnaeus established a new primate order, which included humans—*Homo sapiens*—alongside *Homo troglodytes* (a creature illustrated as a hairy woman, classified in the same genus as humans), a genus for monkeys and apes, one for lemurs and colugos, and one for bats.[5]

The scientific naming of animal classes within Linnaeus's system performs two roles: it both identifies the individual animal and locates its place in relation to other classes. What underlies the Linnaean naming system, furthermore, is the assumption that all living things can be systemically compartmentalized into hierarchical categories. Such categories can then be named and presented as mutually exclusive and exhaustive—constituting a system that is consistent and complete.[6] Moreover, through classification, the relationship between various animals, and between animals and humans, is rendered scientific and even natural. Naturalization thus lies at the heart of the classification project. In the words of history of science and feminist scholar Donna Haraway,

> The role of the one who renamed the animals was to ensure a true and faithful order of nature, to purify the eye and the word. The "balance of nature" was maintained partly by the role of the new "man" who would see clearly and name accurately. . . . Indeed, this is the identity of the modern authorial subject, for whom inscribing the body of nature gives assurance of his mastery.[7]

Classifying Species

The responsibility of naming animal species rests today with the International Commission on Zoological Nomenclature (ICZN). Founded in 1895 with twenty-eight members from nineteen countries, the ICZN is dedicated to achieving "standards, sense, and stability for animal names in science."[8] The ICZN decides whether to assign an animal a new scientific name and then how to name it. According to registrar Jean Miller of the Buffalo Zoo, "They consider chromosomes; they consider structure, habits, range; they consider all of those factors in deciding whether or not they are the same or a slightly different animal."[9]

Miller explains the use of scientific naming in the context of zoos. In her words, "It's a way that people . . . across the globe, across disciplines . . . can talk about a particular thing without seeing it. If somebody says that they are going to send us *Panthera tigris altaica* . . . you know exactly in your mind the description of it, you know its size, you know its normal range, [and its] gestational period."[10] In these few sentences, Miller captures what lies at the heart of modern governance: the need to know populations from afar, without actually seeing or experiencing them on a physical level. In Michel Foucault's words, "Each group can be given a name. With the result that any species, without having to be described, can be designated with the greatest accuracy by means of the names of the difference groups in which it is included. . . . In this way, a grid can be laid out over the entire vegetable or animal kingdom."[11]

Beyond its capacity to enable the collective use of information systems, the process of scientific naming also enables the replacement of physical bodies with their corresponding abstract representations. Classification, in other words, weakens the materiality of the classified subjects.[12] In the case of zoos, classification and abstraction are the means by which animals and their wildness are harnessed into an orderly system within which they can be observed, objectified, and dematerialized. Though this process, wild animals become more manageable.

The classification of zoo animals into scientific categories such as species and subspecies presents itself as scientific, stable, and solid. This, however, is not exactly the case. In fact, the definition of many species is still hotly debated within biology circles and among conservationists.[13] Certain debates have significant implications for conservation and breeding in the zoo world. The classification of tigers is a good example. In the 1990s, a scientific debate began over the delineation of tiger species and subspecies according to their geographic origins. Although any of the tigers could produce viable offspring, biologists argued that each subspecies should be bred and conserved separately in order to preserve specializations that would enable them to survive in each unique regional habitat. The debate resulted in the designation of a single species—*Panthera tigris*—with six living and three extinct subspecies.[14] Because thousands of tigers were already crossbred in captivity, the new classification meant that these now "generic" tigers were useless for conservation. As a result, the Association of Zoos and Aquariums (AZA) decided to prohibit their breeding in captivity,[15] the Animal Welfare Act withdrew its protections,[16] and hybrid cubs were euthanized in Germany.[17]

The reclassification of tigers into distinct subspecies illustrates the importance of classification to the everyday operation of zoos. The tigers were reclassified to ensure their naturalness, their potential to survive in their original habitats, and thus their value for conservation. Hence, the Bali, Caspian, and Java tigers are now considered extinct, while the South China and Sumatran subspecies are designated as critically endangered.[18] Zoos debated: if they were to classify all tigers as one species and breed them as such, there would be plenty of genetic diversity in captive populations and little immediate risk of extinction. However, they eventually decided to follow the scientific classification and to consider tigers as separate subspecies. As a result, tigers with mixed origins have since been phased out of the population by preventing them from breeding.

Listing Zoo Species

The scientific classification of animals is also extremely important for the design of zoo exhibits. Indeed, exhibiting a wide variety of species in the same exhibit space—also referred to by zoo professionals as biodiversity in display—is one of the criteria used by the AZA for assessing a good exhibit. To this end, the Buffalo Zoo documented the animals and plants that live in its Rainforest Falls exhibit when applying for the AZA award for this exhibit. The list compiled for this purpose demonstrates the zoo industry's practice of classifying animal and plant collections according to their common and scientific names (the latter presented in italics) alongside their conservation status (US Endangered, CITES I, CITES II[19]) and program management type (SSP, PMP,[20] studbook). What follows is the full list of animal species at this exhibit, courtesy of the Buffalo Zoo:

Pink-toed tarantula, *Avicularia magdelenae*
Brazilian red and white tarantula, *Lasiodora cristata*
Brazilian salmon tarantula, *Lasiodora parahybana*
Colombian giant tarantula, *Megphobema robustum*
Blue poison dart frog, *Dendrobates azureus*, CITES II, PMP
Bumblebee poison dart frog, *Dendrobates leucomelas*, CITES II, PMP
Red piranha, *Pygocentrus nattereri*
Giant South American river turtle, *Podocnemis expansa*, CITES II, US
    Endangered, studbook
Yellow-spotted Amazon river turtle, *Podocnemis unifilis*, CITES II, US
    Endangered, studbook
South American red-footed tortoise, *Geochelone carbonaria*, CITES II
Dwarf caiman, *Paleosuchus palpebrosus*, CITES II
Green crested basilisk, *Basiliscus plumifrons*

Monkey-tailed anole, *Polychrus marmoratus*

Green anaconda, *Eunectes murinus*

Boat-billed heron, *Cochlearius cochlearius ridgwayi*, PMP, studbook

Scarlet ibis, *Eudocimus ruber*

Roseate spoonbill, *Ajaia ajaja*, PMP, studbook

Fulvous whistling duck, *Dendrocygna bicolor*

Sunbittern, *Eurypyga helias*, PMP

White-tailed trogon, *Trogon viridis*

Blue-crowned motmot, *Momotus momota*, PMP, studbook

Chestnut-mandible toucan, *Ramphastos ambiguus swainsonii*, SSP, studbook

Linne's two-toed sloth, *Choloepus didactylus*, PMP, studbook

Six-banded/yellow armadillo, *Euphractus sexcinctus*

Giant anteater, *Myrmecophaga tridactyla*, CITES II, PMP, studbook

Southern tamandua, *Tamandua tetradactyla*

Brown capuchin, *Cebus apella*, CITES II, PMP, studbook

Common squirrel monkey, *Saimiri sciureus*, CITES II, PMP, studbook

White-faced saki, *Pithecia pithecia*, CITES II, PMP, studbook

Black howler monkey, *Alouatta caraya*, CITES II, PMP, studbook

Capybara, *Hydrochaeris hydrochaeris*, PMP, studbook

Vampire bat, *Desmodus rotundus*, PMP

Ocelot, *Leopardus pardalis*, CITES I, US Endangered, SSP, studbook

Collared peccary, *Pecari tajacu*, PMP, studbook

This list was submitted to the AZA along with a much longer list of plants, which I will not include here.

The various lists compiled by zoos in the process of forming their collections demonstrate the human desire to thoroughly order and know all animal species, thereby rendering human knowledge of the world complete. The foundations of this knowledge lie in the capacity to scientifically name a species, which then manifests into processes of listing and mapping. Contemporary zoo collections are also measured according to their success in displaying an optimal number of species. The more diverse the species display is, as implied in the rainforest example above, the more valuable it is. The reorganization of animals and plants within zoo exhibits thus not only imitates nature but also provides a more thoroughly ordered and dense arrangement of this nature.

Selecting Zoo Animals

The days of Noah's Ark, zoo people tell me, are long gone.[21] Nowadays, zoos do not have the unlimited boarding capacity of the legendary ark, said to hold a pair of each animal species on the planet. As a result, they must frequently make difficult choices as to which animals to exhibit and which to exclude. In making these decisions, zoo personnel consider a range of factors. Certain animals are perceived as more charismatic and more popular with the zoo-going public. These are the "flagship species," such as the Bengal tiger, the giant panda, the golden lion tamarin, and the African elephant. Then there are the physical limitations: the size of the exhibit, the availability of the animal, and the cost of exhibit design. Zoos also consult with AZA's relevant animal programs to determine which animals are available from other facilities and which animals are considered a priority by the association. Using the AZA's criteria, animal programs form recommendations on how many animals of each species to keep and which animals to breed. According to Ape TAG chair Tara Stoinski, "You apply all these different criteria—how healthy the population is, how many spaces you have, what their status is in the wild, if there's a possibility to do genetic exchange with Europe or with a habitat country. When you do all those numbers it's . . . a pretty clear divide of what we should keep and continue in zoos and what we shouldn't."[22]

As mentioned by Stoinski, the status of a given species in the wild as endangered or threatened often affects zoos' decisions about which animals to select for captive breeding. Moreover, the legal definitions of endangered and threatened are used to justify and prioritize the captive state of these animal species in zoos. The correlation, however, is not as straightforward as Stoinski implies; it is often complicated by other factors, including changes in species definition and the dynamic state of animals in the wild. For example, polar bears used to be considered endangered because of excessive hunting, and thus many zoos designed exhibits to save the polar bears. But after the five countries with polar bears (Canada, Greenland, Norway, the United States, and Russia) came together and established hunting quotas, the polar bear population grew from five thousand to twenty thousand. At that point, many zoos decided to phase out their polar bear exhibits. Randi Meyerson, Polar Bear Species Survival Plan (SSP) coordinator, explains this decision and what has unfolded thereafter:

No one knew the ice was going to be melting. [So] a lot of people closed their polar bear exhibits, or planned on phasing out. . . . But then climate change became such a big issue, and polar bears were the face of it—they [were] such a good ambassador for it. Then a lot of people decided, "Oh, we have to do our polar bear exhibit again." And then you try to turn "on" your polar bear breeding. But by then, a lot of your younger bears had aged, so you're not having bears that still have reproductive capacities.[23]

The consequences that flow from deeming an animal endangered are also susceptible to change. Whereas in the past, the endangered status of animals would irrefutably qualify them for breeding in zoos, the AZA is currently reconsidering its priorities. In fact, animals may be phased out from today's North American zoos precisely because they are so critically endangered that zoos cannot feasibly sustain them. An animal population is considered demographically sustainable if it is able to retain a high amount of gene diversity (larger than 90 percent in relation to the founding zoo population) for one hundred years or more. As of 2011, species populations with fewer than fifty animals— some of them the most endangered populations in the world—are identified by the AZA as "red" populations and deemed unqualified for collective management by zoos. This recent redesignation of animal programs is further discussed in Chapter 7.

Are Captive Animals Wild?

Although a captive-born giraffe has probably never set eyes on Africa, the Linnaean classification system identifies this giraffe with the giraffe that roams the African savannas thousands of miles away. Indeed, neither the geographic origins of these animals nor their surrounding habitats make much of a difference when considering their identity—it is only their genes that matter. Along these lines, distinct geographical regions can result in a separate species classification if genetic differences can be proven. For example, gorillas are divided into two species: eastern (*Gorilla beringei*) and western species (*Gorilla gorilla*), each of which is further subdivided into two geographically separated subspecies: eastern mountain (*G.b. beringei*), eastern lowland (*G.b. graueri*), western lowland (*G.g. gorilla*) and western Cross River (*G.g. diehli*). *G.g. diehli* occurs only in the upper reaches of the Cross River on the Cameroon-Nigeria border.[24] This scientific classification identifies both free roaming and captive gorillas by their genetics and associates them with their geographic origins in Africa, regardless of the fact that some of them may have been bred on another continent.

Likewise, the English term "gorilla" applies to both captive-born and free roaming animals; the animal's actual habitat, in other words, makes no difference to its common nomenclature. The zoo's frequent use of the terms *in situ* and *ex situ* further establishes that it is the very same animal that is situated either at the zoo (*ex situ*) or in the wild (*in situ*). In this fashion, the Gorilla SSP website discusses the natural range of gorillas, following it up with a link to where one can find gorillas in AZA zoos.[25] This image reflects and reinforces the idea that North American gorillas are also wild.

But the definition of zoo animals as wild is not shared across the board. Certain scholars have argued, for example, that zoo animals are not domesticated but are also not wild; that they are not hybrids, at least not in the sense of cross-breeding, but that they also never fully embody their species. These scholars define zoo animals as body doubles, as stand-ins for the real animals, as ambassadors for their conservation,[26] and as "a living cemetery of all that is diminishing."[27] Scholar Susan Willis further explains that the zoo cheetah "may look like a wild cheetah, and its genetic code may be similar to one, but released into the wild it cannot in fact be one: its cultivation has failed to include all the skills, practices, and awareness that cheetahs in the wild acquire in order to live in the savannah."[28] Journalist Vicki Croke agrees. "Imagine having to teach a monkey how to eat a banana," she says. "Those are plastic monkeys."[29] Scholar Randy Malamud argues similarly that "a better appreciation of the multifaceted magnificence of nature and animals [can arise] by not seeing a zoo's giraffe [rather] than by seeing one."[30] He then suggests that the zoo animal is a flesh-and-blood representation of the stuffed bears and cheetahs that zoogoers buy at the zoo's gift shop and that it is altogether different from the wild animal.[31] When asked whether or not captive animals are wild, David Hancocks, formerly Woodland Park Zoo director and currently director of the Open Range Zoo at Werribee, Australia, echoes these sentiments:

> No, not in any sense. Wild animals are bound by many factors, but they are essentially free agents. This is an especially important factor for large, social, intelligent species, which is what zoos typically like to own and display. Zoo animals, in contrast, have every aspect of their lives regulated: when to eat, what to eat, where to sleep, who to cohabit with, when to be outdoors, and so on. Also, the longer a species remains in

captivity, the more it biologically diverges in many important ways from a wild species, until eventually the individual animals cannot even survive in the wild.[32]

Yet within the professional community of humans who care about animals, Hancocks's opinion is the exception. Rob Laidlaw of Zoocheck Canada explains, "Although they wouldn't survive in the wild, most zoo animals are still wild animals. . . . What makes zoo animals wild? That they've not been bred to live in an environment created by humans. They don't do well."[33] Laidlaw is arguing, in other words, that zoo animals are wild because their genetics have not been modified by selective breeding and husbandry; even if they have been born in captivity, zoo animals have not been domesticated.

Ron Kagan, Detroit Zoo director, explains how wild domesticated animals can be. A feral animal (a domestic animal released or escaped into the wild) easily loses its docility, he says; it "loses some of its comfort in terms of living with people or being around people. . . . [And] that's how fast domestication to some extent can be undone."[34] Kagan, too, defines captive zoo animals as a subset of wild animals, rather than as their own distinct category. In what follows, he explains what he believes is the source of the confusion between the terms wild and captive:

Clearly, the vast majority of animals that are in zoos . . . [are] wild animals. . . . And the thing that is different now [from] fifty years ago is that the vast majority of animals . . . were born in captivity. . . . These animals are not domestic, but they never lived in the wild. So when you say wild animals, people assume that means that they used to live in the wild. No—their forefathers did, they didn't.[35]

Alternatively, wild animals are defined as those animals that remain dangerous for humans. According to Randi Meyerson,

We train them to open their mouth to take a look to see what's going on with their teeth. They're trained to actually sit up and put their claws up—we can trim their toenails. But if we have to actually have our hands on them to do anything, then they [must be] immobilized. We never go in with them. We work with them on the other side of a fence.[36]

Although they may train wild animals in order to facilitate their care, zoo personnel oppose the training of wild animals to practice domestic tasks, effectively self-imposing limits on their power to train and discipline animals. More broadly even, the AZA vehemently opposes extraneous training of captive animals for "unnatural" behaviors, such as training bears to dance on street corners and chimps to perform in television advertisements.[37] Tara Stoinski explains that seeing a chimpanzee on television undermines the zoo's conservation mission because people mistakenly believe that if they see an animal on TV, then it must not be endangered in the wild.[38]

Naomi Rose, a marine mammal scientist for the Humane Society International, agrees that while zoo animals may be tamed in certain ways, they can never be domesticated. "Tame is different from domesticated. Tame is a behavioral thing," she says. "You've taken a wild animal and you now habituated it to human presence and human handling. That's tame. Domestication is when you're deliberately breeding them for selective traits—[ones] that go from wolf to dogs."[39] When I ask her whether zoo animals are wild, Rose replies:

> To me it's not really a debatable question. . . . A wild animal is any animal that is evolutionary in its natural state. There's been no selection—no artificial selection—for traits to domesticate. A domesticated animal is an animal that has been bred specifically by human beings with artificial selection breeding for traits that you desire to create in that animal. *If . . . people are not selecting for traits—in other words, if the breeding is just sort of random, because you're just trying to get them to breed at all, for instance—then they're still wild animals.* . . . And in fact, [zoos] are actively avoiding artificial selection . . . partly for real reasons and partly for public relations. They're presenting themselves as arks, as depositories for wildlife in case everything goes perishing in the wild—[so that these animals] will be alive and be safe until we put them back into the wild at some point in the future.[40]

Although Rose and Laidlaw work for organizations that generally oppose holding wild animals in captivity, and Kagan and Meyerson work for institutions of captivity, they all share the assumption that a zoo animal is wild. This shared assumption is based on a genetic definition of the animal that is mostly concerned with whether or not the animal has been selectively bred for certain traits by humans, a practice that both zoos and their adversaries reject for wild animals. According to this definition, wild animals are clearly different from domesticated animals. As Rose has pointed out, it is precisely the wildness, or the non-artificiality, of the zoo animal that lies at the heart of the institution of captivity.

Indeed, the incarceration of zoo animals—and the concurrent freedom of their genetically similar, if not identical, body doubles in the wild—is what makes these animals so fundamentally attractive. Without wildness, there would be nothing exciting about captivity; the zoo would be as domestic as a barnyard. Indeed, domestic dogs are not usually perceived as captive because they are not seen as wild in the first place. If zoos decided to display only pet animals, they would not attract the public in the same way they do by exhibiting wild animals. The zoo's institutional survival thus depends on the survival of both captivity and wildness. In other words, captivity and wildness are codependent: if not for freedom, incarceration would make no sense. The wildness of these animals, along with the presentation of their captivity at the heart of the modern city, is the zoo's main appeal—and also the core of the heated debates about its existence as such.

Animal protectionists, too, rely on the assumption that zoo animals are wild. This wildness is at the core of their argument against contemporary zoos: zoo animals are wild, and thus are either born or meant to be free, or at least free roaming. The wildness of zoo animals thus serves both to legitimize their captivity, by zoo people, and to delegitimize it, by animal activists. Remove the shared assumption about the wildness of zoo animals, and the battle between pro-zoo and anti-zoo people becomes meaningless. Under these assumptions, Naomi Rose warns against some of the dangers in blurring the distinctions between wild and domesticated:

> If you're not careful about maintaining genetic diversity and not selecting captivity traits—docility or small size or any of these things that you might want in a zoo animal, but not in a wild one—if you're not careful to avoid that sort of artificial selection and work really hard to keep the genetic diversity diverse, then you're going to end up with a zoo-adapted animal that is hopeless in the wild.[41]

But what will happen if and when the wild, as currently perceived, ceases to exist? Will zoos then disappear, or become wilderness reservations? What would be the purpose of saving wild animals in the absence of wilderness? With regard to some animals, this is no longer a hypothetical question. Aside from its existence in several European zoos, the Alaotran gentle lemur's range is now limited to the marshland surrounding a single lake in Madagascar, and it continues to be threatened there by burning and habitat destruction.[42] The polar bear's dependence on Arctic sea ice means that its habitat is disappearing because of global warming,[43] and the western and mountain gorillas are succumbing to hunting, disease, and habitat loss due to agriculture, deforestation, and mining.[44] Other species have been more fortunate. For some, wild animals can be maintained in captivity while their wild ranges are restored. The last wild Arabian oryx were hunted to extinction in the wild in 1972, but since then, effective prohibition and regulation of hunting has enabled captive breeding and release programs to reestablish a wild population of over six thousand in Saudi Arabia, Oman, Israel, Bahrain, and Qatar. According to Phoenix Zoo's director of conservation and science Stuart Wells: "We called it 'Operation Oryx.' In May 1962, an expedition was sent to Oman to catch and bring the oryx here. Only seven of these animals reproduced, and these were pretty much the founders of the entire population that exists in the world today."[45]

Shifting Bodies

The definition of zoo animals as wild draws a metonymic link between the captive animal at the zoo and the "real" animal—that which roams free in the wild. Bronx Zoo director Jim Breheny stresses the importance of this link:

> It's really pretty simple. You want to go to the zoo to see the animals. We like those animals. Well, these animals are endangered; they might be extinct in your children's lifetime. Well, that's a shame. . . . How do we not let that happen? You can't just save the animals without saving the environment. When you look at the environment, it's really a community of animals that function together in a habitat situation—and that's why we have this whole thing about arks and zoos and whatever . . . yeah, but only if you're going to use it as a tool to save *the real thing*. People used to talk about saving species, but you can't save species without saving habitat.[46]

According to Breheny, zoo animals are the hooks for saving their counterparts in the wild and thus also for saving the wild itself. Through experiencing a bond with zoo animals, human zoogoers are disciplined to care for wild animals and, by extension, for wilderness at large. Zoos, then, function as pedagogical institutions: they entrust their public with the power of care and, alongside this power, with the responsibility for saving nature.

Although zoos need captive wild animals to attract the public and to instruct them how to save wilderness, it is illegal to take endangered animals from the wild. Moreover, the AZA strictly prohibits accredited zoos from taking *any* animal—endangered or common—from the wild. "Zoos should be net producers of wildlife, not net consumers," says Dan Wharton, former director of Central Park Zoo.[47] Tara Stoinski explains the implications of this prohibition on her work with apes:

> We're dealing with a fairly small number of species across the globe. . . . Most of these species are endangered or critically endangered, and so we do not bring in animals generally from the wild. [We] have a population here—a historic population—that

we're dealing with. So we don't have a lot of options to say, "Well, we also want to have mountain gorillas in zoos," because that's just not a possibility. We wouldn't want to contribute to their further decline, and it would be politically impossible to bring mountain gorillas in. . . . We're a pretty closed population, and so there's not a lot of decisions we're making about which species to have and not have at this point. I kind of inherited what was already present in zoos, and we're just focused on maintaining that.[48]

However, the on-the-books prohibition against taking animals from wild habitats is somewhat more fluid in practice. Stoinski provides an example of when such takings are actually possible: "There are some gibbon species that are in sanctuaries in Asia that have been rescued from the pet trade or lost their land and have been rescued from deforestation. And so, in theory, in the future, there could be the possibility of bringing in one or two animals from the captive facility in Asia to help increase the genetic diversity."[49] Randi Meyerson describes another possibility for working around the prohibition against taking from the wild when non-endangered animals are concerned:

[As] for the black bears and the brown bears . . . we do not breed those bears in captivity. We use our space in zoos as rescue space for nuisance bears or orphans. So those populations aren't managed like we do for the other species, but we have registries. Fish and Wildlife or the state game departments call up and say, "Hey, we have a nuisance bear that we have to bring in, or we have these orphans, you know, can you help us place them?" And then we talk to zoos and try and find places for them.[50]

Clearly, zoo people see themselves not only as caring for zoo animals but also as caring for wild animals anywhere. Dan Wharton says along these lines that "there are some species that are always taken from the wild for humane reasons." The raccoon is one example. "There is no reason to have a raccoon [breeding] program," Wharton says. "They have larger populations than their environment can handle. They are a pest species." When a vulture is found with one of its wings damaged, Wharton adds, the zoo can lawfully rescue it from the wild. This vulture's offspring may later be reintroduced into the wild. As a result, "what would otherwise be a dead animal is still contributing to the vitality of the wild population."[51]

These instances demonstrate the zoo's position that by taking from the wild, zoos are actually saving this wild. It follows, then, that zoos cannot import a wild animal unless someone else has already destroyed its habitat, trapped it for trade, killed its mother, or otherwise endangered it. The take must be for the purpose of caring, not profiting. This rationale also applies in the context of endangered species: the San Diego Zoo imported a whole family of elephants from Swaziland, where they were slated to be culled due to overpopulation in the area.[52]

Whereas the transfer of animals from the wild into zoos is usually considered problematic and is thus highly regulated, the opposite movement—from zoos into the wild—is not only considered legitimate but is also highly desirable and, as such, publicized widely by zoos. Although in truth they are quite rare, the transfers of animals back into the wild—what zoo people refer to as "reintroductions"—are considered the pinnacle of zoo conservation and a direct illustration of the inherent interconnections between the conservation of *in situ* and *ex situ* animal populations. This context highlights another important aspect of Conway's phrase "buying time for wildlife"—but whereas the focus in Chapter 1 was on the "buying" part of this phrase, here my focus is on "time." According to Conway, zoos function as a limited version of Noah's Ark, containing the animals safely until the storm passes and the animals can be returned to their reestablished habitat. The eventual possibility of reintroduction ensures that the zoo animal, even if captive born, is always potentially wild.

Critics of zoos challenge the importance of reintroductions by zoos, arguing that they are better for the zoo's public relations than for actual conservation. For example, Laidlaw of Zoocheck Canada highlights the practical limitations of such reintroductions:

> [Most people] don't realize that the SSPs are essentially breeding animals for zoos, and that almost all [zoos] . . . have no mechanism whatsoever and never had any intention of ever putting animals back into the wild. And yet . . . you go anywhere and it's wishy-washy wording that creates the impression, certainly amongst the people who visit the zoo, that these animals are part of this founding population [and] that their progeny are being released to the wild and are repopulating the wild.[53]

The rhetorical and actual shifting of animals is not limited to their movement from wild to captive and vice versa. Wild animals are also used for the exotic pet trade, defined as the trade and keeping of wild animals as pets. Illegal trafficking in exotic animals is a global business, worth close to $20 billion each year. According to the U.S. Fish and Wildlife Service, the profit made from illegal trade in wildlife in the United States ranks second only to that of illegal drugs. Each year, countless numbers of exotic animals are purchased as pets across the country. Sugar gliders, hedgehogs, and prairie dogs are just a few of the exotic species that have recently gained popularity in pet stores. Others, such as nonhuman primates, tigers, and even bears, are readily obtainable from private breeders and dealers.[54] The regulations that pertain to these animals vary by state, municipality, and species, and in many areas of the United States it is still legal to keep exotic wild animals in private captivity.[55] The federal government regulates international and interstate trade and release of wild animals into the environment, but as of 2011, fifteen states still allowed the keeping and trading of wild animals within their jurisdiction.

Whereas zoo professionals often portray the boundaries between zoo and wild animals as fluid and dynamic, they perceive the boundaries between zoo animals and exotic pets as being clear and inflexible. Dan Wharton describes the relationship between the pet and zoo industries as a "one-way street." On limited occasions only, he says, zoos may rescue wild animals from the pet trade. For example, following the October 18, 2011, incident in Zanesville, Ohio, where fifty-six exotic animals were released from a private farm, the Columbus Zoo rescued three leopards, two Celebes macaques, and a grizzly bear.[56] The rest of the animals were killed by local authorities out of self-defense and public safety.[57] Even before the incident, Ohio zoos were actively trying to prevent such a situation by promoting legislation to control the exotic animal trade in this state.[58]

The movement of animals in the opposite direction—namely, from zoos to the exotic pet trade—is even more strictly forbidden. In fact, AZA's Code of Ethics prohibits sending animals to people who cannot properly care for them. Under very strict conditions, Wharton says, certain animals may be moved to private hands, provided that they are not part of the pet trade. In the case of SSP animals, this requires that the receiver be a certified AZA facility; for non-SSP animals, the decision is made on a case-by-case basis.[59] Wharton explains that "it is better to euthanize animals than [to] send them to hands that may not be able to take care of them properly."

Rob Laidlaw tells a very different story about the boundaries between zoo and exotic pet animals. He says that although accredited zoos indeed regulate the movement of animals from the wild into captivity and from captivity into the pet trade industry, there are many ways around these regulations:

The exotic pet trade . . . is basically a recipient of a lot of animals from the zoo industry. . . . A lot of the bigger zoos either have instituted policies to control how they dispose of animals, or they insulate themselves by going through accredited brokers who then can disperse animals almost anywhere they want. But certainly, there are a lot of animals going from accredited to unaccredited zoos, and . . . who knows where they go from that point—there's no passport system for animals.[60]

Furthermore, Laidlaw implies that the zoo industry benefits from the existence of the exotic pet trade. "Many zoos have a predictable annual surplus that they have to get rid of every year," he says. "It's huge, and that's why there's like twenty thousand pet tigers in the United States. . . . [But] very few zoos ever take in animals from the pet trade."[61] Although it is not my purpose here to accurately quantify the wild animal trade and its relation to zoos, I present these contradictory portrayals to illustrate how passionate pro-zoo and anti-zoo people can be in their struggle to be the exclusive spokespersons for the animals.

Domesticated Zoo Animals

At the periphery of their wildlife exhibits, North American zoos also exhibit domesticated animals. Such domesticated animals are, however, usually restricted to a particular space: the children's zoo or the petting zoo. The Philadelphia Zoo opened the first children's zoo in the country in 1938,[62] establishing a national precedent for the inclusion of domesticated animals in zoo collections. In Buffalo, the Delta Sonic Heritage Farm opened in 2010 to replace a conventional petting zoo with a re-created historic farm. Berkshire pigs, a Devon cow, Southdown sheep, Dominique chickens, turkey, and a mule are exhibited there to reflect the way they were raised and fed in western New York in the 1860s.[63] In a concerted effort to maintain historical American breeds from over one hundred years ago, the Buffalo Zoo specifically utilized heritage breeds of domesticated animals. Similarly, in today's Philadelphia Zoo, "Chickens of many breeds, including rare and endangered breeds, display their many colors proudly!"[64] If the loss of genetic diversity has become a problem for zoos in the context of wild animals, now the loss of genetic biodiversity in *domesticated* animal breeds is also becoming a concern. This concern manifests itself in the design of petting zoos that play a role in maintaining the biodiversity of domesticated animals.

The zoo's exhibition of domesticated animals is quite different from that of wild animals. Whereas the zoogoer is commonly allowed only to look—not to touch—wild animals, visitors of children's zoos, especially children, are encouraged to pet the animals. Moreover, touch is a central feature of these animal exhibits. The Lincoln Children's Zoo in Nebraska encourages hands-on learning in its Firsthand Farm and Critter Encounter exhibits. According to the zoo's website, new animals are brought for the public to view and touch every hour. "This one-on-one interaction makes lasting memories—and inspires children of all ages to not only care about nature, but to take action to protect our environment."[65] Indeed, zoos increasingly present themselves as providing urban children with what might be their only opportunity to physically connect with nature, now broadly defined to include all nonhuman animals that have been driven out of the modern city.[66] At San Diego's Children's Zoo, "The popular Petting Paddock allows kids a chance to feel the wooly coat of a sheep or comb a gentle goat's hair."[67] At the Bronx Children's Zoo, visitors are invited to "climb into a bird's nest, hop like a wallaby, and feed a goat! There's plenty for little fingers and big eyes to touch and see in this cozy, three-acre setting full of kids' activities. Experience firsthand various types of animal habitats, locomotion, senses, and defenses. . . . Touch velvety noses and furry ears. Feed a handful of grain to goats, sheep, and llamas at the barn area."[68] Finally, at the Phoenix Zoo—"Voted One of the Nation's Top 5 Zoos for Kids"—children can pet and feed Cownose stingrays, ride camels, and encounter giraffes.[69]

The visitor's ability to feed the animals at the children's zoo is yet another element that distinguishes this exhibit from the rest of the zoo. Some have suggested that the zoo's general prohibition from feeding wild animals deprives visitors of an opportunity to interact with, and therefore to practice care for, wild animals.[70] This human desire to care for animals through feeding finds a partial relief at the children's zoo. Instead of the purely visual and therefore limited experience of wild animals in the general zoo exhibit, a more comprehensive sensory interaction with domesticated animals can thus emerge in this space.

At the same time, the division between human and animal at the children's zoo is strictly supervised and sanitized. During Buffalo's Heritage Farm's visiting hours, one or two zoo instructors are present on site to guide children as they pet or feed the animals. Sinks and hand sanitizing devices are situated at central locations, along with signs that encourage visitors to wash their hands after touching the animals. The ability to touch domesticated animals in the petting zoo—alongside the constant reminders to wash hands thereafter—maintains and reinforces the status of the wild animals as "untouchable" elsewhere.

Other distinctions between wild and domesticated animals also exist at the zoo. In contrast to the multiple projects of naming and exhibiting wild animals by scientific classification and zoogeography (see Chapter 1), domesticated animals are not assigned geographic color codes, nor are they affiliated by scientific names or habitat. Instead, these animals are typically identified by their common name, such as cow and chicken. Even when zoos use their scientific names, these names are often distinguished with a subspecies designation as domestic, or by using the domesticated animal's Latin name: *Equus ferus caballus* (horse), *Sus scrofa domestica* (pig), *Bos primigenius taurus* (cow), and *Canis familiaris domesticus* (dog), to name a few. Moreover, a search of various zoo websites reveals that domesticated animals are usually listed separately from wild animals, if at all.[71] This, Fernandes instructs me, is meant to simplify the exhibit for its target age group: two- to five-year-olds. Whatever the reason may be, the result is that the animals exhibited at children's zoos—mostly domesticated animals—are presented quite differently from the wild animals of traditional zoo exhibits.

Unlike wild animal exhibits, domesticated animals are presented in the context of things that humans can do with these animals, or how they can use them. In its Heritage Farm, the Buffalo Zoo uses interactive signage to demonstrate the uses of domesticated animals. Children are asked: "What products come from this animal?" and are instructed: "leather shoes," "meat," and "milk" come from cows, "pigskin football" and "meat" from pigs, "pillow feathers," "meat," and "eggs" from hens, and "wool yarn" and "meat" from sheep. Such distinctions in animal displays serve to reinforce the social and cultural categorizations of animals into domesticated and wild.

However, whereas humans may kill domesticated animals for their daily consumption—and the zoo's mission in this context is thus to teach children "that bacon and ham come from a pig and not Wegman's [supermarket]"[72]—humans are prohibited from consuming or using wild animals, especially endangered or threatened, unless they can obtain proper permits and licenses. The separate status of domesticated animals at the zoo underscores the special protections for wild, and especially for endangered, animals. More broadly even, by distancing the farm and its animals from the wild nature of, say, the rainforest, the zoo reifies the nature-culture binary and its underlying idea of "first nature." The farm exhibit is thus the negative image of the idealized nature displayed in other zoo exhibits.

Conclusion

The human need to organize and classify animals is projected onto the space of the zoo, resulting in the separation of domesticated animals from wild animals. Additionally, companion animals (or "pets") are prohibited from entering the zoo. For example, a sign at the entrance to the Buffalo Zoo stipulates what can and cannot be brought into the zoo, stating that "pets," along with "radios, skates, frisbees, scooters, grills, alcoholic beverages," are not allowed inside. Along these lines, zoo professionals have often advocated against the blurring of categories between wild animals and exotic pets, as in the fight against lax exotic-animal laws in Ohio, and the Bear TAG's public statement (discussed in Chapter 1) against keeping black bears as exotic house pets.

Zoos also present other instances for exploring the rich interconnections between various animal categories. For example, rats, mice, crickets, and other small animals—although typically bred for labs—are raised in this context to feed zoo animals. Companies that specialize in zoo food thus offer an interesting variation on farm-raised animals for human consumption.[73] The RodentPro.com advertisement referred to in Chapter 1 illustrates how zoos facilitate the relations between the various animals. In the shadow of the zoo's publicly noble dealings with wild animals, other animals are produced in captivity to be consumed by the captive-bred zoo animal population. These other animals are an important part of the zoo world, yet they are mostly invisible to the public eye.

The distinctions between wild and domesticated animals are reflected and reinforced in their exhibition. In zoos, wild animals are displayed in a "state of nature"—*ferae naturae*, in the legal terminology—and thus in a potentially predatory or competitive relationship with humans. For safety, wild animals and humans are separated by invisible barriers—which enable the thrill of the spectacle to occur. Yet the wild animal can only be gazed at in its naturalized enclosure from a safe distance, thereby reinforcing its untouchable status. By contrast, domesticated animals are exhibited as tame and as relatively harmless—safe even for children to touch and feed, so long as they wash their hands afterward.

Although safety concerns are indeed a major reason for separating humans from wild animals, additional factors contribute to the centrality of the visual—or scopic—regime at the zoo. Most important is the cultural framing of the zoo as a museum that displays living animals rather than inanimate artifacts.[74] At the heart of this approach is the belief that humans may gain access to the beautiful through an undistorted *vision* of it—the creation of enlightened optics not clouded by interests or emotions.[75] Indeed, the museum is "a space of seeing that constitutes subjects and objects in certain ways through a history and geography of optic relations."[76] The idea of the optic as paramount to the haptic—that which is experienced through touch—serves an important purpose in the zoo context: it furthers the institutional ability to govern zoo collections.

CHAPTER THREE

Seeing Zoo Animals

People look, and take sight, take seeing, for life itself. . . . Sight and seeing, which in the Western tradition once epitomized intelligibility, have turned into a trap: the means whereby, in social space, diversity may be simulated and a travesty of enlightenment and intelligibility ensconced under the sign of transparency.

Henri Lefebvre, *The Production of Space*[1]

At the zoo, direct physical contact between zoo animals and zoogoers is not only discouraged but also physically prevented.[2] Fences, moats, cages, and separate air and water systems ensure that animals and humans cannot touch one another, and to a lesser extent, that they cannot smell one another. Sight—the strongest, safest, and most sanitary of human senses—emerges as the only possible contact between the two populations.[3] Of all the senses, the zoo's preference toward sight is not incidental, nor is it unproblematic.

Humans have long constituted both subjects and objects in optic relations that are characteristic of particular histories, geographies, and technologies of seeing. These configurations of subjects and objects and their visual relations may be referred to as scopic regimes.[4] Under modern scopic regimes, humans taxonomize, manage, and objectify the world through a visual system of cartography and from the geometric perspective of an unblinking, unbiased observer who can see the truth.[5] Although the scopic is often synonymous with the optic— as it is in museums, zoos, and other institutions where the visual regime reigns supreme and is accompanied by a prohibition against touching the exhibited artifacts—it may also incorporate other senses, especially touch, albeit in a way that still interprets these senses through the framework of vision.[6]

Zoo designers and architects face unique challenges in their construction of scopic regimes. They must bridge the inherent contradiction that the very act of seeing wild animals undermines their wildness, which is intensified by the

fact that wild animals at the zoo are surrounded by humans and human artifacts. In the wild, animals are practically never seen by humans except by their
traces—at most, "they are fleetingly glimpsed at as they scurry or bound away."[7]
Zoo designers overcome the challenges of designing exhibit spaces for seeing
wild animals by using a suite of spatial tricks, including glass panels, temperature controls, vanishing mesh barriers, and the elevation of exhibit spaces. Still,
visitors often complain about their restricted view of zoo animals.

One rarely hears such complaints about the zoo's restriction of animal smells.
Quite the contrary, "A lot of people complain about [the gorilla] area because . . .
it's kind of stinky," says Gwen Howard, Buffalo Zoo architect.[8] "But that's what a
gorilla smells like. They smell like a men's locker room."[9] Animal smells are indeed quite a bit more pungent than zoogoers realize. At Buffalo Zoo's Rainforest
Falls exhibit, for example, powerful ventilation systems were installed to separate animal and human airways.[10] The restrictions on smell at the zoo highlight
an important property of immersion design: to ensure that humans are brought
close enough to *see* but not to *smell*, or to pass on germs. Indeed, whereas the zoo
experience is all about seeing, and to a lesser extent hearing, it is much less about
smelling. Moreover—as is the case with traditional museum displays[11]—touch is
also strictly prohibited at the traditional zoo exhibit and is confined to the petting or children's zoo.

Even as exhibits are designed to dampen smells and heighten visibility, it is
equally important for zoo designers to make entire sections completely *invisible* to the public eye. In fact, many zoo animals spend the bulk of their time
away from public view. The most intense project of managing animals takes
place in these invisible spaces, referred to by zoo professionals as "holding
areas." Exhibit spaces and holding areas are situated on opposite ends of a spectrum: the visible, cageless naturalistic exhibit stands in stark contrast to the
explicitly artificial, functional, and cage-style design of the invisible holding
area.

Invisible elements also exist within the space of the zoo exhibit, the most obvious of which are human-related. Earlier, I have mentioned that in order to
maintain the human-nature divide that is so essential to the routine function of
zoos, the human work that is performed there must be rendered invisible. Another aspect of this invisibility is the absence of humans as subjects of the gaze in
zoo exhibits. This, however, has not always been the case. Human zoos—zoos

that exhibited humans alongside animals according to their regions of origin— existed in the United States well into the twentieth century.

Seeing Humans

Alongside his infamous bar-less zoo design discussed earlier, Carl Hagenbeck also played a pioneering role—albeit a much less famous one—in the modern zoo's display of humans alongside animals. This practice can be traced back to one of the earliest known zoos, that of the emperor Montezuma in Mexico, which exhibited not only a vast collection of animals but also unusual humans, for example dwarfs, albinos, and hunchbacks.[12] In 1874, Hagenbeck exhibited Samoan and Sami people as "purely natural" populations.[13] Similarly, both the 1878 and the 1889 Parisian World's Fair presented a Negro Village. Visited by twenty-eight million people, the 1889 World's Fair displayed four hundred indigenous people as a major attraction.[14]

Human zoos were not only successful in Europe. In 1906, the Bronx Zoo exhibited Ota Benga, an Mbuti pygmy from central Africa, as an example of an emblematic savage from a primitive race.[15] At first, he was free to move around the zoo and help keepers feed and communicate with the animals. Soon, however, he was confined to a cage, with a parrot and an orangutan to keep him company.[16] While this exhibit was fairly controversial, it is nonetheless illustrative of the debates of the time. It was not simply who was and who was not human that worried westerners at the turn of the century, but "who was more human and, finally, who was the most human, that concerned them."[17] In this sense, the human zoo of the nineteenth century did not see itself as exhibiting humans per se, but rather as displaying animalized humans.[18] Such humans were typically represented as the still-living examples of the earliest stage in human development, the point of transition between nature and culture and the missing link necessary to account for the transition between animal and human history.[19] Human zoos were, in effect, exhibitions of the Darwinian rhetoric of progress as well as visible demonstrations of colonial power.[20]

This historical and racial account might serve to explain why the topic of exhibiting humans in zoos is handled so gingerly by contemporary North American zoos. For the most part, humans are missing from today's naturalistic exhibits. They exist only as background, for instance in signs that refer to human consumption as a major cause for environmental destruction, or conversely as a vehicle for saving this nature. Humans are rarely displayed as an integral part of nature. The human-animal separation performed at the zoo reinforces the zoo's construction of a separate "first nature" in the wild, which remains unmodified by humans.[21]

Lee Ehmke, Minnesota Zoo director and president of the World Association of Zoos and Aquariums, explains his objection to the inclusion of humans in zoo exhibits beyond the abstract depiction of their responsibility for both destroying and saving nature. According to Ehmke, one of the confusions that arise from building animal exhibits amid, say, a miniature Taj Mahal, is that it results in the misunderstanding that "humans and animals can coexist just fine."[22] For Ehmke, the explicit inclusion of humans in a zoo exhibit reinforces such a misguided view of nature. For this reason, he believes, it is best to leave humans out of the zoo story altogether.[23]

A former exhibit in Seattle's Woodland Park Zoo provides an example of the underlying tensions caused by exhibiting humans, especially when these humans are indigenous.[24] The exhibit, displayed in 2007 and 2008, included a replica of an African village with vernacular architecture. The zoo also hired Kenyan Maasai tribesmen who resided in Seattle as interpreters of this nature. The zoo's literature stated that "understanding the wildlife of East Africa also means knowing about the people who share the land. The Maasai are a herding culture living primarily on the savannas of southern Kenya and Tanzania. Several Maasai have joined us to present stories of their lives and the impact that wildlife has on them."[25]

A lively debate ensued. "It became a huge controversy," says Ehmke. "Somehow, [it] seemed like these people were being kept in the zoo as [part of the] exhibit." One of the Maasai cultural interpreters was quoted defending the program: "We're not out there holding monkeys,"[26] he said, recalling images of Ota Benga's display at the turn of the twentieth century. In a statement to the press, the zoo defended its exhibit: "It is essential to note that saving animals and their habitat and saving human cultures go hand in hand."[27] Despite the fact that the Maasai interpreters considered themselves to be ambassadors representing Kenyan wildlife and people, they soon found out that at the zoo, only animals can be ambassadors for the wild. Although they were not part of the animal exhibit per se, the transgression of the human-spectator/animal-subject divide and the mixing of "first" and "second" nature by the Maasai interpreters were considered intolerable by many zoos and the public.[28] Thus, most zoos avoid integrating humans in their exhibits altogether.

Seeing Nonhuman Animals

You have to try to design your zoo so . . . that people can see the animals.

Paul Harpley, Toronto Zoo[29]

[People] want to see animals, and they want to see them doing stuff, living their lives.

Susan Chin, Bronx Zoo[30]

The visual display of nonhuman animals is central to the zoo's construction of nature. This visual display also exposes an inherent contradiction in the mission of contemporary American zoos: in contrast to the old-style cage exhibits, where animals were fully and constantly exposed to the gaze of the public, a convincing nature display inevitably renders less control over the animal and thus over what zoogoers will see. Moreover, the very act of seeing animals, which is an essential component of the zoo's mission, already undermines the animal's wildness and thus the authenticity of the zoo's message.

In light of the near-consensus among zoo professionals about zoo animals being wild, how do they explain that wild animals can actually be seen in zoo exhibits? According to Tom Mason, Toronto Zoo's curator of birds and invertebrates: "The animals here allow themselves to be seen. They wouldn't allow themselves to be seen by humans, their number one predators, in the wild. But here they feel safe to show themselves. Otherwise, there would be much less sense in keeping them in captivity."[31] In other words, Mason assigns agency to the zoo animal by describing its willingness to submit itself to human inspection. Ironically, then, the animal's choice to expose itself to humans is what reifies its wildness. Clearly, this same depiction can also be interpreted as contesting the animal's wildness. These different interpretations again illustrate the zoo animal's existence in between the domesticated and the wild.[32]

Designer Susan Chin of the Bronx Zoo articulates a similar idea when explaining why her design powers are always much more limited than visitors believe. "The animals are going to do whatever the animals want to do," she says. "You can't control them, nor should you. These are wild animals. They do what they want."[33] Chin's perception that animals will only let humans see them if they wish to works around the same paradox: the paradox of wild animals displayed in captivity, seemingly the very opposite of wild. This articulation of the zoo designer's restricted powers thus reaffirms the wildness of zoo animals, while establishing that the most effective way to actually view animals is at the zoo, where various tactics and tricks make this possible.

Generally, North American zoos use three different viewing styles.[34] Stadiums for shows, by offering a spectacle for mass viewing, are the most efficient way to see zoo animals. In contrast to impersonal stadiums, museum-like displays and dioramas bring viewers up close, offering a controlled intimacy with the animal. Finally, zoo designers often break up the landscape into small niches, creating a sense of casualness that enables what feel like incidental looks that relieve the organized gaze of the stadium. Each viewing style discreetly manipulates animal and human movement to facilitate the human gaze.[35]

Alongside these general viewing styles, zoo designers have come up with an array of spatial tricks to bridge the inherent contradiction posed by the fact that seeing wild animals undermines their wildness. Architects Jones and Jones, a firm based in Seattle that specializes in zoo design, propose a number of general "viewing guidelines." These include:

1. Ensure that the animals are seen as only a part of the surrounding landscape which they co-occupy with the viewer;
2. Provide selected views only into the exhibit;
3. Augment the sense of anticipation by sequential staging of approach views before the animals are actually seen;
4. Screen out the cross-viewing of other people and exhibits;

. . . .

8. Eliminate views of animals from outside the zoo and from parking and entry areas.[36]

Ultimately, the exhibit is designed from the zoogoers' perspective—and with an eye toward optimizing viewing capacity.[37] Take the award-winning Gorilla Forest exhibit in Louisville as an example. Here is how this exhibit is described by one of its architects:

> The large wraparound porch of the Gorilla Sanctuary extends to invite you into the first expansive view of the gorilla by looking up the hill you just traversed. . . . The animal entrances into the sanctuary were purposely collected right in front of the fourteen foot tall, 1½" thick glass windows, so that the visitors can have a prime view of the

troop even when the gorillas are ready to call it a day. . . . You reach your destination under a two-story hexagonal atrium, as you are now aware of gorillas all around you through the fourteen-foot tall glass walls.[38]

The glass panel is a central feature of the Louisville exhibit and one of the more common tricks used by contemporary North American zoo designers. Adapted from aquarium design, glass panels enable visitors to get "real close, literally face-to-face, with the animal."[39] The glass also enables a variety of vantage points and a level of visual domination that could never be achieved with the old-fashioned barred cage. Animals can now be viewed from the front, side, and back, topside and bottom, thus creating a controlled intimacy between observer and observed.[40] At the same time, glass panels demarcate an absolute separation between the human and animal worlds. It is an internalization of the camera that turns animals into images.[41] The glass lets humans see without having to touch or be touched, without having to smell or be smelled. Large signs posted on glass panels throughout the Buffalo Zoo instruct visitors: "Do Not Tap on Glass"—indicating that the threat of disturbance goes both ways.

Vanishing mesh is yet another trick used at zoo exhibits to enable heightened vision. "Vanishing™ Coil Mesh—Second only to nature," reads the slogan of one of the companies that manufactures these expensive and finely woven fences.[42] While permitting an unobstructed view for zoogoers, the mesh also maintains a physical barrier to movement between various animal species and between animals and humans.

An additional tactic for the enhancement of seeing involves the placement of temperature-controlled places at strategic viewing points. This tactic attracts animals to use these spaces, in turn exposing them to the eyes of visitors. For example, exhibit designers use light to attract lizards to high visibility locations and comfortably heated resting spots for certain primates and large cats where they can be seen by visitors. Additionally, the animals' hiding places—secure niches and nesting spots—are often designed to be near windows and viewing points. According to Gwen Howard, "it's really a kind of staged reality. You force them to do the thing they would naturally do, [but to do it] in a prime viewing spot."[43]

But there is more to exhibit design than the closeness and convenience of seeing. Zoo designers create some exhibits with the intention of fostering a sense of awe and respect toward zoo animals, especially primates. This is achieved by elevating the exhibit spaces so that the human gaze is directed upward rather

Figure 6. Through the looking glass: polar bear and human family. Courtesy of Andi Norman / Toledo Zoo.

than downward. "[When] you're looking down on something, you're not fully appreciating what they are," explains designer Chin.[44] This is also important for the animals, Chin adds. "If they're up there it's really hard to get eye contact with them. But some animals, like leopards, feel better up high, so you want to give them that, you want them to feel comfortable."[45] The visual dynamics between humans and animals at the zoo are designed to promote a sense of wonder toward a remote nature that cannot be touched nor looked directly in the eye, a nature that can only be known through managed observation.

Some zoos even explicitly prescribe the sort of looks that visitors should and should not perform. A sign posted at Buffalo Zoo's gorilla exhibit instructs visitors that "staring a gorilla in the eyes is considered a threat." The sign also suggests that "if a gorilla looks your way, nod and lower your head, glance away [and] don't stare! Crouch or kneel down, so the gorilla is above or across from you, this posture puts them at ease."[46] Indeed, of all animals at the zoo, the silverback male gorilla is most likely to return the gaze.[47] Other animals tend not to return the gaze of humans that look at them. For this reason, John Berger questions the very possibility of humans to actually see animals and be seen by them at the zoo.

> The zoos cannot but disappoint. The public purpose of zoos is to offer visitors the opportunity of looking at animals. Yet nowhere in a zoo can a stranger encounter the look of the animal. At the most, the animal's gaze flickers and passes on. They look sideways. They look blindly beyond. They scan mechanically. They have been immunized to encounter, because nothing can any more occupy a central place in their attention.[48]

Despite the fancy viewing tactics and tricks, Berger believes, at the end of the day the zoo can offer no real connection between humans and animals.[49]

Seeing Through Cameras

Cameras are becoming increasingly popular in zoo design. An installment of simple web cameras, for example, can provide instantaneous and constant views of the everyday life of zoo animals. At the Toronto Zoo, the black-footed ferrets have cameras pointed at them to monitor them in their nest boxes. According to Eldon Smith of the Toronto Zoo, this form of monitoring serves conservation, education, and behavioral purposes.[50] Cameras will also be installed in Toronto's new polar bear exhibit, "so we can monitor the bears in the exhibit and see what's going on," Smith says. "You want to be able to see even though you're not there."[51] Beyond exposing animals to constant surveillance by zoo staff, cameras enable their exposure to the constant gaze of an anonymous public. For instance, the San Diego Zoo website contains live video streams from the panda bear, polar bear, elephant, and ape exhibits.[52]

The camera's vantage points and angles are configured to maximize the illusion of naturalness. It is a hidden observer that does not elicit a response from the animal filmed, but produces images as though there was no observer.[53] It follows, then, that the camera also violates the animal's normal capacity for stealth, depriving it of its own ability to see the gaze and of its agency to choose whether or not to expose itself to it.[54] As such, the camera embodies the inherent tension between authenticity and artifice. Does this mechanical reproduction result in a broader, more egalitarian, and less intrusive appreciation of animal and wildlife, or does it turn animals into yet another spectacle for the benefit of consumer culture?[55]

The reliance on enhanced forms of vision in displays of nature is not unique to zoos. It also happens, for example, in wildlife documentaries, although some have argued that seeing at the zoo is more "real." According to film and television scholar Brett Mills, for example, "There is a sense in which the narrative which commonly drives wildlife documentaries is one which is *less* realistic than that of the zoo, because such documentaries require animals to *do something*," mostly excluding "lengthy sequences of animals sleeping or sitting around."[56] Ape TAG chair Tara Stoinski comments along these lines that she often hears people express their empathy for zoo animals because they "look like they have nothing to do and are just lying around," failing to realize that "in the wild, too, these animals may take a rest after eating."[57] Cameras and television have thus transformed the way we see animals at the zoo, which is increasingly more event-driven and focused on instantaneous gratification. They have also influenced the zoo's exhibit design in myriad ways. For example, signs posted at the Buffalo Zoo instruct zoogoers where they should stand to get a good "shot." Indeed, beyond seeing with their own eyes, zoogoers increasingly see animals through the lenses of their cameras, turning the mundane urban visit into a memorable touristic event. Well-composed scenes will later remind zoogoers of their wild experience and the underlying instruction to care for nature; poorly configured visibility will shatter the illusion of wilderness.

In order to more fully understand how zoos manage the visibility of animals in their exhibit spaces, one must also take into account what happens behind the scenes: in those places where the routine human work with animals takes place.

Invisible Holding Areas

Holding areas at the zoo are strictly off-limits for zoo visitors and generally invisible to the public eye. In what follows, I examine why, in the highly visual institution that is the zoo, holding areas are nonetheless inaccessible and invisible.

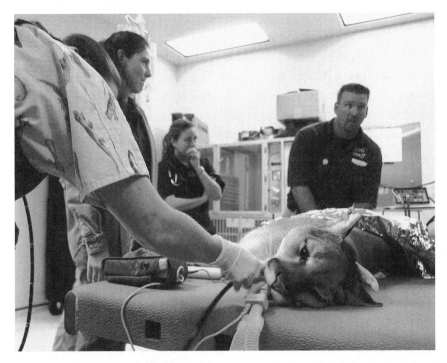

Figure 7. Behind the scenes: cougar "going under" for a routine physical exam by veterinary staff. Courtesy of Tom Gillespie / North Carolina Zoo.

Lee Ehmke of Minnesota Zoo explains that holding areas are "critically necessary [areas] for keeping the animals healthy and happy and safe in the zoo."[58] Toronto Zoo's Tom Mason explains the purpose behind the design of holding areas in more detail:

> We want to be able to lock them up at night. That's better for their own safety as well as the safety of visitors. We don't want any Joe that just happens to wander in to be attacked. We bring in birds at night, for example, otherwise other predators will eat them. I am not talking about zoo predators, because the birds are protected from those by fences and moats. I am talking about wild animals. These animals wouldn't show their face around here when there are humans around. They would come in at night only, and then we are not here to protect the animals.[59]

Zoo animals are wild, but also vulnerable to predation at night from the even wilder animals of the urban environment, necessitating nightly care and protection by humans. The zoo animal thus emerges yet again as a hybrid that exists somewhere between the categories of wild and domesticated.

Whereas the zoo's publicly visible spaces have transformed over time to exhibit naturalistic features, its invisible holding areas have arguably not changed much since the turn of the century.[60] "There is a very functional animal management routine that used to be part of what you would see in a zoo," says Ehmke.[61] "You know, the classic cat-house with an outdoor cage and an indoor cage. . . . That all still exists functionally in these new habitats, but the outdoor spaces have become much more naturalized, bigger, and more theatrical because of the message for the public."[62] An American Zoological Association conference paper dated 1995 states additionally that, "It is still the rule rather than the exception for most zoo animals to spend the greater part of each day in concrete cubes of cages."[63] A bifurcated space is thereby constructed: a visible stage outdoors, which follows a naturalistic design that hides human features, and an invisible backstage indoors, which does nothing to conceal such human management. Designer Jon Coe explains: "Consider the theatre. The public isn't allowed to see all the backstage activity because it distracts from the effectiveness of the story being told. Nor are the actors on view in their dressing rooms as they are being made up and costumed. I believe zoo animals also have a right to reduce the stress of the vast public gaze when they choose, including not having strangers invade their semi-private night quarters."[64]

The most intense form of human management that occurs in the holding areas is animal training by zoo staff. In Ehmke's words, training zoo animals

> is very important for managing the animals because the idea of just letting the animals out in a big naturalistic space is not so great. What happens when you need to check its teeth or give it a booster shot? It used to be that the only thing you could do was really stress the animal out by capturing it, or darting and immobilizing it. Today, a lot of that management comes through getting the animals to voluntarily give a blood sample or to show their teeth—[all] for a positive reward. It's a much less stressful existence for the animal [and] much less stressful for the veterinarians and the animal care staff. We do that a lot behind the scenes in zoos.[65]

Animals holding their tail out of a cage for a shot to win a positive reward in the form of a blueberry muffin are not exactly the image of wild nature that visitors expect to see at the zoo. Indeed, such everyday scenes of animal training are made invisible to the eyes of the zoo-going public. Ehmke explains that "all the management facilities—the holding areas, and the spaces for keepers—are parts that distract from the message of an animal in the environment. So I think it's basically about emphasizing the message of animals as a part of a habitat that leads to the desire to hide the infrastructure."[66]

The most striking features in holding areas are the cages, which physically dominate this space. Gwen Howard explains that whereas exhibits are made to seem boundless, holding areas are much smaller and more confined. In her words, "We design a lot of that support space almost like a battleship or submarine [so] that every inch means something. I don't want to have a luxurious mechanical room and holding area. I want to spend my five hundred dollars per square foot on stuff the public is going to see."[67] Howard's submarine image illustrates the level of functional planning, as well as the spatial and financial constraints that zoo architects must consider when designing holding areas. The physical difference between the submarine-like compactness of holding areas and the spaciousness of exhibits also illustrates another, less apparent, feature of zoos: that the naturalistic exhibit is not so much for the well-being of the animal—which spends much of its time inside the holding area anyway—as it is for the well-being of the zoo's human visitors. Roby Elsner, formerly Timmy the gorilla's keeper at the Louisville Zoo, tells me that zoo animals often prefer the enclosure of holding areas even when presented with the choice to stay in naturalistic outdoor exhibits. Timmy, for example, "preferred indoors almost always. Maybe this was a remnant of his past in Cleveland."[68]

Beyond their compactness, holding areas are also different from exhibit spaces in their routine use of artificial features. When my class visited the zoo's rainforest holding area, for example, one of the keepers explained the existence of a broom brush in some of the cages: "We put treats in [the brush], like cereal and stuff like that. It mimics a plant that they'd have to go through all the different leaves to grab different fruits or vegetables or seeds."[69] At the zoo's gorilla holding area, which we were not allowed to enter, a television set and a fish tank take up a considerable portion of the hall. "They were very interested in the fish tank for a while," the gorilla keeper informed me, "but as the novelty of it wore off, they would only look at it occasionally." As for the television, it "seems to catch their interest when there are cartoons or animal shows on, but the 'people shows' don't interest them as much."[70] The invisibility of holding areas thus enables their construction as a creative hybrid ground, where the rigid separation between humans and nonhumans is both intensified (cages) and eroded (television for gorillas).

Figure 8. Television and aquarium, gorilla holding area, August 26, 2009. Courtesy of Cyndi Griffin / Buffalo Zoo.

Because exhibit and holding spaces differ in function, two distinct professions assume responsibility for their separate design: exhibits are designed by landscape architects, and holding areas by "technical" architects. Architect Howard describes some of the manifestations of this professional and spatial split: "The exhibit architects are really good at exhibit design, [but] they are not technical architects. . . . They're not necessarily good with holding areas, [nor with] mechanical rooms and all that. . . . They couldn't do a set of stairs to save their lives. They don't know how stairs go together, they don't understand the order that things get built."[71] For the most part, Howard paints a congenial picture of the relationship between the two sub-professions. However, at times a critical tone creeps into her descriptions. "They are very talented people," she says about exhibit designers, but "they kind of treat us like we were their blue-collar cousins." In more ways than one, Howard implies, holding areas are built in the shadow of public exhibits. They exist to support the exhibit. They are the "blue-collar brothers" of the zoo's richer, larger, and publicly oriented naturalistic exhibits. Mostly as a result of their different degrees of exposure to the public eye, these two spaces also accommodate very different animal-human dynamics.

Underlying the discussion about holding areas is the assumption by zoo personnel that these areas must remain inaccessible to the public. Fernandes confirms that generally "we don't allow members of the public or press into holding areas."[72] "This is particularly true of primate holding areas," she says, "due to the risk of contamination of our primate collection with human-borne illnesses and vice versa."[73] Other North American zoos enforce similar restrictions. According to Jim Breheny of the Bronx Zoo, "For a number of reasons—including safety, security, and creating a low-stress environment for our animals when they are off exhibit—we do not permit visitors to these areas."[74] Similarly, William Rapley, executive director of conservation, education, and research at the Toronto Zoo, explains that "we generally do not take people into the holdings to reduce stress to animals from strangers, etc. In some cases, such as primates, we have disease restrictions in place. This is to prevent colds, flu, etc. from getting into our collections."[75] The fear of human-animal contamination with zoonotic disease also engenders the degree of human-animal separation that exists at the zoo exhibit. Simultaneously, the desire to immerse the visiting public in intimate experiences of nature engenders various architectural tricks to make this separation invisible.

Despite the restrictions, zoo personnel will occasionally allow public access to certain holding areas, which is how my class was able to see the broom brush at the Rainforest Falls exhibit. Toward the end of the same tour, one of my students commented that encountering the lion face to face in the holding area had been the most humbling experience in his life and that every human should have the opportunity to encounter wild animals in such proximity. Ironically, this proximity to wild animals—whereby one comes face to face with the animal's wildness with no separation but cage bars—is rarely achieved at the zoo's naturalistic public exhibit, despite all the tricks. In this sense, the older, less naturalistic, zoo exhibit might have been more effective in bringing visitors closer to wild animals and thus to nature.

Figure 9. Lion holding area, Buffalo Zoo, October 2009. Photo by author.

The Power of Seeing

In his article "Zoos and Eyes," Ralph Acampora compares the project of see-ing animals at the zoo to pornography. Zoo and porn participants, he argues provocatively, are both visual objects whose meaning is shaped predominantly by the perversions of a patriarchal gaze.[76] In Acampora's words, "Zoos are por-nographic in that they make the nature of their subjects disappear precisely by overexposing them."[77] For Acampora, the wildness of animals is negated by their observation in captivity, where their wildness cannot be expressed.

One need not adopt such a radical approach to recognize the importance of the gaze at the zoo. Michel Foucault situates the gaze at the nexus of knowledge and power. He famously applies Jeremy Bentham's panoptic design of a model prison[78] to various institutions that practice order and power over *human* bodies—for instance, the military base, the asylum, the hospital, and the school—demonstrating how these institutions use the gaze to discipline their subjects.

The gaze, Foucault asserts, is embedded within the institutional architecture so that it may function automatically. Here, from Foucault's interpretation of Bentham's panopticon:

> Hence the major effect of the Panopticon: to induce in the inmate a state of conscious and permanent visibility that assures the automatic functioning of power. . . . In view of this, Bentham laid down the principle that power should be visible and unverifiable. Visible: the inmate will constantly have before his eyes the tall outline of the central tower from which he is spied upon. Unverifiable: the inmate must never know whether he is being looked at any one moment; but he must be sure that he may always be so. The Panopticon is a machine for dissociating the see/being seen dyad: in the peripheric ring, one is totally seen, without ever seeing; in the central tower, one sees everything without ever being seen.[79]

Curiously, Bentham's architectural model was inspired by the design of Louis XIV's menagerie at Versailles, where animal stalls were enclosed by three walls, with bars facing a central pavilion from which the animals could be viewed.[80]

Is the panopticon a relevant lens through which to look at the zoo? Is the zoo yet another institution—alongside prisons and asylums—that practices power through panoptic design? Many scholars believe that the answer to both questions is no. Some even claim that vision at the zoo triggers the opposite effects of those sought by the panopticon model: through being exposed to the human gaze, animals are disciplined to *ignore* the gaze rather than to internalize it. Moreover, scholars suggest that zoos make an effort to display their animals as if they were not in captivity, so that they may engage in behaviors that spectators imagine them performing in the wild. The ultimate goal of the zoo gaze, these scholars believe, is to acculturate animals sufficiently to ignore their human spectators.[81] At the same time, the inward-focused gaze established by the panopticon might seem meaningless in the context of animals, since, unlike humans, they purportedly cannot ever be the full, realized subjects of discipline.[82]

The rhetoric of punishment associated with human prisons, too, does not fit so well in the context of zoos. "Do you think we like seeing wild animals held in captivity?" curator Mason asks me in an interview. "The animals are deprived of their individual freedom in order to save the rest of their species and even their entire habitat," he says. The animals are, in other words, subject to a collective form of incarceration: collective not in the usual sense, but in the sense that they are individually imprisoned in the name of their particular animal collective and for actions performed by another collective: humans. This form of sacrifice recalls the essential paradox of Foucault's pastoral power: the shepherd who must mediate between the needs of the individual and those of the entire flock. Finally, unlike human prisoners, who are disciplined to act normatively and rewarded when they do so, the behavior of zoo animals typically does not make a difference for the course of their captivity. As ambassadors for their species, the animals have no say in the process of their incarceration.

For these reasons, some have suggested moving beyond the paradigm of the panopticon into that of the "zoopticon"—namely, "a kind of panopticon turned inside out."[83] Others have suggested using a different framework altogether: the exhibition.[84] The exhibition model entails the transfer of bodies and objects from restricted private domains into progressively more open and public arenas. Through the exercise of power to command and arrange things and bodies for public display, exhibitionary technologies seek to enable people, en masse rather than individually, to see rather than to be seen and to know rather than to be known. At the exhibition, then, the focus is on the observer instead of on the observed. Tony Bennett further articulates this idea: "Not, then, a history of confinement but one of the opening up of objects to more public contexts of inspection and visibility: this is the direction of movement embodied in the formation of the exhibitionary complex. A movement which simultaneously helped to form a new public and inscribe it in new relations of sight and vision."[85] The exhibitionary gaze is panoramic: it focuses on how those who gaze are influenced and disciplined. Instead of the many being inspected by the few, the panoramic gaze affords the inspection of the few by the many. Thomas Mathiesen refers to this system of control of the few by the many as a "synopticon."[86]

Although both the panopticon and the exhibition (or the synopticon) models tell important parts of the story, neither fully accounts for the complexity of the human-animal gazes at the zoo. Rather than juxtaposing the panoptic and the exhibition, zoos demonstrate their interconnectivity. At the zoo, the two gazes work simultaneously. First, the traditional Foucauldian (or panoptic) gaze focuses on the body of the animal for the purpose of governing it. At the same time, the gaze is also panoramic, reflecting back upon the human masses that visit the zoo. In the context of accredited zoos in North America, the exhibitionary technology (or the synopticon) enables 175 million zoo visitors to observe 751,931 zoo animals every year.[87]

The disconnect in scholarly literature between disciplining the subjects of the gaze and disciplining those who perform the act of gazing is very much a result of Foucault's interpretation of Bentham's panopticon concept as confined to the former project. However, Bentham himself had both purposes in mind.[88] This was illustrated by Jacques-Alain Miller, Foucault's contemporary. In Miller's words, "the house of calculations, the whole of the vast, efficient system, was designed to be a school for mankind. The public was welcome to view the spectacle."[89] Miller notes five utilities that arise from the single project of opening up the prison to the public: the public receives moral education in the form of deterrence; the public receives education in economics and rationality by witnessing the functioning prison; the public's gaze into the prison acts as a form of inspection into the prison system and its guards; the public in effect becomes a multitude of guards, producing a super-control by thousands of inspectors over the prisoners; and finally, the public observation accelerates the moral improvement of prisoners as they are observed and shamed not only by guards in a distant prison colony, but by the public masses at the heart of the city.[90]

Whereas the traditional focus by the vast majority of panopticon scholars has been on disciplining the subject of the gaze, the zoo brings to the forefront the public education of the masses and their disciplining into a certain philosophy of nature and conservation. In the case of the prison, the public's gaze upon the panopticon functions through the power of deterrence and shame. By contrast, the spectacle of the zoo is meant to be powered by care and sympathy for the animals. Just as prisons in Bentham's model were located at the heart of cities where the public could observe them, zoos are located in cities so that the disciplinary power of the gaze can more effectively reach the public. David Hancocks speaks about the power of zoos to bring conservation education and ethics from the distant wilderness to the heart of the city:

> Monkeys have traditionally been represented in rows of cages . . . so that people could make comparative observations of the physical form of different species. It is within a wider definition of education that the best and most viable reason for the continuing existence of zoos can be found. They have enormous potential to shape public opinion, to encourage sympathetic attitudes toward wildlife, and to educate the public about ecology, evolution, and wild animals. Zoos can open windows to a world of Nature that people could otherwise experience only via technology.[91]

Do zoos in fact educate—or, in Foucauldian terms, discipline—their publics? Twelve AZA institutions participated in a study on the impact a zoo or aquarium visit has on the conservation knowledge and behaviors of visitors.[92] Released in 2007, the study found that the zoo visit does indeed reinforce positive feelings toward animals and the environment and helps to link caring for animals with action. The study also found that although most visitors do not necessarily leave zoos with more knowledge of conservation and ecology, they do leave with motivation to conserve nature.[93] Whereas once zoos were in the business of entertainment through taxonomic exhibitions, now they discipline the public into caring about nature.

Conclusion: Seeing and Care

Kristen Lukas, Gorilla SSP coordinator and curator of conservation and science at the Cleveland Metroparks Zoo, describes the conversation she held with her son after watching a heart-wrenching National Geographic documentary about gorillas. Acknowledging the power of this medium, she found herself wondering about the role of zoos in today's society, and so she asked her son,

> "If you were going to tell someone else about how incredible gorillas are, would you have them watch this movie or would you take them to the zoo?" Without hesitating, he said, "I'd take them to the zoo." And I said, "Why?" And he's seven, and he was like, "when you're watching them on TV, you're seeing them through someone else's eyes, but when you're at the zoo, you're actually seeing them with your own eyes." I was, like, "Wow."[94]

This discussion highlights the intense connections between the zoo's project of seeing animals and its mission of caring for animals and nature. At the zoo, heightened vision is a tool for disciplining zoogoers into a particular conservation etiquette that relies on carefully drawn associations between zoo and wild animals, and between the conduct of zoogoers and that of an abstract human collective. By inspiring their visitors to care for wildlife, zoos also delegate their own power of care to the public. And as care by zoos is bestowed upon both individual animals and the flock, the public, too, is educated to care for both the single animal subject and the entire flock. Human zoogoers are thus disciplined by the zoo's institutional gaze to become caregivers—or, in Foucauldian terms, shepherds. In the words of Pat Thomas, general curator at the Bronx Zoo: "Seeing and hearing and smelling an animal and seeing it interact with others of its own kind, or [with] other species in some instances, can inspire care in a way that no reading about it in a book or seeing it on TV will ever do."[95]

Although zoogoers and zoo personnel probably experience the act of seeing animals in similar ways, their interpretations of this act and its manifestations beyond the moment of vision are fundamentally different. For zoogoers, seeing is typically either an end in itself—a mere spectacle—or a necessary stage toward education. For zoo personnel, however, seeing is always more than a spectacle: it is the foundation of effective knowledge about zoo animals. Specifically, seeing is a precursor to a comprehensive project of management by zoos that includes naming the animal, identifying it, documenting its properties, registering it into various databases, and, finally, making decisions about the animal's life and death. Seeing the body of the animal is thus fundamental for its scientific governance by the institution of captivity.

CHAPTER FOUR

Naming Zoo Animals

To observe, then, is to be content with seeing—with seeing a few things
systematically. With seeing what, in the rather confused wealth of
representation, can be analyzed, recognized by all, and thus given a name
that everyone will be able to understand.

Michel Foucault, The Order of Things[1]

And out of the ground the Lord God formed every beast of the field, and
every fowl of the air; and brought them unto Adam to see what he would
call them: and whatsoever Adam called every living creature, that was the
name thereof. And Adam gave names to all cattle, and to the fowl of the air,
and to every beast of the field.

Genesis 2:19–20[2]

The shepherd manages his flock through a systematic gaze that translates into
knowing each sheep individually and, in turn, naming it. In the Bible, the power
to name all animals was given to Adam by God—the ultimate shepherd—who
created and physically brought to Adam all of the animals for a daylong naming
ceremony conducted under his direct supervision. The zoo's comprehensive
naming practices can be viewed as an extension of Adam's task and as one of the
prerequisites for the capacity to care for and, at the same time, manage and control the animal kingdom.

At the zoo, however, naming is not an end in itself. The animal's name serves to
abstract it beyond the particular space and moment of its encounter with humans.
The link between the animal's body and its name is established through the project
of identification. Once identification has occurred, information can be recorded
and managed efficiently, extending beyond the individual animal and even beyond
the zoo it inhabits. Specifically, animal bodies can then be translated into abstract
data entries and inscribed onto two-dimensional formats, based on which a sys-

tematic recording of relevant information can be achieved. Finally, zoos can reapply this information to the animal body as part of their power of care.

The power of the shepherd to care for his flock—pastoral power—is only possible when the shepherd is in close proximity to a manageable number of sheep. Such proximity promises a direct, intimate, and individualistic form of care that is different from the "politician's rule." In Foucault's words, "Do you think that the politician could lower himself, could quite simply have the time, to act like the shepherd, or like the doctor, the teacher, or the gymnast, and sit down beside every citizen to advise, feed, and look after him?"[3] According to Foucault, this capacity to care on an individual level is also what distinguishes pastoral power from the power of the sovereign.

In addition to caring for their animals individually, zoos must also know their populations on a collective scale. The flock of animals housed in accredited North American zoos is vastly more complex than the traditional shepherd's flock: in September 2011, the zoo flock contained not only sheep, but 6,000 unique species and 751,931 individual animals, dispersed in 225 institutions throughout the United States and six other countries.[4] In order to execute such an intimate project of governance on this large scale, zoos must collect information about their animals and translate this information into legible records that can then be transferred between them, apart from the animals' bodies.

Record keeping is a constantly evolving process. Since 2010, accredited North American zoos have been transitioning from the older Animal Records Keeping System (ARKS) database to the new Zoological Information Management System (ZIMS). ZIMS is a sophisticated computer software system that is intended to "create natural order" through a systematic organization and centralization of information about zoo animals worldwide.[5] The move from ARKS to ZIMS represents both a technical and a qualitative shift: it marks the entry of zoos into a new and different form of surveillance,[6] one that focuses on simulation, on the replacement of actual with virtual processes and on various devices for encoding and decoding information.[7] Through this change, zoos have also shifted their center of calculation—namely, the location where the accumulation, synthesis, and analysis of observations takes place[8]—into a more abstract, centralized, and globalized domain. By the same token, the body of the captive animal is increasingly supplanted with its coded records. Through enhancing the ability of zoos to collaborate on a global level, ZIMS thus provides an effective tool for the globalization of animal bodies. Borrowing from discussions of human surveillance, the detailed form of surveillance established through the collection, maintenance, and management of data is referred to here as "dataveillance."[9]

Naming Humans and Racehorses

It has long been acknowledged that the governance of large human populations by nation-states requires assigning individuals with uniquely identifiable names.[10] Historically, the requirement for first and family names, or personal names, originated as a prerequisite for the execution and expansion of the modern tax system.[11] In addition to their function as official identifiers for human individuals, personal names are often embedded with intimate information about relationships and circumstances.

In his work *The Savage Mind*, Claude Lévi-Strauss points to the categorical meaning of personal names—or what he calls "proper names." Lévi-Strauss suggests that these names "form the fringe of a general system of classification: they are both its extension and its limits."[12] Indeed, proper names are similar to species names in that they serve not only to classify but also to mark the outer boundaries of classification. But unlike species names, proper names signify a class with only one member.[13] Mary Phillips argues, accordingly, that "in using proper names, we socially construct individuals and create a narrative account of the meaning of their lives."[14] Increasingly, the process of naming has become the foundation for a much broader and more elaborate assemblage of identification regimes. To overcome the difficulties of distinguishing between individuals with identical proper or personal names, a parallel use of corresponding numbers—for example, social security, date of birth, and credit card numbers—now forms the basis for the contemporary project of governing humans.[15]

Not unlike humans, animals have long been subjected to various types of naming regimes.[16] Racehorses provide a particularly good example of an elaborate use of naming and registration. In the United States, thoroughbred horses—a breed best known for their use in horse racing—are required to have precise genealogies and unique names documented in a centralized registry. The act of registration draws a genealogical connection to a history of sires, dams, and births in particular moments in time and space. All modern thoroughbreds can trace their pedigrees to three stallions, originally imported into England from North Africa and the Middle East at the turn of the seventeenth century, and to a larger number of foundation mares of mostly English breeding. A fifteen-point list enumerates types of inadmissible names, including those over eighteen letters or those that end in a horse-related term.[17]

In Canada, the Canadian Horse Breeders Association ensures diverse and unique names by requiring a three-name convention. First, the foal is assigned a registered herd name, which refers to the breeding program and is commonly the farm name. Second, the horse is assigned a sire name that is similar to that of the siring stallion. Finally, the foal's given name is designated with a letter for the year in which it was born: 2011 foals will start with Y, 2012 with Z, and 2013 with A. Thus, any Canadian horse breeder could infer a horse's birthplace, sire, and age from its name.[18] North American zoo professionals prefer to refer to proper or common names as "house names." As in the case of thoroughbred horses, the naming and registration process performed by zoos aspires to trace zoo animals back to their founders from the wild.

Naming Zoo Animals

Any living thing that has been found, and seen, and identified has a name.

Jean Miller, Buffalo Zoo registrar[19]

Alongside the scientific classification of zoo animals within their taxonomic categories, such as species and subspecies (as discussed in Chapter 2), zoo animals are also subject to individual naming systems, which include house names and a variety of identification numbers. These different forms of naming operate simultaneously and serve different purposes in that they offer distinct types of information about the animal on different scales. As with human names, proper or house animal names are a way to both confer relational and contextual information about the animal and to identify individual animals.

Many zoo animals are given house names, whether by staff to differentiate between animals, by the zoo to entice the public to relate to the animals, or even by the public to increase interest in the zoo and raise donations. When keepers give animals their house names, the purpose is to make remembering and referring to certain animals easier. Fernandes of the Buffalo Zoo explains that "house names are typically used to simplify communication among individuals (keepers, curators, vets) who might find it difficult to remember lengthy individual accession numbers for all specimens, e.g. a keeper reporting to the vet that Sydney had loose stool that morning."[20] Although insufficient for animal identification in formal records, and thus ineffective for governing zoo populations on a larger scale, house names are popular features in today's zoos. This popularity serves to illustrate that naming is not merely a technical process, but that it also holds powerful emotional properties for the humans involved. Rachél Watkins Rogers, registrar at Zoo Miami, offers another reason why zoos use house names: "The public loves it. They want to see Fluffy the tiger. They want to see Jojo the lion."[21] Jean Miller, the Buffalo Zoo's registrar, suggests similarly that "the gorillas, the elephants, the rhinos, the giraffes—as well as the very public tigers and lions—they get [house] names because the public can relate to them much better this way."[22]

The curators or keepers usually decide the animal's house name, which expresses their intimate bond with the animal. This, for example, is how a new gorilla at the Buffalo Zoo received its name: "We called her Aunt Bumpy because when she first came in she was just getting over chicken pox so she had bumps all over her face—so she was the bumpy one. They then decided to call her *Aunt* Bumpy because she became the aunt of the offspring of her sister here. So before she had offspring of her own, she was the aunt of the other ones."[23] In this example, the house name derives from the animal's particular physical features (bumpy), as well as its anthropomorphized family relations (aunt). Performed by zoo personnel as an intimate act, this form of naming makes the most sense to them and to their affiliates at the zoo.

However, zoos may also choose names with a meaning that is intended for zoogoers and the public. In 2009, the Buffalo Zoo named its new baby giraffe Malia, after the oldest daughter of President Barack Obama. According to Fernandes, "The young female calf was the first daughter born to mother Akili and arrived very close to the inauguration date of the new president. The zoo's intent was to honor the first family, since giraffes are a symbol of grounded vision and farsightedness."[24] Despite the zoo's respectful intentions, many people were upset by this decision. Typical of the comments was, "I don't think the First Lady and President of the United States of America gave their children names that should be transferred to a four-legged animal." The zoo responded by saying that many animals have been named after famous people and that two other giraffes were named after Goldie Hawn and Clint Eastwood. However, in light of the intense responses, the zoo eventually retracted the name.[25]

Until recently, it was customary to give animals common American names, such as Timmy and Kate for gorillas. Nowadays, however, it is fashionable to give zoo animals names that evoke an association with their wild origins. For example, most of Timmy's offspring were named in Swahili: Ngoma (drums or celebration) was the name given to the first of Timmy's twins, and Kumi (ten) was the name given to his tenth offspring. Likewise, San Diego Zoo's elephants were given names derived from South African languages, accompanied by nicknames and pronunciation guides: Mabhulane the Proud Papa, Swazi the Fearful Leader, Umoya the Spitfire, Litsemba the Drama Queen, and Umngani (oom-Gah-nee) the Diva.[26]

In addition to its function in associating the zoo animal with its purported wild origins, public participation in zoo animal naming is a common way to raise interest and funds. The San Diego Zoo houses three giant pandas with Chinese names: Yun Zi, Gao Gao, and Bai Yun. Yun Zi's name (Son of Cloud) was chosen from a list of five by 17,521 votes from zoogoers and is a tribute to his mother, Bai Yun (White Cloud). His naming ceremony was an excellent opportunity for public relations and diplomacy with invited guests from the Chinese consulate.[27] In another example, this time from the Toronto Zoo, over eleven thousand people cast their votes as to what the zoo's baby gorilla should be called. The zoo stipulated that the name had to start with the letter N, which is the first letter of his mother's name, Ngozi. Zoo staff and kids whittled nearly five thousand different names down to a list of ten. Then the public voted to shorten the list to five: Nassir, Neo, Nico, Nigel, and Nsambu. The five selections were placed at separate stations, each containing a treat, for father-gorilla Charles to choose from. Under the observing gaze of a large and rapt audience, the suspicious gorilla finally "selected" the name of his first son by taking a treat from the closest station.[28]

At the Tennessee Aquarium, more than eight hundred names were submitted during a contest for naming the youngest female gentoo penguin born at the aquarium. In January 2011, the aquarium's aviculturists decided to name the animal Shivers and publicized this decision alongside information on limited penguin "encounter" tours for fifteen dollars.[29] Similarly, the Los Angeles Zoo offers "animal naming opportunities" to the public: for donations of one thousand to fifty thousand dollars, the zoo will name certain animals according to the choice of the donor. From the zoo's website: "A program of imperial distinction, the animal naming program provides groups and individuals an opportunity to develop a deeper connection with a Zoo resident while supporting the Zoo's animal acquisition fund, which promotes vital wildlife preservation and breeding projects here and around the world." The website further suggests that donors can name their own "wild child."[30] A list of the already named animals includes "Dauna Borska: A flamingo, named in honor of her life love, her aunts, uncles, and cousins."[31] A final example of naming zoo animals is from the Bronx Zoo. In 2011, this zoo came out with a "Limited-time Valentine's Day offer." Using the banner "Flowers wilt. Chocolates melt. Roaches are forever," the zoo was able to persuade almost six thousand people to name its Madagascar hissing cockroaches after their loved ones for a nominal fee.[32]

What can be learned from this human fascination with naming zoo animals? Four points come to mind. First, that the selected names often hint at the animal's perceived origin in the wild—for example, Shivers (presumably because penguins originate from cold climates), and Nassir (an Arabic name that connotes the African origin of the gorilla). Despite their exotic names, however, most of these zoo animals have never set foot (or flipper) outside the United States. Using animal names that are associated with the animal's region in the wild thus serves to both assert and naturalize the connection between the captive and the wild animal. Naturalize, in this sense, means to make the connection seem as if the named captive animal is simply and directly connected with the animals in the region from which its name is derived. The choice of geography-oriented names may also explain why some people took offense at the Buffalo Zoo's naming of an African American giraffe after an African American girl, in this case the U.S. president's daughter. The comment cited here suggests that it is offensive to conflate humans with animals, especially if the two have the same perceived geographic origin.

A second reason for the popularity of house names for zoo animals is the *paternal* relationship of care and power established through the act of naming, as implied in the Los Angeles Zoo's project of naming one's "wild child." By enabling their visitors to name these wild animals / children, zoos attempt to draw the visitors closer both to zoo animals and to the wild. This act fulfills two needs: it promotes the zoo's educational message, and it raises money. Indeed, caring for the animal occurs through knowing, classifying, and consuming it, all packaged together through the act of buying its name. Naming, in other words, is an instance of caring for the animal and thus of exerting pastoral power over it. Furthermore, the donation-by-naming scheme serves to extend the pastoral power of care for an animal from the zoo's caregivers to the naming public. By participating in the naming event, then, the public gets to experience the satisfaction that comes from this intimate act of control over animals.

Third, the Toronto Zoo's attempts to democratize the naming process exemplify the deep human desire to anthropomorphize animals. In this instance, the zoo involved not only the general public but also the animal itself in the selection of its baby gorilla's name. The father gorilla was portrayed as exercising agency by naming his son, albeit within the confines of the five options given to him. Since naming is considered a profoundly human (and divine) prerogative, the assumption that the animal would want to name its own offspring is a projection of human conceit onto the animal world. In some instances, however, animals have failed to cooperate. For example, the National Zoo's octopus neglected to grab any of the names offered to it in plastic balls.[33]

Finally, the act of naming zoo animals with house names can establish a bond between the human caretaker and its animal. In many instances, animals that are assigned house names can respond to their names, seemingly confirming this bond. Mary Phillips observes, "we produce biographies for some animals, and these are the animals we name: pets, race horses, prize bulls, Bambi."[34] Miller points out along these lines that a herd of roan antelopes will probably not be given house names as "they don't come when you call their names."[35] Indeed, zoos do not name every zoo animal. According to Fernandes, "House names are generally given to species that can be easily distinguished (facial features, coat patterns, or large identifiers such as ear tags). It is simply harder to distinguish individuals in a tank full of cichlids or [in a] case full of cockroaches."[36] The Bronx Zoo episode provides a humorous twist on the traditional act of naming in zoos. In this instance, cockroaches were presented as being just as nameable as giraffes, penguins, and gorillas. This is the exception, though, as smaller or less popular animals—such as fish, spiders, frogs, and cockroaches—are typically not assigned house names. This does not necessarily reflect a value judgment, only a different method of ordering these animals.[37] The animals too numerous to be named are instead counted and numbered.

Naming Through Numbers

Unlike giving animals house names, naming by numbers is not an expression of intimacy but rather a formal way to codify the animals for the purpose of their accurate identification, recording, and tracking in the zoo's institutional records. According to Jean Miller, the first number identification system used by North American zoos was based on a sequential count of female and male zoo animals. "For a while, the record was always based on tag number such and such, in the right ear. [But] you ran out of tag numbers, you ran out of tag colors. So they decided—well, maybe we'll call this 'number 1 male.' And that's the way our system evolved. . . . From about the 1960s to the 1970s that's how they were identified here: m1, m12, f5—down the line."[38] However, in light of the growing numbers of animals at zoos, the simple sequential numbering system soon reached its limit as well. According to Miller, "They saw this record for m1, [but] is this the gorilla record or is it the roan antelope record? So they thought, 'ugh, this isn't going to work.' You know, because you've got a piece of paper lying there, 'keeper reports that m1 did such and such.' [But], which m1 are you talking about? *So we needed something more.*"[39] This "something more" was the addition of certain letters—*b* for bird, *r* for reptile, etc.—to the previous male/female numbering system, thereby applying a limited version of Linnaean taxonomy to classify the animal.

The process of digitizing information by zoos has given rise to yet another naming/numbering system. Until recently, the most comprehensive computerized database system for zoo animals was the Animal Records Keeping System (ARKS) designed by the International Species Information System (ISIS). Founded in 1973, "ISIS provides world-standard zoological data collection and sharing software to more than 800 member zoos, aquariums and related organizations in almost 80 countries. The ISIS global database for the zoological community contains information on 2.6 million animals—10,000 species—and is constantly growing."[40] An ARKS record has two parts: the zoo's name and the animal's assigned number; so, for example, an animal at the Buffalo Zoo or the Bronx Zoo "is always identified as Buffalo123 or Bronx123."[41]

But basing animal identification on an institutional name proved to be problematic in the new zoo world, where multi-institutional breeding projects require that captive animals be made more mobile and more identifiable than ever before. As a result, a comprehensive system of naming and recording zoo animals is currently in the works: the Zoological Information Management System (ZIMS). ZIMS is supposed to eventually replace the ARKS institution-based naming system of animals with "a randomly generated [and global] nine-digit number."[42] This form of naming is referred to as a "global accession number."

Even prior to the development of ARKS, the studbook provided an elementary database for the collective management of zoo animals. Still today, a zoo animal studbook details the lineage, location, transaction history, and even the reproductive capabilities of each collectively managed animal.[43] The studbook is developed for a single animal species, and the studbook keeper assigns each animal in that species a unique studbook number. Certain captive animals may be given a number for an AZA studbook and another number for an international studbook managed in cooperation with other zoo associations around the world. The AZA and international studbook keepers often cooperate so as to generate identical studbook numbers and to ensure data consistency. Nowadays, the registration in studbooks serves mostly to calculate the degree to which the zoo animal's genes are related to the genes of other individuals within its species.

Despite the house names, codes and numbers for institutional records, veterinary records, and studbooks, zoos and zookeepers would still not be able to determine which animal is which without asserting a clear link between the name and the particular body it inscribes. These acts of translation from the animal's body to the record, and vice versa, are referred to here as "identification."

Identifying Zoo Animals

At the zoo, naming is tied to the ability to identify and thereby to record and track zoo animals. For a name to function as an identifier, a link must somehow be made between the written record and the physical animal to which this record applies. The material body of the animal is thus still a necessary component of its abstracted inscription.[44] Judith Block, registrar emeritus of the Smithsonian's National Zoo, further addresses this point:

> I always tell the story of the time I went over to the monkey house and asked which one was [the] mom, and one person called her "Spook" and the other one called her "Martha" and someone else called her something else. . . . They couldn't match up this animal with that record because the culture was all verbal. [Indeed, if] you didn't identify the animal with some tag or unique identifier what would happen is you would lose track of what animal went with which record. . . . *You needed to have something that matched the record with the animal.*[45]

As long as both keepers and animals were relatively stationary and the project of governing zoo animals was performed on an institutional scale, the personalized identification process sufficed: the link between name and body was made on a personal level and was based on direct forms of observation. The use of physical identifiers, such as scars or particular hair length and color, was then an effective form of identification. According to Jean Miller,

> Male lions have different manes, and some of them will have tufts of hair that stick up in this place or that place [and] that don't in other ones that you see. And you have to remember that you're looking at your collection. You're not looking at every single lion in North America. If you were looking at a facial photo of each gorilla, you may be able to identify one from the other.[46]

However, the changes in inter-zoo relations and the increased movement of zoo animals between zoos rendered this personalized form of identification ineffective. As part of their move toward global conservation in the last several decades, zoos have thus begun to create a more reliable link between the written record and the animal body. For Shivers and the other penguins at the Tennessee Aquarium, this entails wearing red flipper bands to enable the tracking of individuals and genealogies. This form of identification facilitates the surveillance of reproduction in a group of similar animals by accurately identifying and selecting the one pair of penguins with suitable genetic diversity to breed, which results in replacing the eggs of all other pairs with artificial replicas.[47]

But even the enhanced identification system proved insufficient for the global collective management system. Zoos wanted an identification system that would be more reliable than flipper bands or other external tags, which can be lost or misread. RFID, or radio-frequency identification, was thus introduced into the zoo world. This technology consists of a coded microchip, which is inserted into the body of the animal and read by means of a hand-sized "reader" device. The chip's number is entered into the record by the institution that inserted it, and the same chip stays with the animal for as long as it lives. "You're told not to reuse them on a different animal," explains Miller. "You don't ever want to risk the chance that [microchip] such and such that was in a fish is now in a turtle."[48] RFID technology thus enables unmistakable animal identification by securing a match between the animal and its data.

In another animal context, concerns over the identification of high-value animals and over food security and contamination have prompted the application of multiple animal identification technologies. Companies such as Global Animal Management offer centralized databases for life histories, ownership, and immunization records linked to RFID tags in everything from catfish to cattle.[49] Tags are also increasingly used for family pets, gaining publicity with stories of lost dogs being found and identified after years astray.[50] These applications have not been overlooked by ZIMS, which is currently being designed to incorporate inventories of RFID chip numbers.[51]

Recently, the use of RFID has expanded from the project of governing animals of various types to that of governing humans in certain situations. Specifically, RFID has been applied to scrutinize the movement of human employees and to monitor money transfers, medical records, and passport details.[52] Precision Dynamics Corporation makes RFID wristbands for children to wear in theme parks, enabling them to purchase food and beverages with money deposited into an account linked to the wristband and to be identified if they are lost.[53] At the same time, such bands also make it possible to track the children's movements through the park.

In the human context, the microchip is commonly inserted into a keycard or an identification card rather than directly into the body, but there are indications that this might be changing. In 2004, the VeriChip Corporation (since 2009, the PositiveID™ Corporation) received approval from the U.S. Food and Drug Administration to market a human chip implant in the United States within specific guidelines.[54] In 2007, it was revealed that nearly identical implants caused cancer in hundreds of laboratory animals. This discovery had a devastating impact on this corporation's stock price.[55] In 2011, the corporation had completed development of an "implantable RFID glucose-sensing microchip" called GlucoChip, "which will accurately measure glucose levels in individuals with diabetes," paving the way to use RFID not only for identification purposes but also for acquiring biological data on individuals.[56]

The use of RFID technology demonstrates two interrelated points. First, it illustrates the dependence of current surveillance systems on machines to inscribe discrete observations.[57] Indeed, machines increasingly replace the earlier forms of panoptic technologies analyzed by Foucault, which relied more heavily on direct visual observation by humans. Second, the RFID example shows that although surveillance technologies may be perceived as benign in the animal context, once developed for animals they can easily creep into more problematic human contexts.[58] Improving technologies in the world of animal surveillance can therefore set the stage for similar projects in the context of human surveillance. Scholars have pointed to the inevitable consequences of this technological creep: "In the face of multiple connections across myriad technologies and practices, struggles against particular manifestations of surveillance, as important as they might be, are akin to efforts to keep the ocean's tide back with a broom . . . while the general tide of surveillance washes over us."[59]

Despite its reliability, RFID technology is usually not used in large groups of small animals such as frogs or fish. "You have to remember that this chip costs a dollar or two," Miller points out.[60] "Plus, that keeper or vet [doesn't always have the] time to catch the fish, to handle it properly, and to inject the transponder. You could do that, but we don't, normally."[61] The alternative technique used for counting large groups, Miller notes, "is to take a photo, blow it up, and then have somebody count the animals."[62] The identification of smaller animals thus usually takes place on a broader, less intimate scale that is mostly concerned with determining quantity and group patterns rather than individual behaviors. As technologies improve, however, RFID projects are becoming more prevalent and are even available to the public in aquarium displays:

> The Virginia Aquarium & Marine Science Center . . . names each fish swimming within its 45,000-gallon Chesapeake Bay tank. . . . With an RFID system now in place, . . . aquarium visitors can [identify] such individuals as "Ted the black drum fish" and [view] where that particular fish was collected from the wild, its size and growth history, and its species characteristics—all displayed on a 23-inch video monitor as the fish drifts by within the tank.[63]

Although ostensibly technical and neutral, the application of different identification technologies to different animals belies a certain value-based categorization of these animals. The more important the individual animal is to the zoo, the more heavily named, identified, and subject to surveillance it will be. Similar to the work of classification, the technology by which this naming operates valorizes certain animals over others. In the human context, too, surveillance scholars have warned about categorical choices that, although purporting to be merely technical, are also inherently ethical.[64]

Dataveillance: From A(RKS) to Z(IMS)

> Computers have made coding, viewing, storing, and recalling information
> on persons, events, and everything in general, faster and more efficient,
> and as each day thousands more computers are added to the existing web
> of networks, sharing and comparing information becomes easier.
>
> William Bogard, *The Simulation of Surveillance*[65]

> ISIS hopes to revolutionize worldwide animal conservation efforts with the
> introduction of a Web-based animal knowledge management tool.
>
> ISIS Newsroom[66]

In the past, animal record keeping by zoos—when it existed—was mostly an internal endeavor performed by individual zoos. As such, it focused on the individual animal and varied from zoo to zoo. Increasingly, however, advances in computer database systems enable a more global and standardized animal record. For the past several decades, the collaboratively produced ARKS served as the central animal database among zoos from around the world. Each ARKS entry contained basic information about the captive animal: its scientific and common names and identifiers, its sex, and its birth date. Recently, this database was fully incorporated into ZIMS and, as of 2011, it contains records on 2.6 million animals (374,000 currently living), comprising more than ten thousand species.[67]

Under the previous system, zoos could record as little or as much as they wanted, and there was no way to inspect the reliability of this information. Also, it was up to the recording zoo to decide whether to make the institutional record of the animal available to other zoos, as the records were stored locally. When the zoo did make information available, it was usually transmitted through hardcopy reports that were shipped together with the transferred animal. Nonetheless, the ARKS database enabled global electronic access to basic information on zoo animals worldwide. For example, anyone with access to this system could find out, in a matter of seconds, how many gorillas were held at a certain point in time in zoos around the world (but not much more than that).

Alongside the ARKS animal database, ISIS also maintains the Medical Animal Records Keeping System (MedARKS) database, which supports animal health and treatment data, and the Single Population Animal Records Keeping System (SPARKS) software, which supports studbook management and species analysis used by hundreds of studbook keepers worldwide. Miller says about ARKS and MedARKS that "you have two separate databases, and they don't really talk. I can't import information medically into the ARKS record. They can't import information about the animals . . . to the MedARKS."[68] More broadly, zoo administrators became frustrated with the fragmentation and incompatibility of databases from individual institutions as well as the division of functions and records among the three separate systems: ARKS for institutional records, MedARKS for veterinary records, and SPARKS for studbooks and population analysis. ISIS project managers also criticized these programs, saying that "although ISIS is dedicated to serving the zoological community, it is a small, member-owned non-profit organization that has not been able to keep pace with the technological advancements in information management and does not have the resources to ensure the accuracy of the records it receives."[69]

In recent years, this system of record keeping has become too cumbersome for the collective global management of animals. ZIMS was designed to integrate both the institutional databases and the separate functional systems into modules within one centralized and global database system. For example, a veterinary module in ZIMS will soon replace the MedARKS database.[70] ZIMS will thus centralize what were previously separate databases for institutional records, veterinary records, and studbooks. With ZIMS, Rogers says, "you'll be able to see *all* the systems in *one* record."[71]

After extensive delays and institutional changes, in March 2010 the first stage of ZIMS was released for use by a test group of eighteen zoos. According to ISIS, all member zoos are scheduled for ZIMS deployment by January 2013.[72] Here is an early definition of the project and its significance by some of the zoo professionals involved:

> Our zoological institutions are very reliant on information to provide adequate animal care and participate in conservation programs. We cannot afford to lose any more time in bringing our information technology and data management practices up to speed. *It is extremely important to the management of our collections that we share data globally and that we have confidence in the quality of the data.* . . . What is needed is the immediate development of a *global animal management database* that is Web-enabled and contains up-to-the-minute information that is *both accurate and secure.* Although the database must be flexible enough to meet specific regional needs, there must still be a central, "core" database that allows free and easy exchange of information between all participants.[73]

The above quote highlights the urgent need for change in animal database management. Indeed, zoo personnel interviewed for this project have described the new ZIMS database as potentially transformative, even revolutionary, for their work. For example, Rachél Rogers of Zoo Miami excitedly notes that with ZIMS, animals will be recorded "in real time."[74] By this she means that information will be updated on the software directly rather than through the zoo's institutional records.[75] Such a move toward a direct system of management will provide instant global access to animal documentation—an expansion and acceleration of the geographies of documentation and control of animals.

ZIMS records will not only be available in real time, they will also be available in full to all institutions connected to the database, greatly simplifying animal transfers between these institutions. Additionally, the animal's identity will no longer be created by registrars at particular institutions and tied to the animal's physical presence there (as in "Buffalo123"), but will instead be established through a fixed global accession number that will accompany it through life. In other words, rather than depending on individual institutions to properly identify and transmit records for each animal transfer or loan, zoos will now have an international form of identification for their animals—a global passport, if you will. This improved procedure will more closely track and thus facilitate the increasing movement of animals between zoos, while eliminating any gaps of knowledge that previously existed along the way.

Jean Miller suggests that ZIMS will also dictate certain data standards, resulting in a more reliable and ready-to-use system.[76] Finally, ZIMS will offer a range of graphic options. "We will be able to link photographs, digital photographs, and digital X-rays to their master record," Miller says, adding that "right now we have to wait for a birth in order to create a record. . . . But with ZIMS we'll be able to track that fetus for the twenty-two months [of being in the womb]. . . . You'll [also] be able to upload, store, and link to sonograms. So when you first see a baby elephant by sonogram, that will be the start of that baby's record."[77] This example illustrates how technological advancements in data management affect the nature of record keeping at the zoo, extending not only the geographies of animal management but also its temporalities.

The globalization of digital data records and physical animal bodies is expected to open up new prospects of collaboration between zoos worldwide, hence adding to the ever-increasing globalization of these animal bodies. Whereas previously, international collaboration required using informal means to acquire information (for example, a telephone call to the Copenhagen zoo to follow up on rumors that they own genetically relevant cheetahs),[78] it will now be possible to obtain all necessary information about the identity, location, and genetic and demographic properties of zoo animals worldwide by a simple click of a mouse. "If, for example, we need new cheetahs in our North American zoo collection," AZA's vice president Paul Boyle tells me, "we check on ZIMS and find out that Copenhagen has a large group of cheetahs."[79] Once mostly confined to animals in North American and European zoos, the project of naming, identifying, and finally recording zoo animals is expanding to include all major zoos in the world.

Some zoo personnel are daunted by the regulatory hurdles involved in trans-ferring animals on a global scale. "In my vision of the future," Boyle says in re-sponse, "zoos will be exempt from this complicated permit process because they work for the public good and for conservation."[80] But even streamlined permit systems and instantaneous data access will not make the task of transferring a four hundred-pound silverback gorilla long distance much easier, nor will they help acclimate him to a new environment and social group. However, with the current pace of scientific progress, it may soon be unnecessary to move the entire body of the animal in order to breed it: freezing and transferring its gametes may suffice.[81]

The extensive reliance on databases and computer systems by modern proj-ects of governance has attracted the attention of surveillance scholars, who have coined the term "dataveillance" to describe this shift in the mode of sur-veillance.[82] Until now, this term has only been used in the human context, thereby ignoring its applicability to governing nonhumans. The human con-text can nonetheless provide some insight as to the nature and dangers of in-tensified dataveillance in the context of captive animals. Some scholars have warned, for example, that an intense reliance on computerized data systems might lead to new and more serious prospects of error: "Dataveillance relies on conscientious and accurate data input by a widely dispersed and uncoordi-nated network. . . . Each keystroke contains possibilities of errors, some of which can have monumental consequences."[83] Depending on one's viewpoint about the moral status of animals vis-à-vis humans, this prospect of error may or may not be alarming.

Zoos have come up with various recommendations on how to circumvent such errors. "Despite the best intentions," reads the Standards for Data Entry and Maintenance of North American Zoo and Aquarium Animal Records Databases©,

> individual identification sometimes becomes muddled. For example, naked mole rats or antelopes may lose their tags. Another common scenario is waterfowl and softbill birds on large ponds or big aviaries, where some individuals disappear . . . some lose bands, and some unbanded birds are added through birth. When the error in indi-vidual identification rises above 5–10% of the specimens in the enclosure, and proba-bly can't be resolved in a reasonable amount of time, it is best to move all unidentifi-able specimens to a group record.[84]

Database administrators and small-population biologists recognize the fallibility of human record keeping, tagging, and banding, and the tendency for animals to hide nests and eggs in an enclosure. They know that erroneous data, generated due to uncertain identities and genealogies, can undermine small population analysis and breeding programs by inadvertently allowing the inbreeding of animals or incorrectly estimating the birth, reproduction, and longevity of a species. Therefore, they advise keepers to leave gaps in data or aggregate records for individuals into groups, rather than entering guesses or estimates.

Conclusion

In a study on lab animals, scholar Mary Phillips shows how these animals can either be nameable or unnameable, stating that when they are unnameable they are typically assigned unique numbers. "For scientists," Phillips says, "these are mutually exclusive categories."[85] Only those lab animals with histories and biographies that extend beyond the necessities of experimentation are given names. At the zoo, however, the nameable animal acquires multiple names: the same animal serves as a specimen of a particular species for the scientist, as an endeared house animal for zookeepers and the public, as a number for the registrar and studbook keeper, and as a much larger and randomized set of numbers for international database administrators.

The zoo's multilayered naming system is a result of the historical development of animal names in the zoo world. Animal names began as personalized house names that referenced the genealogy, individual characteristics, and geographical origins of zoo animals. They were then abstracted to codes referencing their gender, institutional environment, and sequential birth or acquisition numbers. Finally, animals were recently assigned abstract numbers within a global database record. To promote accuracy, these multiple naming and identification techniques are used simultaneously. In Miller's words,

> Some of the hoof stock have transponders, they have ear tags, they have house names, they have an accession number. They have four pieces of identification on one animal. That's a very valuable thing so you can crosscheck. . . . I noticed just the other day [in a] keeper report that someone said "red ruffed lemur number such and such and name such and such." [But] the number was wrong. . . . One is prone to more mistakes if it's only one number or name.[86]

At the North American zoo, keeping track of animal names, identities, and records is the task of the registrar, who also administers the zoo's complex array of spaces, employees, visitors, activities, and legal requirements. The recent transition from multiple institutional systems to one integrated global system, ZIMS, promises zoo registrars an era of greater collaboration, accuracy, and sophistication of record keeping.

CHAPTER FIVE

Registering Zoo Animals

> The surveillance analyst should not necessarily look for an observer gazing out the window, but rather for the bureaucrat located in his office, behind piles of papers and other inscriptions.
>
> Christopher Gad and Peter Lauritsen, *Situated Surveillance*[1]

> As a registrar, nobody bothers you. They don't want to know what you do because it will give them a headache. They would rather be out there, getting chased by an animal or getting dirty or bloody or something.
>
> Rachél Watkins Rogers, registrar, Zoo Miami[2]

The world and work of zoo registrars is largely an understudied topic, even within the zoo itself. While their counterparts in the museum world have received some scholarly attention,[3] no scholarly account of zoo registrars has been published to date. This may not be surprising, as the literature on zoos has had far more dramatic topics to focus on, such as the future survival of wild animals and the ongoing conflicts between pro- and anti-zoo people.[4] The work of zoo registrars is also not as exotic or romantic as that of zookeepers, who interact with wild animals on a daily basis. Zoo registrars, by contrast, are administrators. They sit behind desks, insert figures into computers, fill out forms, and attend numerous meetings, all of which have very real legal and material implications for zoo spaces and animals. If the zoo is a place of spectacular exhibits,[5] the work of zoo registrars is precisely its opposite: an administrative routine that is carried out behind the scenes, without the glow and glitter of the zoo's exotic displays.

So why bother studying zoo registrars? Even some of the registrars interviewed for this project have wondered about this choice, surprised to be in the spotlight. I contend that it is precisely the invisibility of registrars to the public and the perceived monotony of their administrative tasks that make their work so important to unravel. Just as laboratory technicians and notebooks are essential actors in the construction of science,[6] so registrars and databases are essential for the physical, social, legal, and scientific construction of modern zoos.

Specifically, there are three major reasons to study zoo registrars. First, registrars perform central administrative and legal roles at the zoo. In the midst of the zoo's wildness, the registrar is the embodiment of classification and order. She (registrars are typically women) manages the procedural components of the zoo: a junction between data management and micro-scale legal administration. Second, the work of the registrar is uniquely situated on the border between the inside and the outside of the zoo. The collective management of captive animals depends upon frequent animal loans and transfers between individual zoos. Typically, the registrar sets up the official and legal connections between her zoo and other institutions and between her zoo and the relevant regulatory systems. Third and finally, more than any other zoo professional, the work of registrars is the result of the significant transformations that have occurred in North American zoos over the last several decades. As discussed earlier, since the 1970s zoos have been undergoing a paradigmatic shift: from entertaining the urban elite to conserving wild animals and educating the general public on their behalf.[7] The zoo registrar's routine administrative tasks are at the heart of the ambitious conservation project of contemporary zoos.

The registrar's work entails two major and interrelated responsibilities: the registration of zoo animals and the administration of the zoo's legal requirements. The registrar's first responsibility is to record information about animals into the relevant databases, as well as to track these records. For this to occur, she must routinely sort through and organize the available information about her zoo's animals, usually from piles of paperwork and handwritten forms. This administration of data is foundational for the management of animals. The registrar's second major task is to manage the zoo's everyday legal operations. The eclectic and fragmented state of zoo laws—discussed in Chapter 6—translates in this context into a regulatory labyrinth of permits and licenses. Much of the registrar's work involves providing the legal prerequisites for the transfer of captive animals between zoos. Despite the legal obstacles, in this era of collaborative animal programs such transfers are standard zoo procedure.

The two arms of the registrar's work—information management and legal administration—are closely related. Essentially, both are classification systems. Hence, at their core, they relay not only the powerful human urge for order, but also a strong assumption that the world *can* be neatly and exhaustively ordered. At the zoo, the responsibility for ordering lies with the registrar.

Registrars in Zoos: A History

I'm a paper girl, absolutely.

Andrea Drost, curatorial assistant, Toronto Zoo[8]

The need for "paper girl" registrars in North American zoos is relatively new. It was born and has evolved alongside the mushrooming of animal population management programs toward the end of the 1970s and the parallel rise in the digital dataveillance of zoo animals. Today, the registrar is a central node in the zoo network, linked indirectly to the animals by keepers, veterinarians, and their reports. What are some of the reasons behind this emergence of the registrarial role in contemporary North American zoos? Judith Block is registrar emeritus of Smithsonian's National Zoological Park, commonly known as the National Zoo. By her account, she invented the position of record keeper at this zoo during the 1970s.[9] Block reflects on zoo practices at that time:

> It was kind of by accident that records were kept, and they were probably kept [only] for certain purposes. [For example,] when one of his snakes died, a curator [of ours] pulled the record of the oldest animal, so that he ended up with some really good longevity records. . . . For him, what was important was having the longevity record—that was a big deal back then. . . . So the records served a lot of purposes. [But] this was a long, long time ago.[10]

At the time described by Block, the individual identities of snakes and other animals were largely unknown and so the records were kept with a bias toward reporting zoo successes, rather than in a strictly scientific manner.[11] Nowadays, Block says, the manipulation of longevity records would be considered an ethical breach as the modern zoo's conservation mission requires accurate and detailed record keeping. Block emphasizes, "you report everything because *you need to know*; you need to know your reproductive rates and you can't really look at success without knowing. Nowadays that's just standard."[12]

The elaborate record keeping system compartmentalizes information into data variables that then serve as the basis for the zoo's knowledge about its animals. "Without keeping records you really don't learn anything about the animals you're taking care of," Block explains.[13] Contemporary North American zoos "employ a whole cadre of people whose job it is to keep records."[14] Block believes that this shift toward institutional record keeping is a result of the increased attention to the public role of zoos. In her words,

> Most zoos are public: zoo animals belong to the zoo, but they really don't. In the same way that a great painting doesn't belong to a museum, it belongs to the people. And as part of that trust *you need to know the most you can about the animals.* You must keep records of their breeding, eating, [and] all the things you would need to know [for] husbandry and management. . . . The type of record that I'm talking about is an everyday thing. . . . That's the thrust of record keeping.[15]

Block believes, in other words, that zoos are publicly responsible for producing scientific knowledge about animals. For Block, this responsibility is founded upon the public's trust in zoos as institutions that care for captive animals as a common natural heritage. Although Block's ideas about the status of zoo animals as natural heritage may not be widely accepted among registrars, or among other zoo professionals for that matter, her statements do represent what zoo personnel typically perceive as the primary purpose of governing zoo animals: the advancement of scientific knowledge for the dual purpose of educating the public and saving the animals.

Record Keeping

Block divides record keeping into two distinct categories: inventory-based and husbandry-related—with registrars managing both:

> There's the kind of record keeping that says, "we've got fifteen wildebeests, and this and this wildebeests are the parents of these wildebeests, and these three we got from Joe Shmoe." . . . [In this case we ask:] "Where and when did you get it? What kind of animal is it? How old was it when you got it, and on what terms?" These belong to the institution and are accountability records. . . . And then the other kind of record keeping [looks at] . . . how much the [animals] eat and their physical condition. These things are more husbandry-related, and the responsibility for that [information] is an overlap between the curators and the keepers. The registrar ends up being the de facto record keeper for both types of records.[16]

Animal keepers are probably the main source of information for the second type of records: those detailing the minutiae of animal husbandry. Keepers spend the most time with the animals and are usually required to write daily reports about the animals under their care. In the words of Rachél Watkins Rogers, registrar for Zoo Miami: "The keeper report is the most important thing. . . . What keepers capture on a day-to-day basis from the animals that they work with is the basis for all of our knowledge about [animals] in zoos. If the keeper makes a mistake and picks the wrong animal [as] the father or mother, it could genetically ruin a breeding program."[17] Yet obtaining information from zookeepers is not always easy, especially because it requires them to conform to the process of report writing, and, according to Rogers at least, "zookeepers are notorious for not writing things down."[18] The job of zoo registrars thus includes the task of herding keepers to write their reports.

The animal's records must also reflect the needs of a range of professional disciplines and purposes. This requires the registrar to successfully negotiate between various zoo personnel. Rogers explains:

> It's very difficult to get [keepers] to understand [the importance of reporting]. Their focus is the animal. The vet's focus [is] on the medicine and medical records, the curator's focus [is] on the collection, [and] the director focuses on the zoo. There's all these various disciplines of people [who] make up the zoo. The difficult part is getting everybody to collaborate and work together and come up with a good product: to have accurate records capturing information that's important to capture.[19]

As expressed by this quote, zoo personnel in different roles practice care for the animals through different sets of professional perspectives and routines. "The registrar is the glue in all of that," Rogers says.[20] "We grab onto what the curator talks about, we grab onto what the zookeeper says, we grab onto what the vet says, we grab onto the information in the keeper report and see what really needs to be in there."[21] Rogers further elaborates on the glue metaphor and on how it plays out in the registrar's everyday work:

> The glue permeates things, it binds things together. It synergizes things. [Similarly,] no matter what is the quality of the data that we get, [we need to] either accept it, correct it, or reject it. It's either good enough, or it's not right, or it's very important. You have to assign a value to it. *If you don't assign a value to what's put in the record, the records are of no value.*[22]

Essentially, Rogers is saying that even when the registrar is handed accurate information by the various parties that care for the zoo animal, she must still sort through this information to distinguish the valuable from the useless, in effect actively gluing the record together.

How do registrars decide what information to include in the records and what to discard? Some information is required by law, such as the requirement by the U.S. Department of Agriculture to record all mammal movement between zoos. Other information is required by zoo scientists: for example, precise birth, death, and reproduction data are needed to estimate the viability of small populations over time. However, in most instances there is no strict law or hard science for the registrar to follow when deciding what information to record and what to leave out. Whereas a range of credible information is important for a good animal record, a cumbersome record is as good as no record at all. The registrar must therefore strike a balance between a record that is too thin and one that contains too much information.

Each zoo currently maintains its own record system and makes the relevant decisions internally. "I have a program here on my computer that lets me do stuff only for Buffalo," Buffalo Zoo's registrar Jean Miller says.[23] Consequently, every zoo registrar enjoys broad discretion about what to register in the institutional records, or more specifically, in the animal's specimen report.

Naturally, certain topics are more likely to be included in the specimen reports than others. Lynn McDuffie of Disney®'s Animal Kingdom tells me that in the past, only births and deaths were recorded, but that things have changed significantly during her tenure as registrar.[24] The staff at Disney, for example, has agreed that all "central life events" should be in the records.[25] According to McDuffie, these consist of the animal's acquisition and disposition information, as well as its identifiers, behavioral issues, training, and group composition. Basically, she says, "this is the type of information that will help you manage the animals down the road."[26] By "down the road," McDuffie is probably referring to the periodic analysis and planning performed by AZA's relevant animal programs (discussed in Chapter 7), in which small population models predict breeding success and mortality rates.[27] Such predictions can only be made by entering extensive data for each of the animal's major life events. Even within generally accepted parameters, however, the line between valuable and nonvaluable information is not always clear. "The road is not always known in advance," McDuffie acknowledges.[28] "You can't really just be a technocrat," Rogers adds. "You have to look at the animal's life and choose what needs to be there."[29] Indeed, a good animal record must include a wide yet limited range of credible information.

Timmy the gorilla's specimen report illustrates the vast amount of information that registrars insert into the zoo animal's institutional records. Just for the first month of his stay in Louisville, Timmy's report includes thirty-three pages of data, documented in an eight-point type size. The report records the minutiae of Timmy's feeding habits, his relations with other gorillas and with each of the keepers, and the basic medical details of his everyday management. Here, for example, is a short excerpt from the records for Timmy's first day in Louisville: "Timmy investigated door #1 for a moment, and then returned to 1 for his kiwi smoothie and the rest of his cantaloupe. He received his PB&J with antibiotics as well."[30]

Specimen reports typically start with the birth of an animal and end with its death. Yet even here the line is not fixed, as the record is actually never hermetically sealed. Jean Miller illustrates this point:

> When [an animal] dies, that's when the record closes. [But] you can still change the record. . . . Say we have two prehensile tail porcupines out on loan to the same institution. They get them mixed up and say, "Emma died and Adelaide is still alive." Then, later on, somebody says, "Oh, they have transponders, we should read the transponders." And then they say, "Oh, it was Adelaide that died. Emma is still alive here." I can resurrect that record. But it takes a lot of finagling. It's a mess when a mistake like that is made.[31]

In unusual cases, then, records can be reopened even after they are sealed. In other cases, records may begin even before the animal's birth, for example by recording thermal images of a panda fetus during gestation or tracking penguin eggs as they incubate.

Tracking

In addition to identifying and documenting information about the zoo animal, the registrar must also be able to track this information. Rachél Rogers defines successful tracking as a situation in which "when I look at [something], I know where the information came from, I know who put it in, I know when it was put in."[32] She emphasizes the importance of this process: "Tracking is the main thing I do with everything. I have to track where pieces of paper go. . . . Every time I put a note in a record, I put my initials next to it. I put the initials next to the person who gave me information because the other thing about the records [is that] anything that's in there, I am accountable for."[33] For registrars, the meaning of tracking is thus very specific: it refers to tracking the human trail of information in each particular registration instance. In information systems, such data about data—or metadata—allows for enhanced accountability in management.

Some of the registrars state, additionally, that their work is rather disconnected from much of the other work that goes on at the zoo. "I'm my own monitor," Jean Miller says. "I monitor myself because nobody else is monitoring me."[34] But although their work is rarely supervised, the registrars are the ones held responsible when anything goes wrong with the zoo's records. Consequently, registrars frequently express feelings of seclusion from the rest of the zoo staff. "It's a lonely life out there," comments Judith Block.

A second, perhaps more common, interpretation of "tracking" relates to the physical ability to trace bodies through space and time. Whereas the scholarly literature on surveillance focuses on the *human* body as the central locus of observation and tracking, the zoo animal provides another example of how the observed body is broken down through its abstraction from the physical body and its placement, only to then be tracked and reassembled elsewhere through a series of data combinations. "The result is a decorporalized body, a 'data double' of pure virtuality," surveillance scholars Richard Ericson and Kevin Haggerty suggest.[35] As data comes to stand in place of the animal, the animal's body increasingly disappears from human view.[36]

The registrar does not need to physically leave the space of her office in order to gain access to a wide range of information about zoo animals—she only needs to know how to activate and operate the relevant databases. She also does not need to leave her office or have any physical contact with zoo animals in order to translate their bodies and behaviors into virtual inscriptions accessible to zoo professionals around the world. For example, the Virginia Aquarium's registrar may have never seen sea turtles directly, but she may nonetheless be the one assigning the code attached to each turtle's radio frequency identification chip and recording the keeper's reports about this animal, thereby deciding what information to include and what to leave out. Using this database, the turtle's records can then be observed by another zoo registrar on the opposite side of the country or the world.[37]

Legal Administration

The registrar is the conscience of the zoo.

Judith Block, National Zoo registrar emeritus[38]

Alongside her various administrative tasks as the zoo's record keeper, the registrar must also perform the vast majority of the zoo's mundane legal tasks. Because the registrar is usually the person responsible for obtaining the zoo's permits and licenses, she must decipher the relevant city, state, federal, and international laws, regulations, and industry standards that pertain to each situation, ensuring that her zoo complies with these legal norms. Specifically, the registrar's work typically includes filling out permit requests from the myriad agencies that govern and inspect zoos, seeing to it that the AZA's acquisition and disposition policies are adhered to, and assuring that the zoo complies with animal shipment standards.

The registrars I interviewed for this project have mentioned how difficult it is to stay on top of the growing number and intensifying details of the legal norms that pertain to contemporary zoo operations in North America. McDuffie of Disney and Rogers of Zoo Miami explain, for example, that in Florida new regulations are enacted literally every day, making it impossible to master the legal norms at any given time.[39] McDuffie testifies, moreover, that at one point she applied for over forty types of permits pertaining to various animals at her zoo.[40]

To perform her role as the zoo's legal liaison, the registrar must also be conversant with the scientific classifications adopted by various laws, such as the distinction between cold- and warm-blooded animals in the Animal Welfare Act of 1966, or between an African and an Asian elephant for the African Elephant Protection Act of 1988. The zoo depends on its registrars to work through the intricate webs of legal classifications, regulations, and exceptions that have come to dominate almost every aspect of its operations (as discussed in Chapter 6). This recalls Michel Foucault's depiction of the king of the city-state—whom he likens to a ship captain that navigates his ship through reefs and storms to safe harbor.[41] Likewise, the zoo registrar must take care to ensure the zoo's adherence to order by navigating through the quagmire of official laws, regulations, industry standards, and guidelines.

Transferring Animals

Just over fifty years ago, nearly half the baby gorillas Dr. Pickett collected in Cameroon died in transit, and two were transferred like human infants with Pickett in the cabin of the plane. Today, such a scenario would be close to impossible. The vast majority of animal transfers to North American zoos originate from other zoos in this region, rather than from the wild, and transfer conditions are closely regulated and scrutinized to ensure legality and care. Moreover, most of today's animal transfers are triggered by the frequent breeding recommendations drafted by animal programs under the supervision of the AZA.

Figure 10. Sanya, a great Indian rhinoceros female born in Toronto Zoo, 1999, is seen here during a 2004 transfer to the Wilds in Ohio upon recommendation by the Great Indian Rhinos SSP. Indian one-horned rhinoceroses are listed as vulnerable in the wild and are assigned to a yellow SSP program by the AZA. Courtesy of Ken Ardill / Toronto Zoo.

Bronx Zoo registrar Nilda Ferrer elaborates on the frequency of animal trans-fers: "We have a lot of animals coming in and out. . . . We just imported a red bird of paradise yesterday from Chile, and we exported one to Chile last week. So we do a lot of exchanges with other institutions."[42]

To be effective, the breeding and transfer recommendations issued by AZA's animal programs are translated into a routine practice of drafting animal loan agreements, obtaining permits, building physical containers, shipping animals, and administering quarantine and medical tests before and after shipments. Such a transfer of zoo animals, especially across state or international boundar-ies, requires sorting through a maze of institutional procedures and myriad legal requirements. Whereas the registrar is normally not involved in deciding the conservation or breeding status of zoo animals, her work is fundamental for the implementation of these decisions.

The first formal step in the transfer of a zoo animal between AZA-accredited zoos is the drafting of a loan agreement. A zoo can also donate the animal or lend it out for exhibit purposes only—but these are rare occurrences.[43] Most often, the transferred animal is assigned an "on loan" status. While the receiving zoo physically holds and manages the animal according to the contractual agreement, the loaning zoo still formally owns the animal. Jean Miller explains this relationship from the perspective of the lending institution:

> If [the animal] goes out on a breeding loan, normally it will not move unless there's an agreement specifying who is responsible for everything, [until] there's a written, signed contract. We also have a signed breeding loan separate from the contract, [which] specifies who gets what [and] who is responsible for care. [For example,] in the event that there is a surgical procedure that has to be done, if it's elective, we have to approve it; if it's an emergency, it's exempt. We have to be informed within thirty days of the death [because] we own the carcass. That's all written out beforehand. And sometimes it's very difficult to negotiate these details.[44]

Despite the collegial spirit of collective animal management programs and conservation, behind the scenes the registrars must still untangle complicated legal arrangements concerned with ownership and institutional responsibilities. Andrea Drost, registrar for the Toronto Zoo, says about her zoo's customs pertaining to "on loan" animals:

> If we lent out the female [for breeding], we will get the first female and the second male. The third female will be ours, the fourth male will be ours. So it alternates back and forth between the two sexes, and it alternates back and forth between the two zoos. [But] sometimes, instead of being a division of females, it's just a division of viable offspring, [with] no sex at all. If a turtle lays its eggs and five turtles successfully hatch out, three go to one place, and two go to the other, regardless of sex.[45]

Miller further clarifies that underlying the collective spirit of loan agreements there is still a core of individual ownership:

> [It used to be that] the female was always more valuable because she had offspring. . . . And the male was with her [only] for a few minutes and that's it. . . . So the owner of the female usually got the female offspring, the owner of the male usually got the first male offspring, and the holding institution got the third. . . . This was the norm within zoos. However, it's being recognized more now that the holding institution is putting all of their time and effort into it. So the thinking is shifting. . . . The norm, I think, is

going to change in favor of the institution that holds the animal. . . . So the owner of
the female, the owner of the male, these are all terms that [need to be] worked out. . . .
It's a gamble of ownership.[46]

In economic terms, zoos are shifting from a framework whereby owners of animals on loan collect "rent" in the form of offspring, to one whereby the host institution benefits from the labor and care it invests in breeding. This new emphasis
mirrors the shift in the zoos' mission from entertainment and profit to conservation and care.

The story of Timmy the gorilla reflects the complexities of such loan agreements between zoos. Timmy was first owned by Cleveland Metroparks Zoo, then
transferred to the Bronx Zoo and later to the Louisville Zoo. Because the last
transfer involved three zoos, Timmy's was a three-way loan agreement: it stipulated, accordingly, that the receiving institution shall own the first viable offspring, the owner of the male shall own the second viable offspring, the owner of
the female shall own the third viable offspring, and so on. In effect, as the receiving institution, the Louisville Zoo owns one-third of Timmy's offspring; as the
owner of the male, Cleveland owns one-third of Timmy's offspring, and the owners of Timmy's mates own the rest. The language of Timmy's breeding loan—and
of breeding loans more generally—suggests that despite the increasingly collective work between zoos, they still seek to gain institutional advantages from this
practice.[47] Moreover, animal loan exchanges between zoos are still based on the
institutional ownership of animals.

Upon the successful draft of a loan agreement between the relevant zoos, the
registrars typically obtain all the necessary permits and licenses for transferring
the animal. For example, shipping containers must follow a detailed set of instructions that depends on the type of animal shipped and the various geographies involved. Both the AZA, regulating care of animals in zoos, and the CITES
treaty, regulating international trade of endangered or threatened species, require adherence to the Live Animal Regulations of the International Air Transport Association (IATA). For gorillas, "Container Requirement 34" stipulates
that the holding container must be large enough to "allow the animal to turn
around completely and easily . . . to stand fully upright with its head extended,
and . . . to lie down in the fully prone position."[48] It also instructs that the frame
must be constructed of welded metal with a layer of smooth wood and support
braces, the front must be made of "strong iron bars spaced in such a manner that
the animal cannot push its arms through the bars," and that there must be a

sheet of welded mesh 7.5 centimeters in front of the bars. Furthermore, "a wooden shutter with slots or holes for ventilation must cover the whole front in order to reduce the amount of light inside the container as well as to reduce the disturbance to the animal and to protect the handling personnel." Additional requirements prescribe the construction of sides, floor, ventilation, and feeding and watering containers within the holding container. Finally, strict quarantine requirements must be adhered to before and after transfer.

The laws that pertain to zoo animal transfers vary according to the geographic origin and destination of the animal (namely, the country, state, and region of both loaning and receiving zoos), the type of animal, and the physical facilities that the animal has come into contact with. Nilda Ferrer of the Bronx Zoo says more about the legal aspects of animal transfers:

> It all depends. You can't write a single rule that covers everything because it all depends on [the] mode of transport, the location, [and] the origin of the species. So you have to know all these things before you can get an animal. If I am importing mice, I need permits from the Centers [for Disease Control], depending on what the species is. . . . You have to know what you're getting and where you are getting it from. [You also need] to know and understand the regulations that go with each transport. So each transport is carefully looked [at] to see what the requirements might be before you can go ahead and ship the animal.[49]

Andrea Drost of Toronto Zoo lends her perspective on the complexities of the legal norms that apply to animal transfers: "Not only is [the transfer] very highly regulated, but it is [also] species specific: the regulations will change depending on which animal you're moving and depending on where you're moving it to. To move a gorilla from Woodland Park Zoo in the Seattle area to here we needed a CFIA [Canadian Food Inspection Agency] import permit, which had eight pages of regulations and testing on both ends."[50] Similarly, Ferrer notes the geographic complexities of the laws that pertain to animal transfers: "You need to know what particular regulations—state-wise, city-wise, international—cover the transport of an animal. When you're transferring something from here to Connecticut, you need to know what are the requirements for Connecticut. You need a license to do anything—you need licenses even to transport rodents—just about anything."[51]

Clearly, then, the registrars cannot rely on a single source of law in their execution of animal transfers; they must comply with regulations from the AZA, IATA, USDA, CDC, CITES, and others, as further detailed in Chapter 6. Judith

Block summarizes the meticulous care that registrars must practice to ensure that every animal transfer and loan is both legal and safe for the zoo and the animal: "The registrar looks at all the aspects of the transaction and makes sure that [they] fit with the policies of this institution, [checks if] the permits are in place, if the person you are getting [the animal] from is legitimate, and if you need a loan agreement and what that would entail."[52]

Registrars as Bureaucrats

Although ostensibly disconnected, the two central functions of the registrar—her role as a record keeper, on the one hand, and her role as the zoo's legal administrator, on the other hand—actually share an important component: the desire for order. As the zoo's central bureaucrat, the registrar systematically implements administrative procedures at the zoo. Zoo registrars believe, moreover, that achieving fair and just results requires affinity with form and process. In the words of Judith Block,

> I think you've got to have some really good policies in place to protect yourself and to help structure your thinking about these things. [Things] need to be hashed out and seen, and, yes, there should be a consensus and a policy that everyone agrees upon that applies to each case and that doesn't differ. Policies [shouldn't be] written off in a corner somewhere; they're usually a collaboration between the administrators and the board and everybody else. That's the reason [they exist]. And you never know what needs to be in the policy until some situation comes up and you think, "Damn, that wasn't covered." And you hash it out and amend the policy.[53]

The work of zoo registrars is not unlike that of bureaucrats in other institutions. As with bureaucrats around the world, North American zoo registrars typically work from the relatively remote location of their offices, which affords them a dispassionate approach amid the heated debates that sometimes ensue among their colleagues at the zoo. Block offers an example:

> The curator can be all excited about getting this wildebeest. [So] the registrar [should be] the one who says: "Think about this, the only place that you can get it [from] is fourteen thousand miles away and there [are] going to be permits and issues like that and does this really fit within the collection plan and with the collection acquisition policies?" . . . The perspective from the registrar would be: "How does this fit?" . . . The register is thinking about the permits, the cost, whether it fits with the collection management policy and with the collection plan, etc.[54]

Based on what she frames as their neutral position, Block proposes that the "registrars are the conscience of the zoo."[55]

Among their fellow bureaucrats, zoo registrars probably share the most in common with registrars in museums. The shared history of zoos and museums is in fact still reflected in both the terminology and the organizational structure of these two institutions.[56] The terms "collections," "curators," "registrars," and "exhibits" are common to zoos and museums alike, as are the recent debates about changing the registrar's title to move away from its technical associations.[57] Moreover, both institutions rely on the scientific ordering of knowledge and on the recording of information through systemic projects of naming, identification, classification, documentation, and tracking. Additionally, both museums and zoos have evolved from a natural history paradigm and share similar commitments to the education of the general public.[58] Finally, to further their mission, the two institutions rely heavily on sight and seeing, specializing in what I have referred to in Chapter 3 as scopic regimes.[59]

An obvious difference between zoos and museums is that whereas museum collections are usually composed of inanimate artifacts, zoo collections consist of living animals. This distinction, however, does not seem to be of much importance to the work of zoo registrars. In fact, registrars often refer to their animals as artifacts and, as such, record them no differently than their museum counterparts would. For example, Block tells me that "you can compare [living collections] to a museum collection in that a painting needs the right humidity, security, and protection from light, stuff like that. The same with a live animal; you have to make sure that it's . . . safe and has the right temperature and humidity."[60] Block further pushes this comparison, suggesting that the zoo animal is less special than the museum artifact. "A wildebeest [is not] so unique that it's irreplaceable in the same way that a Rembrandt [painting] would be. This wildebeest is one of a species and has characteristics that will be useful for the population, but it's one of many [and thus] not so special."[61] "Anyway," she clarifies, "this is all from a registrarial point of view."[62] Although some registrars might disagree with Block's museum-oriented interpretation of the zoo's mission, her comment is nonetheless instructive in that it highlights the registrar's unique point of view within the institution of captivity.

The comparison with museum registrars is also instructive in that it illuminates the connections between data management and law enforcement. Museum scholars have noted about the museum registrar that "although probably sharing the curator's aesthetic or intellectual passion for the museum's collections, the registrar can never permit feeling to eclipse the pragmatic concerns for documentation . . . the arduous tallying and listing without which collections would be essentially unmanaged and of limited benefit."[63]

Museum scholars have also pointed to the close affinity between what they refer to as "registrarial thinking" and the worlds of law, order, and logical systems. They have asserted that "legislators, judges, lawyers, and registrars are professional systematizers, organizers, codifiers, and proceduralists."[64] Hence, "the role of registrars—like that of the institutions they serve—is an evolving one. If the last decade has witnessed augmented respect and understanding of the registrar it is because our colleagues have increasingly learned to value registrarial orderliness in an environment that is frequently pressurized and occasionally volatile."[65] And what is true in the context of museum registrars is even truer in the drama-ridden context of contemporary North American zoos.

Conclusion

The rising importance of the registrar in North American zoos since the 1970s highlights two significant changes that have occurred in the life of these institutions. First, from their previous focus on entertaining the public, zoos have come to focus on conservation through the scientific management of records and databases. Second, zoos are increasingly regulated and standardized by complex official laws, industry standards, software, and databases. Operating in the junction between these two major changes, zoo registrars represent and embody the significance of order, classification, and procedure for the proper functioning of information management systems and regulatory regimes. Their work, in other words, demonstrates the human urge for classification that underlies both scientific and legal systems.

CHAPTER SIX

Regulating Zoo Animals

Who will assume the authority of instructing us in the rules for allowing a
species to die?

William Conway, "The Role of Zoos in the 21st Century"[1]

The institution of captivity encompasses a range of projects, including naturalizing, classifying, seeing, naming, registering, and reproducing zoo animals. To
fully understand these projects, one must study the regulation of animals and of
the zoos that keep them. This entails a complicated journey through a plurality
of legal regimes, including official laws as well as an array of industry-generated
professional standards and animal care guidelines that apply to all accredited
zoos. The term "zoo laws," then, casts a broad net that captures the bricolage of
zoo-related norms—from federal laws and state regulations through case law
and institutional treaties and finally to the zoo industry's standards and guidelines. To distinguish the legal norms enacted by state bodies from those enacted
by the zoo's professional industry—and to assert my position that industry standards are effectively laws, too—I will use the term "official law" when referring to
the first group of laws, and professional or industry "standards" or "guidelines"
when referring to the second.[2]

The long list of official zoo laws is somewhat misleading in terms of legislative intent: in fact, very few official laws have been enacted with the specific goal
of regulating zoos. A close examination of these laws also reveals their inade-
quacy for regulating the hybrid human-animal nature in today's zoos. In practice, zoos are exempt from many of these laws. The zoo industry's professional
association, the AZA, has filled the regulatory gaps (or lacunae) with its own
professional standards and guidelines, which apply to all accredited zoos in
North America—approximately 10 percent of the country's zoos. This is where

the legal story diverges into two adverse narratives: that of zoo professionals, who are frustrated with the complexities and inadequacies of official law and would like to see it replaced with a self-regulatory regime, and that of animal activists, who lobby for the enactment of additional official legal prohibitions against keeping wild animals in captivity.

On the one hand, most North American zoo professionals would argue that their zoos must abide by an eclectic and fragmented body of statutes and regulations that govern their everyday practices and that require a confusing array of permits and licenses. This narrative was clearly expressed by the registrars in Chapter 5. Moreover, zoo people typically claim that official laws are incapable of regulating the complexities of zoos anyway, and that as experts on animal care they should have the authority to self-regulate their industry. According to this narrative, the fragmented legal situation is the *reason* that the AZA has stepped up to enact and administer its high standards of care for animals. In the words of AZA's executive director Kristin Vehrs,

> Basically, we wanted to distinguish ourselves from the 2,600 licensed exhibitors under the Animal Welfare Act, and [from] the regulations under this act, [which are] minimal. And while our standards are not perfect either, we're the experts, we know how to handle animals appropriately . . . and we wanted to make sure that in our goal of advancing zoos and aquariums that we do it absolutely right, as right as we can.[3]

On the other hand, many have criticized the current situation of zoo laws for being overwhelmingly dictated by the zoo industry. Such criticisms vary in scope and source and include critiques from animal protection groups, animal rights activists, and even individual members of the zoo community. The main criticism is that there are few official laws that apply directly to zoos and that as institutions that benefit from captivity, zoos cannot be trusted to self-regulate animal care. The proponents of this narrative call for tighter legal constraints on zoos and even for enactment of a federal zoo law, as several other countries have done.[4] The fragmented state of zoo laws, alongside the heavy reliance on AZA standards, is seen by the proponents of this view as highly problematic for another reason: it leaves unregulated the vast majority of zoos, which are not accredited and thus are not required to comply with AZA's standards and guidelines. The weak state of official zoo laws, critics add, is largely the *result* of the zoo industry's powerful lobby, rather than the cause of it. Here, from the perspective of former Woodland Park Zoo director: "There are precious few laws affecting zoos, and especially their day-to-day operations. For the most part, legislators seem content to let zoos be self-policing, self-administering, self-accrediting. You will find when something goes publicly wrong or when public criticism is applied, the response is very often an assumption that zoos are the experts at what they do. . . . And so the status quo invariably remains."[5] In what follows, I map the various legal norms that pertain to zoos in the United States and the conflicts that have ensued over their enactment and enforcement.

Official Laws and Zoo Animals

There is no one particular official law that addresses the unique properties of zoos and their animals. In fact, most official laws in the United States pertain to zoos and their animals only incidentally. This results in a confusing array of legal norms that apply to some zoo animals on certain occasions and in particular locations. Currently, the legal norms that apply to zoos and their animals are dispersed among numerous statutes and administered by a range of agencies that operate on a variety of scales. While some zoo animals are subject to this hodgepodge of legal norms, many exist outside the realm of official laws, namely in a "state of exception."[6]

The Animal Welfare Act

The most influential of all federal animal statutes is probably the Animal Welfare Act (AWA). Passed in 1966 as a result of public outcry over the research industry's practice of stealing pets to use in medical research, the AWA is administered by the Animal and Plant Health Inspection Service (APHIS) of the United States Department of Agriculture (USDA).[7] The AWA adopts what some have called a welfarist approach to animals, in contrast to a rights-based one.[8] That is, the act provides minimum requirements for food, water, housing, and sanitation for the welfare of animals, but regards animals as subjects without rights.

In total, 8,782 facilities are regulated by the AWA, of which 2,764 are exhibitors.[9] The AWA defines exhibitors as

> any person (public or private) exhibiting any animals, which were purchased in commerce or the intended distribution of which affects commerce, or will affect commerce, to the public for compensation, as determined by the Secretary, and such term

Law	Scale	Jurisdiction	Institution(s)	Exemption(s)
Convention on International Trade in Endangered Species of Wild Fauna and Flora (CITES) (1973)	International (175 parties)	International trade of species designated as endangered or threatened	Fish and Wildlife Service[a] and United Nations Environment Programme CITES Secretariat	Licensed noncommercial trade that does not endanger the species, including transfers of captive-bred wildlife between institutions in a conservation program
Live Animal Regulations	International	Live animals shipped by air	International Air Transportation Association	None—AZA, CITES, and all airlines require these regulations to be met for live animal transfers
Lacey Act (1900 and 1981 amendments)	Federal	Wildlife and fish taken, transported, or sold illegally	Animal and Plant Health Inspection Service[b]	Organizations licensed under APHIS or regulated by other federal agencies
Public Health Services Act (1944)	Federal	Animals potentially carrying human diseases	Centers for Disease Control and Prevention	Certain methods of research
Animal Welfare Act (1966) and Regulations (1989)	Federal	Warm-blooded animals	Animal and Plant Health Inspection Service	Bird, rats, and mice used for research, horses not used for research, and farm animals
Marine Mammal Protection Act (1972)	Federal	Marine mammals in the wild	NOAA Fisheries Service[c]	Public display and educational uses, scientific research, incidental "takes" in commercial fishing, and subsistence use
Endangered Species Act (1973)	Federal	Foreign and domestic species designated endangered or threatened	Fish and Wildlife Service and NOAA Fisheries Service	Incidental "take" permits if in compliance with requirements imposed by the Fish and Wildlife Service or NOAA; nonessential experimental populations of reintroduced endangered species
African Elephant Conservation Act (1988)	Federal	African elephants in the wild	Fish and Wildlife Service	Ivory obtained prior to 1989, part of legally obtained sport trophy, or confiscated in law-enforcement activities

Wild Bird Conservation Act (1992)	Federal	Imports of exotic birds, especially birds listed by CITES	Fish and Wildlife Service	Allowed species, approved foreign breeders, or imports permitted for cooperative breeding programs, zoological breeding/display, and research
State laws protecting animal welfare	State	Varies by state	State and local law enforcement	IA, KY, OH, and WA do not regulate animal exhibitions; MA, NJ, and SC exempt zoos; other states regulate importation, ownership, or licensing
Local laws regulating public displays of wild or exotic animals for entertainment	Local ordinances	Somerville, MA, and many other localities ban public displays of wild animals for entertainment	Local law enforcement	Educational exhibits
Local laws regulating contact between the public and dangerous or exotic animals	Local ordinances	Fairfax, VA, and many other localities ban contact between the public and exotic animals	Local law enforcement	Elephants are excluded; some localities only ban contact with certain animals (tigers, lions, and bears), some localities exclude chimpanzees

Figure 11. Selected laws on zoo animals in the United States. Compiled by the author with data from CITES Secretariat, Convention on International Trade in Endangered Species of Wild Fauna and Flora; Kali Grech, "Detailed Regulation of the Laws Affecting Zoos," Animal Legal and Historical Center (East Lansing: Michigan State University College of Law, 2004); International Air Transport Association, Live Animal Regulations, 36th ed. (Montreal: IATA, 2009); "Digest of Federal Resource Laws," U.S. Fish and Wildlife Service; "Legislation Prohibiting or Restricting Animal Acts," Mediapeta; "Take Action—Progress Through Legislation," Born Free USA; "Wild Animal Circuses," MSPCA.

[a]Bureau of Department of the Interior;

[b]Service of Department of Agriculture;

[c]Service of National Oceanic and Atmospheric Administration, Department of Commerce

includes carnivals, circuses, and zoos exhibiting such animals whether operated for profit or not; but such term excludes retail pet stores,[10] organizations sponsoring and all persons participating in State and country fairs,[11] livestock shows, rodeos, pure-bred dog and cat shows, and any other fairs or exhibitions intended to advance agricultural arts and sciences, as may be determined by the Secretary.[12]

Explicitly included in the list of exhibitors above, zoos are additionally defined by the AWA as—"any park, building, cage, enclosure, or other structure or premise in which a live animal or animals are kept for public exhibition or viewing, regardless of compensation."[13]

For exhibitors, the AWA promulgates standards to "govern the humane handling, care, treatment, and transportation of animals," including "minimum requirements for handling, housing, feeding, watering, sanitation, shelter from extremes of weather and temperatures, adequate veterinary care," and for "a physical environment adequate to promote the psychological well-being of primates."[14] Generally, the AWA requires that exhibitors be licensed; it also requires them to report and record the sex, species, and number of animals on hand, as well as any that have been bought or sold, transported, traded, donated, or that have died.[15]

To be covered by the AWA, a zoo animal must first meet the definition of "animal" within the statute, namely "any live or dead dog, cat, nonhuman primate, guinea pig, hamster, rabbit, or such other warm blooded animal, [which] is used for research, testing, experimentation, or exhibition purposes, or as a pet, but such term excludes: . . . birds [and] rats bred for research; . . . horses not used in research; [and] other farm animals."[16] In other words, the AWA applies only to warm-blooded animals within exhibits. It does not protect reptiles, certain animals used for research (birds, rats, and mice), or farm animals used for food, fiber, or other agricultural purposes.[17] Reserving legal protections mostly to warm-blooded animals confirms the point made by animal geography scholars that "the conceptual placing of animals is first about deciding what is or is not an animal."[18] Indeed, the AWA's standards of care protect some, but not other, animals, effectively creating a hierarchy of "animalhood."[19] As in earlier discussions of how zoos allow certain animals to be used as food, here too "some animals are more equal than others."[20]

Even for those zoo animals that are protected by the AWA,[21] this act's effectiveness is limited, as its standards are considered minimal at best; the bar is usually set at the lowest common denominator: labs.[22] Although an AWA amendment that includes more stringent requirements for primates was enacted, it was never followed up with the necessary regulations required to render it enforceable.[23] Also, the enforcement of the AWA has been criticized extensively, even by the USDA itself: "We found cases where the Eastern Region [of the USDA] declined to take enforcement action against violators who compromised public safety or animal health."[24] In 2005, the Eastern Region did not take action against 126 of 465 violators, including licensees with histories of violations and incidents of primates biting children. Moreover, discounted fines to encourage out-of-court payments resulted in fines so minimal that some exhibitors considered them a normal part of doing business.[25] As of October 2011, APHIS employed a total of only 105 animal care inspectors throughout the United States, an insufficient staff given the quantity and range of exhibitors inspected by the AWA.[26]

The Endangered Species Act

Passed in 1973, the Endangered Species Act (ESA) places restrictions on activities involving endangered and threatened animals and plants to ensure their continued survival. The Fish and Wildlife Service (FWS) of the U.S. Department of the Interior is the primary administrator of the ESA, and the National Marine Fisheries Service of the Department of Commerce shares responsibility for the protection of endangered marine animals. As of January 2012, 1,191 animal species populations have been designated under section 17.11 of this act as either endangered or threatened, including 587 domestic and 604 foreign species populations.[27]

The ESA makes the following activities unlawful with regard to threatened or endangered wildlife: import or export; delivery, receipt, transport, or shipment in interstate or foreign commerce in the course of a commercial activity; the selling or offering for sale in interstate or foreign commerce; and the "taking" of protected wildlife.[28] The definition of "take" in this context includes to harm, harass, pursue, hunt, shoot, kill, or capture, or to possess, ship, deliver, carry, or receive[29]—in other words, "almost anything that negatively impacts a species."[30] Indeed, in *Babbitt v. Sweet Home*[31] the Supreme Court held that even modification of the habitat of an endangered species may constitute a "take." At the same time, the ESA is limited in that it only applies to endangered species and habitats within the United States. Foreign endangered species do not come under the act's jurisdiction unless their bodies or body parts are imported into the United States.

The ESA's jurisdiction is also limited to the list of endangered species and habitats designated by the FWS, which are criticized by many as problematic, even biased. Under section 3 of the ESA "the term 'species' includes any subspecies of fish or wildlife or plants, and any distinct population segment of any species of vertebrate fish or wildlife which interbreeds when mature."[32] Yet species identification, classification, and taxonomy are areas of biology that remain contentious.[33] Although the act requires that decisions over an animal's endangered or threatened status must be made with the "best scientific and commercial data available,"[34] there are no requirements or guidelines for determining if a group of organisms represents a distinct species; furthermore, there is no single accepted method for recognizing species. Inevitably, limited knowledge about the earth's biodiversity results in biased species listings, regardless of ESA priorities.[35] For example, vertebrate groups and certain plants are more likely to be studied by scientists than other taxa.[36]

In 1979, the Captive-Bred Wildlife (CBW) registration system was established as a legal exception to the ESA. This system permits the keeping of wildlife owned and bred in captivity.[37] Specifically, amended section 17.21(g) of the CBW grants a "general, conditional permission to take; export or re-import; . . . any non-native endangered or threatened wildlife that is bred in captivity in the United States."[38] In effect, the regulation creates a blanket permit for taking all nonnative captive-bred wildlife. The FWS has interpreted this regulation broadly to apply to all facilities with "animal husbandry practices that meet or exceed the minimum standard for facilities and care under the AWA . . . breeding procedures, or . . . provisions of veterinary care."[39] Generally, the permits provided under the CBW system are referred to as either "scientific" or "recovery" permits.[40] Many of the CBW permits are issued for the importation of captive bred animals, including those born in foreign zoos. In effect, these permits provide the legal grounds for the routine practices of transferring endangered animals between zoos, an essential component of AZA's collective animal programs.[41] The FWS also issues import permits for animals captured from the wild. Typically, these permits are issued for animals that were taken in the past, for those that were taken by another entity than the exporter, or for those that were deemed by the exporter to be physically or emotionally unsuitable to return to the wild.

To complicate things even further, a federal regulation enacted under the ESA requires importers of threatened species to either add to the geographic area of the animals' habitat or to increase the population of the animals, a requirement otherwise known as "enhancement."[42] The enhancement requirement has proven difficult to fulfill in those cases where the wild can no longer be enhanced, such as in the case of Arctic polar bears. For years, American zoos could bring polar bears into the United States, despite their origin in the Arctic. Some animals were abandoned cubs, while others were "problem" bears. But in 2008, the Interior Department declared polar bears "threatened" under the ESA, effectively blocking further importation of the bears because of the federal regulation requiring enhancement. "These laws were enacted in the 1970s, before global climate change, melting polar ice and diminishing polar bear habitat were anticipated," wrote several House members in a letter to the FWS dated October 2011.[43] "We urge you to grant polar-bear import permits to accredited zoos that meet specific and rigorous public display, animal welfare and conservation standards," the lawmakers added. "Your action would allow these zoos to house rescue bears that otherwise might die in the wild."[44] According to zoos and their supporting legislators, although it was initially enacted to protect wild animals, this federal regulation inadvertently ended up blocking the only realistic option for saving individual polar bears.

Other Federal Statutes

The Lacey Act prohibits dealing in wildlife taken, transported, or sold in any manner that violates any state, national, or foreign law. This act is instrumental in protecting wildlife by making it a separate offense to take, possess, transport, or trade wildlife taken in violation of the ESA and other federal and state laws that offer wildlife protection. However, the act does not apply to persons licensed by APHIS or any other federal agency.[45] Because some zoo animals are regulated under the AWA and thus the zoos that hold them are already licensed by APHIS, these animals are largely exempt from the Lacey Act.[46]

Additionally, numerous taxon-specific statutes offer federal protections or financial support for the conservation of particular species. These include the Marine Mammal Protection Act,[47] the African Elephant Conservation Act,[48] the Great Ape Conservation Act,[49] and the Wild Bird Conservation Act.[50] However, these statutes are intended for *in situ* wild animals and apply only indirectly to the specific characteristics and needs of zoo animals. Moreover, in some cases, zoos are explicitly exempt from these acts altogether. For example, section 101(a)(1) of the Marine Mammal Protection Act exempts public display and educational uses from its protection requirements, effectively exempting accredited zoos.[51]

Finally, zoo animals are regulated in their capacity as pathogen hosts. The federal statute that regulates animals in this respect is the Public Health Service Act, enacted in 1944 and administered by the Centers for Disease Control and Prevention. The act's purpose is to prevent the introduction, transmission, or spread of communicable disease from foreign countries to the United States.[52] The act applies only to those animals that are currently known to threaten human health: turtles, certain birds, rodents, bats, and primates.[53] The applicability of this act thus depends on a definition of certain animals as dangerous or contaminating,[54] or on how closely related these animals are to humans, which may make them more prone to carrying zoonotic disease.[55] Designating certain zoo animals as potential threats to human health under the scope of this law justifies a range of acts, such as quarantines, suspension of imports from particular places, and inspections by health officers.[56]

Other Scales of Animal Legislation

In addition to federal laws, laws on other geographic scales also regulate wild animals and, by extension, sometimes pertain to zoo animals. Most notably, the Convention on International Trade in Endangered Species of Wild Fauna and Flora (CITES) is an international treaty that regulates the international import and export of species threatened by trade, "recognizing, in addition, that international co-operation is essential for the protection of certain species of wild fauna and flora against over-exploitation through international trade."[57] The international trade regulations of CITES include a licensing requirement for the import, export, and introduction of 5,310 listed animal species.[58] In 1975, the United States incorporated CITES through the Endangered Species Act.

In its Appendix I, CITES provides the most stringent protection to 625 of the 5,310 species threatened with extinction, prohibiting the international trade of these species except when the import is not for primarily commercial purposes and is not detrimental to the survival of that species.[59] In these exceptional cases, trade may take place provided that import and export permits are issued. Because most of the zoos accredited by the AZA are legally defined as noncommercial, they have often obtained such permits.[60]

At more local scales of governance, various American states have enacted their own variations on the AWA to prohibit the cruel treatment of animals.[61] Some states, however, including Iowa, Kentucky, Ohio, and Washington, have no state regulation of exotic animal exhibitions. Massachusetts, New Jersey, and South Carolina ban exotic animal exhibitions but exempt zoos; and most other states either regulate the importation or ownership of animals or require combinations of local approval or state or federal license to exhibit animals in a zoo.[62]

Taken together, this bricolage of statutes, each with its own scale, purpose, jurisdiction, and exemptions, can lead to confusion, oversights—or worse. Registrar Rachél Watkins Rogers of Zoo Miami gives a cautionary example of the gaps in official laws that pertain to zoo animals:

> In California, a tiger escaped and killed someone in the public. . . . [It turned out that this] facility had substandard exhibit height, moat depth, and width. How do I explain that this passed the eyes of the inspectors? The Animal Welfare Act is focused on the welfare of the animal. It's not focused on caging standards for safety. . . . Fish and Wildlife is [in some respects responsible for] the safety of the public . . . but I don't think that they do that level of detail. . . . Now, the tiger incident happened because there's all these webs of law that apply to different aspects, but none of them address standards for enclosures by species.[63]

Zoo Animals as Property

The peculiar legal status of zoo animals is not only reflected and created through various international, federal, state, and local statutory norms, but is also manifest in American case law. The first American court case concerning a zoo animal was recorded in the early 1900s: an action in tort for a camel bite injury.[64] In this case, the California Supreme Court appeared to be of two minds about zoo animals: while comparing them to confined, domesticated pets, the court simultaneously presumed them to be generally unpredictable and "naturally ferocious." The few cases on zoo animals published since then express much of the same ambivalence.[65]

Similarly, zoo animals occupy a peculiar place in property law. Current American property law provides that animals that are wild in nature (*ferae naturae*) belong to the state (*res communes*), and no individual property rights exist in them as long as they remain wild, unconfined, and undomesticated.[66] At the same time, the courts have established that "wild animals reduced from the wild state in compliance with applicable law become property of an individual."[67] To the limited extent that the subject has been considered, then, American property cases treat the zoo animal as a proprietary trade good, existing "somewhere above the rank of 'domestic pet' and below that of 'indentured servant.'"[68]

Indeed, zoo animals are almost always owned by zoos (although not necessarily by the zoos in which they are kept, as indicated in Chapter 5). The case of the golden lion tamarin is a remarkable exception to the norm of zoo ownership. According to Cleveland Metroparks Zoo director Steve Taylor, in 1991 North American zoos decided to relinquish their ownership of this animal, instead declaring it the property of Brazil, its country of origin.[69] This, however, is an exception to the general rule: usually, zoo animals—even those that were born in the wild and are critically endangered—are the property of zoos. Moreover, although in this exceptional case the animal is not owned by any zoo, an owner still exists (in this case, the Brazilian government), thereby reifying the significance of ownership for the management of zoo animals.

At the same time, the recent intensification in AZA's collective management of zoo animals has arguably eroded the meaning of the institutional ownership of zoo animals. According to the 2011 International Studbook for Western Lowland Gorilla, only six of fifty-five gorilla transfers in 2010 involved a change of ownership.[70] Owned by Cleveland Metroparks Zoo since 1966, Timmy the gorilla lived in other AZA accredited zoos for over twenty years. The other eleven gorillas displayed with Timmy at the Louisville Zoo exhibit were also on loan from elsewhere, including Atlanta, the Bronx, Cincinnati, Cleveland, Dallas, Chicago, and Philadelphia.[71] "Nowadays, ownership is just a word," says Taylor. "We own several gorillas, but that doesn't mean much, because we believe in the importance of complying with [AZA's] recommendations and transporting them to other zoos."[72] Kristen Lukas of Cleveland Metroparks Zoo states along these lines that although her zoo "technically still owns Timmy, ownership means less and less these days because of how we make decisions through the cooperative management programs."[73] Rather than relinquishing the animal property model, then, zoos have replaced it with a collective form of property administration.

In some instances, however, institutional ownership still matters, even with regard to collectively managed zoo animals. This, for example, was the case in the controversy over the killer whale Ikaika. Owned by SeaWorld©, Ikaika was loaned to Marineland of Canada Inc. pursuant to a breeding loan agreement.

When SeaWorld gave written notice to Marineland of its intention to terminate the agreement upon its expiration, Marineland declined to return the whale. A long trial ensued that ended with the dismissal of Marineland's appeal by the Ontario Court of Appeal in September 2011.[74] Where disputes in the zoo world arise, the model of institutional ownership and loan contracts reemerges as the prevailing legal framework, superseding issues of proper care or the intentions of a breeding program. Ownership also matters in the sense that some zoos still buy and sell their animals, especially those that are not managed collectively (see Chapter 1).

However, the legal status of zoo animals as property is never quite secure. A change of circumstance can easily trigger a change in the animal's legal status into *ferae naturae*, or into something else altogether. In this sense, the animal's "authentic" legal identity as wild always looms in the background, destabilizing its status as a simple matter of property. The most dramatic examples of this destabilization of legal status are unintentional escapes and intentional reintroductions into the wild.

The reintroduction of endangered species onto privately owned land presents a uniquely delicate legal situation. The designation of these animals as "endangered" typically deters landowners from participating in such reintroduction programs, as it normally requires that the land be maintained in its current condition. Therefore, the FWS has been assigning certain reintroduced populations (usually ones that are endangered) the status of a "nonessential experimental population,"[75] which affords landowners certain protections. For example, in 2003 the FWS changed the legal designation of the black-footed ferret in certain areas of the United States from endangered to threatened and finally to experimental.[76] As a result, these animal populations receive less protection than endangered species in the wild, the assumption being that such weakened protection encourages the cooperation of private citizens with the FWS. The reintroduction of captive animals into the wild, especially when this wild is privately owned, is thus as much a legal enterprise as it is a physical and ecological one.

Official Laws for Zoo Facilities and Workers

Because the zoo contains both humans and wild animals in the same space, it must observe the official laws that apply to both of these populations. In the words of geography scholar Gail Davies, "although curtailed by boundaries and unequal separations, you are in a place that is shared between people and animals."[77] In addition to being hybrid animal-human spaces, most zoos are also public spaces, at least in the most immediate sense that they are open to the visiting public.[78] Furthermore, some zoos are partially owned by the public—the city, the county, the state, or a combination thereof.[79] A series of legal consequences flow from the zoo's characterization as a public space. As with other public spaces in the United States, zoos must comply with various laws, including historic preservation laws, state and city building codes, disability laws, and regulations that pertain to the health and safety of workers. Although most of the discussion here draws on the specific example of the Buffalo Zoo, it nonetheless illuminates the on-the-ground frictions between animal-centered and human-centered laws that are characteristic of most American zoos.

Historic Preservation Laws

The Buffalo Zoo—the third oldest zoo in the country[80]—is situated within the Olmsted Parks and Parkways, a registered national historic designed landscape. Three of the zoo's buildings—the Main Zoo Building, the Elephant House, and the Shelter House—are included in the registered listing as original contributing structures.[81] The Buffalo Olmsted Parks Conservancy, the City of Buffalo Preservation Board, the New York State Historic Preservation Office, and the National Park Service thus protect and monitor these structures as well as their surrounding landscape.[82] Donna Fernandes, the zoo's director, explains that the complex set of preservation laws have made it difficult to perform major changes in the zoo's infrastructural design. "Once [a building] is over fifty years [old], it gets protected," she complains.[83] Underlying her frustration is the belief, shared by many zoo personnel, that the preservation of zoo buildings often conflicts with the preservation of zoo animals.

One instance of such a conflict arose over the Buffalo Zoo's Elephant House. The building, one of the oldest of its kind in the country, was completed in 1912,[84] but in 2003 the AZA updated its accreditation standards for elephant care, expanding the required space for each elephant. The Elephant House fell 150 square feet short of the AZA standard. Because of the building's status as a historic preservation site, the zoo had to find a way to expand the inside space without changing the exterior. "We were just caught in the middle," Fernandes says about the difficulties of complying with the two conflicting legal regimes.[85]

New York's Bronx Zoo faced similar issues with its 1905 Lion House. Again, preservation laws prohibited changes to the original footprint of the building, and because of the enactment of more stringent industry standards it became impossible to house lions in the building. The building stood empty for thirty years, until the zoo finally transformed it into the Madagascar exhibit, a region that was chosen because of the small primates found there. The process of renovating the building and designing the exhibit to comply with historic preservation laws cost the zoo over $60 million.[86] Effectively, New York's historic preservation laws, although not intended directly for zoos, ultimately shaped both the physical design of the zoo exhibit and the choice of animals to be displayed there.

Chicago's Lincoln Park Zoo director Kevin Bell speaks more sympathetically about preservation laws. "It took hundreds of millions of dollars to renovate the zoo's old primate house," he says.[87] But rather than seeing historic preservation codes as oppressive, Bell believes that they provide older urban zoos with the opportunity to present themselves as architectural gems. According to Bell, historic preservation and nature preservation—zoo buildings and zoo animals—can coexist, and may even be co-productive in a way that benefits zoos.

The conflict between historic preservation laws and animal care standards reflects the multiple interests at stake in zoos. On the one hand, municipal and state authorities seek to gain protection and recognition for unique historic structures within their jurisdictions. Zoos, as established urban institutions, often house structures that need to be preserved. On the other hand, the AZA advances and enforces minimum standards for animal care and facilities, prescribing changes to the same historic buildings. In other words, this is a conflict between preserving human heritage by conserving the unique architecture of zoo buildings and preserving natural heritage by conserving endangered animals.

Building Codes

William Conway, one of the important figures in North American zoo politics, is often quoted as saying that architects are the most dangerous animals at the zoo.[88] This view evokes the juxtaposition of animals and buildings, which is mirrored in the juxtaposition of animal-related and human-related laws. Building codes are yet another legal regime that influences zoo animals, zoogoers, zoo personnel, and zoo spaces. In this context, however, the zoo is regulated from the perspective of the safety and accessibility of the *human* public. "Running a [zoo] building is like running a small city," says William McKeown who, with Evelyn Junge, serves as legal counsel for the Bronx Zoo. "In every exhibit there is a set of rules and regulations, procedures to be used, and protocols to be followed." "Most importantly," McKeown adds, "physical safety must be obtained."[89] The zoo's legal counselors affirm that human safety is the chief concern of these laws.

Gwen Howard, Buffalo Zoo architect, is all too familiar with the anomalies that arise when human-oriented building codes are applied rigidly to zoo buildings that house animals. As an example, Howard notes the case of a guard railing situated inside the Elephant House, in a space accessed almost exclusively by zookeepers:

> The building code requires that stairs must have . . . guardrails if the drop is greater than thirty inches. . . . Well, I can't make anything elephant-proof, no matter how hard I try. So they [could] take the railings, work them off, and now they are swinging around a railing that could hurt themselves, hurt anybody, hurt another elephant. I was required to put that [railing] in, but I had to go get a variance because I had to explain that it's more dangerous for the zookeeper to keep the railing there.[90]

This quote illuminates a common assumption about law: that the only agents who affect its operations are human. Indeed, laws are imposed on animals and spaces as if they were both passive objects to be molded, protected, and, more generally, spoken for by humans. But the capacity of humans to speak for nature is often problematic and never secure.[91] Animals still have the power to surprise humans and, in this case, elephants can swing around a railing and hurt zookeepers and themselves, thus asserting their agency. Despite their subjugated legal position, animals are nevertheless active subjects that embody a form of agency in their ability to challenge, disturb, and provoke humans.[92] Animals, in other words, can "kick back" at their human protectors, which is how geographer Sarah Whatmore describes nonhuman resistance to human programming.[93] Animals also exercise their own "natural laws," in the sense that they adhere to their basic instinctual and physical constitution.[94] Hence, even after over one hundred years of experience in training and enclosure—designed to keep wild animals confined within the zoo's gates—accidents and escapes still occur.[95] Also, despite the zoos' best efforts to recombine animal social pairings and groups for optimal breeding plans, the animals themselves do not always comply with such matchmaking, as further discussed in Chapter 7.

Beyond the particular absurdities that occur when applying regular building codes to animal houses, architect Howard also points to the rigid attitude of certain zoning officers in the enforcement of these codes. In the case of the Elephant House, instead of granting the zoo an administrative variance—which would have been relatively easy for the zoo to obtain—the enforcement officer insisted that the zoo must apply to the zoning board to obtain a variance to the New York State Building Code:

> We all recognize that the [building] law was not written to protect people from elephants. The law is written to protect people so they can safely get in and out of the building and to control the spread of fire in that building. [But] I had to go through this whole board procedure, which was just process for process's sake. I easily presented the case. . . . They all said "you're absolutely right." They all laughed and sent me on my way. [This happened] because somebody felt they had to follow the rules to the letter.[96]

Following the rules to the letter, Howard implies here, can result in awkward consequences for zoos. This is especially true when laws inadequately address the unique characteristics of zoo facilities and zoo animals. In an attempt to correct some of the obvious absurdities, zoo spaces have often been found eligible for variances and exceptions. However, because these depend on the interpretations of individual inspectors and boards, such variations and exceptions are never secure.

Another example of the tensions that arise when applying human-centered building laws to zoo buildings is the debate that ensued with respect to the inflated Teflon® rooftop at the Buffalo Zoo's Rainforest Falls exhibit. Alongside the complications of accommodating both humans and animals, this exhibit was also designed to create an outdoor experience inside a building. According to Howard, the rooftop material is "an ethylene tetrafluoroethylene [that] lets through 100 percent ultraviolet light, which is healthiest for the animals. Nobody in this country had used that before. So try to explain to a code enforcement official that it is a safe thing to use. . . . We really had to fight to be able to use that building product, because they just didn't understand it."[97] Although the Teflon rooftop violated the relevant energy codes for a human-inhabited building, the zoo eventually received a permit to install it. To work around the intricacies of these codes, the interior of the exhibit space was reassigned from "public assembly" to "U (unregulated) occupancy," the latter defined as "buildings and structures of an accessory character and miscellaneous structures not classified in any

Figure 12. Buffalo Zoo's Rainforest Falls exhibit, classified as a "U" building (an unregulated agricultural occupancy space), June 22, 2009. Courtesy of Eric Lee / Buffalo Zoo.

specific occupancy."[98] Howard explains the reasons behind this reassignment of the exhibit's legal status:

> We decided, as a team, that we were going to call the front part of the building . . .
> "public space," [but] that once you entered the doors into the animal exhibit, that was
> going to be "U occupancy": an unregulated agricultural occupancy under the New
> York State Building Code. . . . We had this kind of tacit agreement that we would call
> this an animal holding building. . . . [So] we didn't have to fire sprinkler it, which
> would have been a big problem to try to fire sprinkler all this space.[99]

Despite its function as a public space, the Rainforest Falls exhibit was thus legally defined as nonpublic through its designation as an unregulated ("U") space. As a result, the zoo was exempt from meeting the requirements of a public space, such as sprinklers.[100]

The Teflon roof example highlights the productive intersections of law and space: legally redefined as a "U" space, this exhibit was better-suited to represent and enable its unique functions of housing and displaying animals. Because "U" spaces are typically applied to agricultural structures, the definition of the exhibit as such enabled certain physical functions that would otherwise have been prohibited (Teflon roofs) or obligatory (sprinkler devices) in strictly public spaces. Again, the various laws and exemptions that apply to zoos effectively shape the zoo's physical terrain and vice versa—the zoo's terrain shapes the relevant laws.

Other odd consequences occur when applying ordinary building codes to animal exhibits. Howard explains that the zoo is required to install a fire alarm system in all of its "public assembly" spaces. But "things like fire alarm systems, which are a required code element, can be really problematic in animal holding areas," Howard says. "Imagine a $250,000 giraffe . . . that's all legs, just wrapping itself around bars and everything because this weird device is going off and screaming in [its] ears. . . . You'd have a bunch of dead giraffes, and if somebody was in there, they would probably be stomped to death before they could get out."[101] Unlike Howard's earlier depiction of the elephant's potentially defiant behavior—characterized by strength, anger, and agency—her description of the giraffe's reaction to fire alarms relays her perception of this animal's helplessness in the face of human technology as well as its lack of agency.

The discussion of building codes demonstrates that official law is ill-equipped to deal with the peculiarity of the zoo as a hybrid place that simultaneously houses both animals and humans. The laws that pertain to zoo buildings and structures may thus be likened to a blanket that is too short: when pulled from the one side (animal safety), it uncovers the other side (human safety). At the same time, this discussion also illustrates how zoo officials have negotiated the often-strict application of building codes and other laws. Legal exemptions provide ways to work around the mismatches between the rigidities of legal classifications and the peculiarities of the zoo. Variances, reassignments, and acts of human discretion enable a more flexible and pragmatic network of zoo laws that promotes the coexistence of humans and animals under the same roof, in turn enabling a space that is "more-than-human."[102] In other words, the various exemptions of the zoo's physical spaces from official laws can provide a legal space that accommodates the unique nature of the zoo.

Americans with Disabilities Act

As a public space, the zoo must also comply with the Americans with Dis-abilities Act (ADA),[103] a wide-ranging civil rights law that prohibits discrimina-tion based on disability. Disability is defined by this act as "a physical or mental impairment that substantially limits a major life activity."[104] Although the space of the zoo is designed around the principle of visibility, the ADA requires that this should not obstruct the right of any sight-impaired person from visiting the zoo. Howard explains:

> Blind people have the right to visit the zoo. I still design for them, whether I think they are going to come or not. [Hence,] there are restrictions as to what can overhang and how far. Like if you had a sign on a pole, the sign can't stick out so far so that if you're walking with a cane, and your cane misses it, then your body hits it. So some of the rockwork things that we did would have been [designed differently if not for this law].[105]

Howard further describes the legal constraints that accessibility requirements impose on her freedom to design the zoo's space:

> We tried to do other things but ended up giving it up because handicap regulations made it more problematic. . . . That's our biggest challenge, handicap accessibility. We could do all kinds of really cool stuff if it didn't need to be handicap accessible. I could really change your perspective on how you view the animals and everything, but it's really hard to make those things handicap accessible. [For example,] in the bat exhibit we wanted to have these little slits in the rock that you could look through, that you would put your face up [to] and peer through. But they weren't chair accessible. [So] we couldn't pull it off. We designed it that way, but it was impossible [to actually do].[106]

Does the zoo's compliance with ADA's ethos of accessibility also present a challenge to its absolute reliance on the eye? In his work on accessibility in mu-seum exhibits, Kevin Hetherington suggests that most accessibility designs still operate within the framework of seeing through the eye rather than creating al-ternative sensory—or haptic—regimes to the scopic or visual ones.[107] In the con-text of animals, such haptic regimes might have included touching, smelling, and hearing animals. As discussed in Chapter 2, such sensory elements are un-derdeveloped in comparison with the heightened project of seeing the zoo ani-mal. In fact, the direct touching, smelling, and hearing of animals contradicts many animal care guidelines and regulations, as examined next.

The Occupational Safety and Health Administration

Direct contact with wild animals is becoming increasingly restricted, even for zookeepers who are employed by the zoo to work with animals. In its Occupational Safety and Health Act of 1970, Congress created the federal Occupational Safety and Health Administration (OSHA).[108] OSHA enforces general safety regulations for the workplace, including zoos. Workplace safety violations for animal keepers at zoos and amusement parks fall within the power of the General Duty Clause, which mandates that each employer provide an environment free from recognized hazards that are likely to cause death or serious injury.[109] Although nothing in this federal law is specific to protecting animal keepers from the dangers caused by wild animals, in recent years OSHA has investigated and fined several zoos and parks for failing to ensure the safety of employees working with such animals.

Specifically, OSHA has recently filed two major suits against zoos for injuries incurred by employees working with animals in allegedly unsafe working conditions. The first major suit was against SeaWorld in Orlando, Florida. During its investigation of the 2010 death of a SeaWorld trainer who was killed by a killer whale during a water show, OSHA determined that SeaWorld regularly exposed its trainers to dangerous working conditions involving the animals at its parks.[110] In August 2010, OSHA fined SeaWorld $75,000 for three safety violations.[111] One of these citations was for a "willful" safety violation—the act's most severe classification—for exposure of employees to "drowning hazards when interacting with killer whales."[112] Most significantly, OSHA recommended the use of physical barriers to prevent SeaWorld trainers from having close contact with the whales.[113] This case has sparked debate as to the safety of animal keepers who perform what zoo professionals call "free contact" work with dangerous animals (in contrast to "protected contact" work).

The free versus protected contact debate was sparked again with the death of an elephant keeper at the Knoxville Zoo in 2011.[114] In a second recent major suit against zoos, OSHA cited the Knoxville Zoo for endangering its employees through the continual practice of free contact between elephants and keepers that resulted in the death of the zoo's elephant-trainer. The investigation determined that there were previous incidents with the same elephant. The Tennessee division of OSHA ultimately fined and issued a "serious General Duty Citation" to the Knoxville Zoo for not placing dangerous animals in protected contact to prevent employees from injury. Following OSHA's recommendation, the zoo has taken steps to improve work safety conditions for its employees by replacing the free contact with the protected contact method. Although OSHA has not called for a sweeping federal regulation that prohibits direct contact between zoo employees and elephants, it acknowledged that human exposure to large animals may pose a serious occupational health and safety concern.

The Tennessee decision prompted the AZA to change its policy regarding contact with elephants. Under the new policy, effective September 2014, elephant keepers in accredited zoos will be required to use the protected contact method, which mandates erecting protective barriers between elephants and keepers and using positive reinforcement, rather than punishment, to train the animals. Animal rights activists have been supporting this move, which they hope will effectively phase out a free-contact training method whereby keepers use the ankus (in the language of zoo staff), or bull hook (in the language of animal activists), to manage the elephants.[115] The Elephant Managers Association sees things somewhat differently, asserting that the new policy contradicts accepted elephant care standards, will compromise elephant husbandry, and will put both elephants and keepers at risk when the animals experience health emergencies.[116]

Industry Standards

> The care of animals is of the absolute, utmost importance in our standards.
> [But] we're also looking at things no one else is looking at, [and that] are
> not all animal related. We're looking at: What's the zoo's financial
> structure? Is there financial contingency? Are there sufficient staffing levels
> for caring for the number of animals in the collection of an institution?
>
> Kristin Vehrs, executive director, AZA[117]

The exemption of zoos and their animals from many official laws, as already noted, is rooted in the political struggles between zoo professionals and animal protection advocates. Indeed, the last five decades have seen intense legal and political clashes between these two groups, grounded in their radically different definitions of conservation. Whereas the animal protection people focus on the rights of individual animals and are less willing to accept compromises to animal welfare,[118] zoos are increasingly moving beyond the welfare model into a new paradigm wherein animals are viewed as part of their wider habitats. As a result, zoo personnel generally believe that compromising the captive animal's individual well-being is justified in the name of the broader survival of the species. According to Kristin Vehrs of the AZA, the battle between animal protection groups and her organization is still as fierce as ever.[119]

But American zoos were not always as organized or successful at making the legal case for self-regulation as they are today. In the 1960s, American animal welfare groups mobilized pressure on Congress, which passed the Animal Welfare Act (AWA) in 1966, with practically no consultation with zoos. It was not until the 1970s that zoos in the United States began to organize seriously.[120] Partly as a response to its failure to prevent the application of the AWA to zoos, in January 1972 the AZA (until then the American Association of Zoological Parks and Aquariums, or the AAZPA) separated from the National Recreation and Park Association to form an independent interest group.

The enactment of the Endangered Species Act (ESA) in 1973 was a milestone in the relationship between zoos and the federal government. While the ESA provided much-needed protection of wild animals—and was therefore initially supported by the network of increasingly conservationist zoo professionals—it also threatened to prevent zoos from collecting or exhibiting wild animals by curtailing their ability to obtain these animals from the wild or to transfer these animals between zoos. Around that time, the animal welfare movement was still lobbying for stricter regulation of zoo animals, and even gained public and congressional support for a federal zoo agency.[121] Faced with this prospect, American zoos, led by the AZA, successfully lobbied for self-regulation and internal policing. Indeed, the newly established professional zoo network advanced the professionalization of accredited zoos and lobbied for exemptions from new laws, including a limited right to take protected animals from the wild.[122] Simultaneously, animal protection groups promoted piecemeal legislation that would apply to zoo animals, to which the AZA reacted by lobbying for further exemptions; and so the cycle of regulation versus exemption continues to this day.

For the most part, the federal government has accepted the nonintervention policy advanced by the AZA, maintaining that zoos and aquariums can more effectively regulate animal care through self-policing than the government has done through rule-making. As a result, American government at all levels generally allows accredited zoos to monitor themselves. As Senator J. James Exon from Nebraska remarked, "America's public display institutions . . . have taken their responsibilities to the public, their animals and future generations very seriously.

Self-regulation among America's zoos, aquariums, and marine parks significantly exceeds the minimum Federal and State standards."[123]

The AZA stresses the importance of self-regulation. Here, from its accreditation guidelines: "Through this process, a profession is judged based on criteria selected by its own members, rather than an outside agency."[124] A senior AZA official suggests along these lines that any legal regimes imposed from the outside are detrimental to the work of zoos, since such outside laws could not even begin to capture the zoo's complicated and nuanced features.[125] One distinct advantage to governing through internal standards, the official says, is the relative flexibility to update these standards to reflect evolving knowledge about zoo animals.[126] Unlike the legislative and administrative processes, he continues, the zoo's industry standards enable an adaptive form of animal management by providing a quicker process of updating and more room for discretion and interpretation. Indeed, AZA's accreditation standards are updated every year, and the standards provided in its care manuals are also updated regularly. So, for example, if a tiger escapes from a certain enclosure, AZA standards for tiger enclosures that apply to all accredited institutions can be fixed accordingly. A second advantage of self-regulation, zoo professionals argue, is its participatory nature. The AZA employs only a handful of in-house staff; zoo personnel from individual institutions voluntarily perform the bulk of the work in animal programs across the country. As a result, the zoo members themselves are responsible for deciding, monitoring, and enforcing association policies. All the working rules, regulations, and guidelines of animal programs thus undergo internal development and review processes, which render them that much more effective.

Although zoo officials have adamantly lobbied for minimal regulation of zoo animals, they have not hesitated to advocate for more stringent legislation of exotic animals in non-zoo facilities. In October 2011, the AZA released the following statement regarding the mass animal escape from a private facility in Zanesville, Ohio:

> The private facility in Ohio, from which animals were released into the surrounding community, was not an AZA-accredited zoo. . . . A number of states regulate the ownership of dangerous wild animals by private individuals. . . . We urge the State of Ohio and others to adopt such regulations. Wild animals do not make good pets. *AZA-accredited zoos have the facilities and expertise to properly and safely care for wild animals.*[127]

A Columbus Zoo press release informs that "the Columbus Zoo and Aquarium has been working with the governor's task force to draft a framework for permanent legislation to enact stronger, enforceable Ohio laws restricting private ownership of exotic animals."[128] This incident thus provided the AZA with an opportunity to proclaim the distinctions between the responsible management of wild animals by accredited zoos and the presumably dangerous management of exotic animals by private facilities.

Animal protection advocates have also used the Zanesville incident to restate their call for official sanctions that apply to all captive animals, whether in private or zoo facilities. According to Born Free USA, the Ohio incident should

> serve as a brutal reminder that wildlife belong in the wild and that no one should ever put the animals or the public at risk by trying to confine them in a zoo, circus, backyard or home, where serious injury or death can occur at any time. Laws have to be created and enforced to stop these potential situations at the source. No one should be allowed ever to 'own' a wild animal. Period.[129]

Zoos certainly disagree, claiming that they abide by strict ethical standards in their care and exhibition of wild animals.[130] For zoos, keeping animals is justified by their dual mission: conserving animal biodiversity and educating the public to conserve nature.[131] This dual mission, zoo officials argue, are evident in AZA's Code of Professional Ethics.

Code of Professional Ethics

All AZA members are bound by the organization's Code of Professional Ethics, which outlines the members' professional obligations and the mandatory standards that pertain to their operations.[132] Originally adopted in 1976, AZA's Code of Professional Ethics states in its preamble that "Members of the American Association of Zoological Parks and Aquariums . . . have an important role in the preservation of our heritage."[133] Additionally, the code states that

> deviation by a member from the AZA Code of Professional Ethics or from any of the rules officially adopted by the Board of Directors supplemental thereto, or any action by a member that is detrimental to the best interest of the zoo and aquarium profession and the AZA, shall be considered unethical conduct. The member shall be subject to investigation by the AZA Ethics Board and, if warranted, to disciplinary action by the Ethics Board and/or the AZA Board of Directors.[134]

The code further distinguishes between obligations, which represent the objectives that every member should strive toward, and mandatory standards, which, if violated, may result in disciplinary actions:

> The Mandatory Standards, to be uniformly applied to all members, establish a level of conduct below which no member may fall without being subject to disciplinary action. The Code makes no attempt to prescribe either disciplinary procedures or penalties for violation of Mandatory Standards. The severity of judgment against a member found to be in violation of a Mandatory Standard shall be determined by the character of the offense and the attendant circumstances.

One of AZA's mandatory standards states, for example: "A member shall make every effort to assure that all animals in his/her collection and under his/her care are disposed of in a manner which meets the current disposition standards of the Association and do not find their way into the hands of those not qualified to care for them properly."[135] Another standard states: "A member shall not knowingly misinform others regarding animal records or specimen disposition, professional information, and advice."[136]

Ethical standards may not be considered legal norms in the traditional sense; they grant broad discretion to board members and the like and, in this sense, are less prescriptive than many official laws. Nonetheless, ethical standards and their prescribed proceedings are framed in legal terms and include sanctions that are likely to influence the practices of accredited zoos as much, if not more, than official laws. Alongside its ethical standards, the AZA has also established an extensive network of accreditation standards and policies.

Accreditation Standards and Policies

AZA's enforcement powers are a result of its effective organizational structure, which is based on accreditation. The AZA maintains two credentialing programs: accreditation for its institutional members, which must conform to AZA's definition of zoos and aquariums, and certification for "related facility members."[137] The AZA defines the type of zoological park or aquarium eligible for accreditation as a "permanent institution which owns and maintains wildlife, under the direction of a professional staff, provides its collection with appropriate care and exhibits them in an aesthetic manner to the public on a regular basis. The institution, division, or section shall further be defined as having as their primary mission the exhibition, conservation, and preservation of the earth's fauna in an educational and scientific manner."[138] Operating alongside AZA's institutional members, "related facilities" are defined as "organizations holding wildlife but not open to the public on a regularly scheduled, predictable basis."[139] These include wildlife ranches, research facilities, breeding farms, and educational outreach organizations.[140] Among AZA's accredited members are also eleven international facilities—including the Toronto Zoo, Parque Zoológico de León in Mexico, and the Bermuda Aquarium and Zoo.[141] These institutions must follow the same accreditation standards that apply to their U.S. counterparts.

The AZA's "Accreditation Standards and Related Policies" are central to the administration and regulation of its members. The standards list the minimum requirements from members (and, with minor changes, from related facilities) on topics such as housing, husbandry, handling, and human-animal interactions.[142] The mission and expectations of conservation and education are articulated in the standards' preamble: "Animals must be well cared for and displayed in naturalistic settings that provide an educational experience for visitors and an appropriate enriching environment for the animals, including proper social groupings. The species included in the collection must be managed on a regional basis to ensure long-term genetic viability of the species, which means careful planning of resource allocation, ex-situ breeding, and ex-situ/in-situ conservation and research."[143] The standards also include minimum requirements from members regarding the collection and documentation of all zoo animals, acquisition and disposition policies, veterinary care, conservation and education, safety and security, quarantine procedures, and human-animal contact.

William Conway provides a historical perspective on AZA's current accreditation system:

> I wrote the AZA's [initial] accreditation program. . . . It was a hell of a campaign, a lot of people didn't want it. I said, "We've got to do a hell of a lot better." So we put a team together and I wrote the damn thing and then we got a team to look at it and agree with it, and disagree, and help to improve it. Then they passed it [and] have kept it ever since. Now I guess it's twenty odd years old, and every year they try to make it better and stricter. It's a lot better than when I wrote it. When we had that, we had a basis.[144]

Conway describes AZA's accreditation program as fundamental for the zoo's institutional existence in the United States. Even so, it was not until 1985 that accreditation first became mandatory for organizations holding wildlife and seeking membership in the AZA.[145]

Pat Thomas, general curator at the Bronx Zoo, speaks about AZA's accreditation routines from an operational perspective:

> Each zoo is reinspected every five years by a team. . . . They're free to go wherever they want. They're free to talk to whomever they want. . . . Certainly, animal welfare is a huge concern, and if they feel that facilities are substandard they can say, "If you don't make these corrections we'll take away your accreditation." If they find something that you are not in agreement with, you have a voice to express your concerns or explain your different views. The team that inspects you is not the team that makes the decision on whether or not you should be reaccredited.[146]

Thomas further stresses the AZA's power to "take away accreditation from a zoo if it doesn't maintain standards."[147] Similarly, Fernandes explains how AZA's sanctions affect her zoo's everyday operations:

> [Basically,] the zoo could continue to operate as such even without accreditation. The only issue is that it's hard to get animals. In many cases our animals are on loan, we don't own all the animals that are here. Zoos from all over the country will send us animals for breeding loan under the assumption that we will take good care of them. And when you lose accreditation, other zoos won't send them, and in some cases they will recall any animals they have on loan to you. So say you had a giraffe on loan, even if your giraffe exhibit was fabulous but you lost accreditation because of some unrelated thing, some zoos would still be inclined to recall their animals.[148]

Because of the strict legal prohibitions against taking certain animals from the wild, American zoos are increasingly dependent on AZA's collective breeding network for an ongoing supply of managed zoo animals. For many zoos, then, belonging to the AZA is not a choice but a necessity. In other words, despite its self-portrayal as voluntary guidelines, AZA's accreditation system is very much the official law when it comes to accredited zoos. Through its accreditation standards, the AZA effectively establishes a legal "zooland," wherein only accredited members may participate in the collaborative conservation project. At the same time, the fact that the vast majority of zoos in the United States remain unaccredited is a testament to the widespread unwillingness or inability to conform to AZA's standards and guidelines.

Animal Care Manuals

In addition to its accreditation standards, the AZA has developed care manuals for ten species—and a dozen additional manuals are currently in progress.[149] These manuals describe the taxonomy of the species, review the current research that pertains to this species, and outline recommendations for its care, including habitat design and containment, transport, social groups, nutrition, veterinary care, reproduction, and behavior management.[150]

The Standardized Care Guidelines for gorillas provide an apt example of AZA's care manuals.[151] In this one-hundred-page document, AZA's gorilla SSP program offers specific guidelines for gorilla care. One of the program's recommendations states, for example, that "elements such as heated perches, shade, and sun pockets should be carefully placed in an exhibit to maximize viewing opportunities."[152] In this one recommendation, the guidelines consider the gorillas' ambient temperature needs, the exhibit's design, and the zoogoers' experience. This recommendation thus differs from official laws in that it simultaneously considers zoo animals, zoo design, zoogoers, and zookeepers. The guidelines also provide detailed recommendations for complex enclosure designs:

> Exhibits with multiple habitats, fully integrated with holding buildings that interconnect each habitat, as well as night quarters, shifts, squeezes, and dayrooms, are necessary to fulfill the concept of a "life-care complex" for an ever-expanding population of gorillas within a singly managed facility. Visual barriers, access to privacy, climbing apparatus, vegetation, nesting material, and manipulable objects are important in reducing stress, social conflict, and boredom.[153]

The gorilla guidelines also recommend designing enclosures that facilitate human management. Specific design features include quarantine spaces, nursing rooms, introduction suites with howdy walls (walls specially designed for gorilla newcomers to see, smell, and even touch each other without the possibility of injury), squeeze cages (where the animal can be contained for medical examination), collection cages (for bodily fluids), and weigh stations. Because the sounds and smells of humans and other animals can affect gorilla behavior, the guidelines also offer specific recommendations for how to create aural and olfactory barriers. Furthermore, the design and materials of the various exhibit features are specified in detail to avoid the likelihood of injury to either gorillas or their keepers.

The guidelines also outline measures to ensure the psychological enrichment of gorillas[154] and to encourage their natural behaviors. The guidelines instruct, for example, that a variety and rotation of different bedding, forage, furnishings, toys, plants, and diet are to be provided and that food must be presented to the gorilla in a variety of forms (e.g., whole unprocessed vegetables and fruits) and challenges (hard-to-reach locations, within puzzles, or mixed with forage). Finally, the guidelines address a wide range of human-animal interactions and associated problems, including zoonotic diseases, safety procedures, training, and the hand-rearing of infants. Some of the most sensitive training for human-gorilla interactions addressed in the guidelines is that between a gorilla mother, her infant, and their human caretakers:

> Infant care training is a priority for animals that are first time mothers. . . . Suggested primary training goals for pregnant females are:
> —*Separation*: In case temporary removal from the group is required or a closer assessment of the infant is needed;
> —*Pick up object*: To develop the behavior of picking up her offspring if she should place it on the ground;
> —*Pick up object and present the object at the mesh*: To develop the behavior of allowing the animal care staff to get a close visual inspection of the infant to assess health status; . . .
> —*Breast manipulation*: To allow animal care staff to assess if the female is lactating, and desensitize the breast to a nursing infant.[155]

From the AZA's perspective, the guidelines that it offers for the care of certain animals are highly detailed and reflect a process of ongoing review and revisions that intentionally integrate animals and humans in the space of the zoo. From an animal rights perspective, however, these guidelines "are often based on hearsay and tradition rather than being objective and scientifically-validated. Furthermore, there is a fundamental lack of basic knowledge in relation to the behaviour and ecology of many species kept by zoos."[156] Regardless of one's position, the fact remains that AZA-accredited zoos are still a minority of captive wildlife facilities in the United States and that AZA's standards apply only within those institutions.

Conclusion

The legal status of zoos and zoo animals is fraught with the tension of human-animal distinctions and correlations, not unlike the tension between animal-human separateness and immersion embodied in the zoo's physical design. The official laws that pertain to zoos almost always ignore either the animal or the human components of this hybrid space. For example, animal-oriented welfare and conservation laws, such as the AWA and the ESA, exclusively target the well-being of animals, disregarding the thousands of zoo employees and the millions of other humans who visit the zoo every year. At the same time, human-oriented building codes are not designed to accommodate elephants, and fire codes are not configured with giraffes in mind. Official laws, moreover, not only reflect the strict animal-human divide performed at the zoo; they also reinforce this divide by establishing it as the prevailing legal norm.

Alongside the differences between laws that pertain to zoo animals, on the one hand, and those for zoo facilities and humans, on the other, the two sets of laws also share something in common: they approach zoos through a regime of exception. Indeed, many zoo animals are exempt from the AWA and from the ESA, from the Lacey Act and from CITES. Similarly, zoo facilities commonly receive variances and benefit from redefinitions. Underlying this state of exception are two recognitions: first, that the zoo is a hybrid space that attempts to bring wild nature to city dwellers, and second, that the zoo animal is unique in its existence between the categories of domesticated and wild. But beyond their nature as peculiar physical hybrids, zoo animals are also peculiar legal hybrids. Official laws handle such peculiarities by creating exceptions to their ordinary application. The particular history of animal law in the United States has also contributed to the special legal status of zoos and zoo animals. Specifically, the political struggles between the AZA and animal protection groups are a major cause of the fragmented state of official zoo laws and their myriad exemptions for zoos and zoo animals.

Alongside official laws, both zoos and their animals are products of complex networks and negotiations orchestrated by the AZA. Unlike official laws, however, AZA standards and guidelines pertain both to zoo animals and to the zoo's facilities, hence addressing more directly the uniqueness of the zoo. The AZA's main focus, in other words, *is* the zoo. Arguably, the AZA fills in the lacunae in official laws, resolving the problems of housing banister-wielding elephants in a one-hundred-year-old room, preventing tiger escapes, transferring a four-hundred-pound endangered silverback gorilla across state lines, and legally accommodating humans and skittish giraffes under the same roof.

Although industry norms accommodate the hybrid nature of zoos, their capacity is limited in terms of power. Indeed, while quite productive in creating standards and guidelines, AZA's voluntary structure, along with its narrow range of sanctions, renders its enforcement powers much less effective than those of official laws. Furthermore, AZA standards and guidelines apply only to its member institutions, which, as I have already noted, comprise approximately 10 percent of all facilities that publicly exhibit animals in the United States. Despite this, the AZA is still an important player in the *legal* constitution of zoo animals. Finally, in its most ambitious undertaking to date, the AZA is orchestrating a highly complex collaborative project for managing selected zoo animals, thereby playing an important role also in the *biological* constitution of zoo animals.

CHAPTER SEVEN

Reproducing Zoo Animals

The aim of captive management is to take a representative "snapshot" of the species' genetic diversity and preserve it in captivity, unchanged, for future use.

C. M. Lees and J. Wilcken, "Sustaining the Ark"[1]

It used to be that you would have two of this species—you know, the Noah's Ark approach. That's not what zoos are about anymore. We have limited space, and so we can't have every single animal represented well in a zoo setting. We want to have populations that are sustainable for the long term—that are able to keep their genetic diversity, [to] keep their population going.

Tara Stoinski, Ape TAG chair[2]

The space of the zoo is limited, zoo people often lament. This means that zoos need to carefully select the animals for display; it also means that they must constantly make reproductive choices for their animals. The project of collectively reproducing and contracepting individual animals—and, moreover, that of adding and removing entire species from zoos—may very well be the most intense form of animal governance practiced by accredited North American zoos to date. Relying on ambitious collaborations and complying with comprehensive industry standards, this technology of governance represents a shift from the mere monitoring of information about zoo animal populations into the very creation of these populations. In effect, the zoo's reproductive project transforms the biblical role of humans from namers into creators.[3] Indeed, modern zoos use genetics and demography to create and sustain their animal populations. An intricate balancing act of life and death thus takes place, with the Association of Zoos and Aquariums (AZA) acting as the shepherd who decides which animal will be sustained and which will expire.

This chapter's focus is on zoo animals that are managed by AZA's collective animal programs. Such animals constitute approximately 9 percent of all animal species kept in AZA-accredited zoos, and are the highest priority of the organization's conservation and education missions.[4] By contrast, the majority of zoo animals in accredited zoos are not assigned to an animal program, which means that they are typically not part of AZA's collective management. These animals are nonetheless subject to the various technologies of governance identified earlier, namely naturalizing, classifying, seeing, naming, registering, and regulating zoo animals. For the most part, it is the individual zoos that employ such technologies. Animals that are not assigned to a program will usually not have a studbook; they are either not bred in zoos or they exist in plentiful enough numbers that breeding can be done on a zoo-by-zoo basis and without requiring collective cooperation and oversight. In certain cases, zoos still obtain animals—especially so-called nuisance or problem animals—from the wild. In other cases, they buy them from private breeders or from the pet trade.

Some zoo professionals believe that the mission of zoos is to serve as a collective ark for sustaining animal populations until such time as they can be returned to the wild.[5] However, emerging technologies may be rapidly transforming the ark into a freezer. For example, the Omaha Zoo and the Audubon Research Center for Endangered Species have developed the technology to freeze the embryos of endangered African black-footed cats and to later reproduce them through in-vitro fertilization.[6] This technology enables the preservation of endangered species' sperm and embryos in a "frozen zoo."[7] At this time, however, these efforts cannot replace AZA's broader project of reproducing live animals and populations. Frozen gametes and embryos develop within a living womb, and frozen zoos are only as reliable as the human societies and infrastructures that build and maintain them.[8] The greater potential of frozen zoos, then, is the capacity to freeze genetic material collected from animals in the wild for breeding in zoos, thereby diversifying their *ex situ* populations.

At present, however, the frozen zoo is mostly a nice idea awaiting future scientific development. The bulk of AZA's reproductive management endeavor currently centers on two activities: breeding and not breeding zoo animals. The AZA operates a structured and specialized network that, among other things, makes collective decisions about animal reproduction. Situated at the top of AZA's animal program pyramid, the Wildlife Conservation and Management

Committee (WCMC) oversees the association's collaborative efforts. One step down in the organizational structure, the Population Management Center (PMC) operates from Chicago's Lincoln Park Zoo, while the Wildlife Contraception Center (WCC) operates from the Saint Louis Zoo—both providing hands-on consultation to animal programs on issues of genetics, demography, breeding, and contraception. Finally, the bulk of routine animal management occurs in AZA's animal programs, which operate on two levels: the Taxon Advisory Groups (TAGs) administer all species in a given taxon, and the Species Survival Plan programs (SSPs) administer a specific species or subspecies.

While the WCMC, PMC, and WCC coordinate and advise, the TAGs and SSPs collectively manage their given species. Specifically, each TAG makes two important decisions about the species under its management. First, it selects the species that will be included in AZA's collaborative project. Second, it decides on the number of animals that accredited zoos across the country will hold per species to ensure that they are neither underrepresented nor overrepresented. Given a target population size for its species from the TAG, the SSP then recommends the specific pair of animals within a species to breed; it also recommends which animal transfers are required for this breeding.

The zoo's project of breeding captive animals has been widely criticized by animal protection activists. It has also raised many questions among zoo professionals themselves: What is the purpose of saving animals through breeding them in captivity? How do zoos choose which animals to save? Can these animals ever be effectively reintroduced into their natural habitats? And what are some of the institutional obstacles that restrict conservation efforts by zoos? The AZA has been struggling with these questions for many years and addressed some of them in its 2010 Action Plan for the Future of SSPs. This plan divides animals into three color-coded groups based on their sustainability within zoos: green for the most sustainable, red for the least sustainable, and yellow for medium sustainability. Whereas green and yellow animal programs are managed collectively by the AZA, red programs are either managed individually on a voluntary basis or are phased out of the collective process altogether. The shift of industry priorities reflected by this newly established tri-level color system provides insights into the "paradox of pastoral power" as it manifests itself at the zoo: the conflict between caring for individual zoo animals, caring for the entire population in captivity, and caring for their counterparts in the wild.

Animal Programs

To better comprehend the breadth of AZA's operations and the range of its influence on the practices of accredited zoos in North America, one must explore the heart of AZA's administration: animal programs. As mentioned, the most prominent animal programs are the TAGs and the SSPs.[9] According to AZA's website, "These Animal Programs, in coordination with significant contributions from AZA's Scientific Advisory Groups, Institutional Liaisons and Institutional Representatives, are responsible for the extraordinary leadership, development, oversight, promotion, evaluation and support of AZA's cooperative animal management, conservation, and scientific initiatives."[10] Bronx Zoo director Jim Breheny describes animal programs as the "lifeblood" of zoos: "We would not be able to have zoo exhibits without this cooperative breeding program. . . . That's the only way we're going to have animals for exhibits; that's the only way we're going to keep captive populations healthy by the exchange of genetic material. . . . If the wild goes extinct, all we have is the captive population."[11]

Animal programs thus serve as control towers for the movement of zoo animals between accredited zoos, in effect shaping the face of zoo exhibits across the country and demonstrating the potentially benign power of the panopticon, as discussed in Chapter 3. Registrar Jean Miller of the Buffalo Zoo explains the influence of animal programs on the zoo's everyday operations: "If it's a new species we're bringing in, the AZA comes into play in that some species are recommended for management in North America and some are recommended not to manage. It would be silly of us to acquire a species that's not recommended for management because then we'd be working with them all alone and you can't maintain a population long-term by yourself. You need partners."[12] Eldon Smith, director of wildlife care at the Toronto Zoo, says similarly, "We have thirty or forty SSPs that we belong to. They dictate to us, [for example,] 'Your male tiger that you have, we need to move him out of your zoo.'"[13] Donna Fernandes of the Buffalo Zoo further elaborates on the relationship between individual zoos and animal programs:

> All of our animals are part of [AZA's] genetic registry. We follow their recommendations. So if they want us to send a female gorilla to Memphis, we do. . . . We now have a baby giraffe. They know we had a baby this year, and some zoo will say, "I'm opening a new exhibit and I need a giraffe," or "my giraffe at twenty-five years old just died so I need a new giraffe, so can I have a giraffe?" And this woman [the SSP coordinator] will

say: "Well, there's a two-year-old female in Buffalo and an unrelated male in St. Louis that we'll send you for that exhibit."[14]

Because zoos can only take animals from the wild on rare occasions, in order to create a sustainable population they must exchange animals between them. Dispersed among zoos across the country, managed animal populations would quickly succumb to inbreeding without frequent, carefully planned transfers for breeding. Human care and breeding and transfer decisions thus supplant the captive animal's own instincts for social grouping, dispersal, and reproductive competition.

Cindy Lee, curator of fishes at Toronto Zoo, explains that the general aim of animal programs is to establish a viable zoo network:

> [AZA's] idea is to save ecosystems and not to save the specific species. This happens through creating a network. Network is the goal. We choose the animals we can hold in captivity by looking into Regional Collection Plans. . . . Having a pair of rare endangered species that no other zoo has won't do us any good. We work with other zoos to make sure that we develop a broad enough gene pool so that if these animals go extinct we could release them into the wild.[15]

TAGs and SSPs are the central nodes in AZA's human-animal networks; they bring together the specialists and caretakers of selected taxa from each AZA zoo for the purpose of sustainably reproducing the taxa's *ex situ* population.

Taxon Advisory Groups

AZA's Taxon Advisory Groups (TAGs) manage animals in the North American region and are chaired and staffed by professional volunteers from across the zoo community. They encourage, supervise, and coordinate regional and international cooperation, as well as research and conservation of the entire taxa—namely, similar animal species grouped together according to their scientific classification.[16] According to the AZA, the mission of TAGs is to "examine the sustainability and conservation needs of entire taxa and . . . develop recommendations for population management and conservation based upon the needs of the species and AZA-accredited institutions."[17] TAG members thus serve as "experts regarding the husbandry, veterinary care, conservation needs/challenges, research priorities, ethical considerations, and other issues applicable to their taxa."[18] The AZA currently manages forty-six TAGs,[19] including Amphibian, Antelope and Giraffe, Ape, Aquatic Invertebrate, Bat, Bear, Canid and Hyaenid, and Crocodilian.[20] Of these, there are fifteen bird TAGs: Anseriformes, Charadriiformes, Ciconiiformes, Columbiformes, Coraciiformes, Galliformes, Gruiformes, Parrot, PAACT (Passeriformes, Apodiformes, Coliiformes, Caprimulgiformes, and Trogoniformes), Pelecaniformes, Penguin, Piciformes, Raptor, Ratite, and Turaco and Cuckoo.[21]

TAGs generally meet once a year and update their Regional Collection Plans, or RCPs, every three to five years.[22] The purpose of an RCP is to "recommend species for cooperative management ... determine the sustainability goals for each recommended Animal Program within its purview, identify objectives (number of spaces, founders, etc.) needed to meet these goals, provide institutions with information relevant to their long-term collection plans, and ensure adherence to AZA's animal management and conservation goals."[23] Based on the RCP, each TAG decides which species within the taxon will be managed collectively by the AZA. Many of the animals targeted by TAGs for collective management are endangered and threatened species, as defined by the Endangered Species Act. However, RCPs also recommend common species for this form of collective zoo management.[24] Of thousands of species assessed by TAGs, they have chosen to collectively manage approximately five hundred species.[25] Each species is either assigned to an SSP program and a studbook, or is tracked and managed with a studbook pending SSP qualification.

Species Survival Plan Programs

Species Survival Plan (SSP) programs have been at the core of AZA's collective management project since they were conceptualized in the late 1970s. The SSPs collaboratively generate recommendations for breeding select animals from across North American zoos.[26] In 2011, the AZA administered 303 species or subspecies[27] through SSPs as diverse as the Addax, the Mexican Red-Kneed Tarantula, the Bigtooth River Stingray, and the Plains Zebra. There are also six different bat SSPs: the Common Vampire, the Egyptian Fruit, the Jamaican Fruit, the Rodriquez Fruit, the Seba's Short-Tailed Fruit, and the Straw-Colored Fruit; and eight different tortoise SSPs, including the Brown Forest, the Burmese Mountain, the Burmese Star, the Flat-Tail Madagascar, and the Pancake. Despite this diversity, the majority of the world's animal species are not managed by the AZA. Sara Hallager estimates, for example, that out of over 10,000 bird species in the world, 107 species are managed through SSPs.[28]

Each SSP is directed by an SSP coordinator and consists of a committee with volunteers from different zoos. Additionally, the AZA assigns a studbook keeper to administer a regional studbook for every SSP. Between the SSPs and the many additional species programs that aspire to become SSPs, there are a total of 537 studbooks.[29] AZA studbook keepers also administer over thirty international studbooks in coordination with the World Association of Zoos and Aquariums and the International Species Information System. Each studbook "dynamically documents the pedigree and entire demographic history of each individual in a population of species."[30]

SSP coordinators work closely with studbook keepers (in fact, they are often the same person), the AZA Population Management Center, and Institutional Representatives (IRs) from participating zoos to develop a breeding plan. These various entities collaborate to recommend which pairs of individual animals should be bred, which animals should be prevented from breeding, and which animals need to be transferred between zoos for breeding or other purposes. The SSP's recommendations are posted on a secure section of the AZA website for comments by its members. After review, these recommendations are formalized into a Breeding and Transfer Plan and released to relevant AZA-accredited institutions. The purpose of the breeding plan is "to maintain a healthy, genetically diverse, and demographically stable *ex situ* population of a particular species through cooperative management strategies among AZA member institutions."[31] Here, for example, are the 2011 recommendations of the Western Lowland Gorilla SSP Population Analysis & Breeding and Transfer Plan: "The SSP is recommending 48 breeding pairs in this management plan with the goal of maintaining 360 gorillas in the population. The SSP has planned 27 transfer recommendations: 8 males and 19 females will move between institutions to permit breeding, fulfill institutional requests, build bachelor groups, approximate composition of species-typical mixed-sex groups, and/or socialize individuals."[32]

AZA's 2011 Accreditation Standards and Related Policies include a document entitled "Policy for Full Participation in the Species Survival Plan Program."[33] Adopted by AZA's board of directors in March 2009, this document mandates participation in SSP programs by all AZA member institutions. Specifically, it dictates that members must assign an IR for each SSP species managed by their zoo. The IR is usually the person in a leadership position who is most familiar with the relevant taxonomic group and with the animal program under consideration. For example, the primate curator in each zoo is most likely to be the IR for the Gorilla SSP.[34] IRs complete annual studbook surveys to provide information and updates on each animal and are invited to the Breeding and Transfer Plan meetings to provide information on their animals and on the particular needs of their institution.[35]

The administrative decision to create an SSP program for certain animals but not for others triggers a series of consequences. Importantly, it determines the identity of the parties that may potentially participate in the collaborative effort to sustain and to save certain species. Until recently, even when a species was critically endangered both *in* and *ex situ*, and even when a non-accredited institution held genetically valuable animals that could save this species from extinction, AZA members were prohibited from collaborating with that institution. Organizational dynamics thus stood in the way of a fuller realization of AZA's broader conservation mission. Pat Thomas of the Bronx Zoo describes some of the underlying tensions that existed until recently between AZA's strict membership standards and the mission of SSPs:

> Not every zoo is necessarily an AZA zoo. There are some zoos that choose not to be. . . . For many years, those individuals were allowed to participate in the [SSP] programs as long as they played by the rules. It's becoming more difficult to utilize those outside partners now because of AZA's regulations and requirements. So there are now private keepers that are left out of the box, [although] they own some genetically important animals.[36]

Thomas explains, for example, how the AZA's previous animal management model affected Amur leopard conservation:

> The Amur leopard is a subspecies of leopard found in the Russian Far East and in northern China. There's a fairly small captive population in the United States. . . . There's an individual who owns a number of very genetically important animals. . . . This guy wanted to participate and [has] made his animals available to [AZA's] program. [But the program] was recently made into an SSP, which means that his animals are now no longer in the program. . . . Because he is not willing to do what needs to be done in the AZA eyes in terms of being part of this particular program, we have to exclude his very important animals from that managed population.[37]

The growing problems associated with the membership-restricted participation in SSPs called for a change in the SSP structure that would enable its participants to work with nonaccredited institutions without weakening AZA's institutional powers. The AZA assigned this mission to a task force and, as of 2012, is in the process of implementing the task force's recommendations, discussed later in this chapter.

Even before these changes, however, AZA members found creative ways around AZA's prohibition from breeding SSP animals with animals of non-AZA zoos and around its strict application of membership access. For example, TAGs and SSP committees often made strategic decisions (and, in fact, still do) about the initial definition of certain animals as SSP animals. Once an animal is not managed in an SSP, zoos have broader discretion as to how to acquire or dispose of it. As Buffalo Zoo registrar Jean Miller points out, another way that zoos used to bypass AZA's strict membership requirements was by defining specific SSP animals as surplus:

> There is a way [to] get around [the SSP]. We can designate those animals as surplus to the SSP population, which means that we can do with them whatever we want. But they can never be bred here in this country because they're surplus. . . . There are all kinds of ways of working this out [so] we're not considered as giving up an endangered species. . . . As long as they are outside the managed population.[38]

Although the framework of surplus may no longer be necessary or relevant in light of the recent evolution in SSP management,[39] the inclusion or exclusion of zoo animals from an SSP program still carries with it a series of drastic consequences for both animals and zoos: it determines the boundaries of breeding, the possibilities of management, and the population viability of each species.

Population Management Center

> What we're trying to do is stop selection, stop evolution. We don't want the populations that we bring in to change. . . . We want to freeze things.
> Sarah Long, PMC director[40]

The Population Management Center (PMC) is an organ of the AZA that consists of a handful of population biologists. Because of their limited resources, these experts produce recommendations for approximately 250—that is, half—of all SSP programs.[41] The PMC helps these selected SSPs maintain accurate databases and studbooks, conduct the genetic and demographic analyses needed to develop population management recommendations, determine the current and future status of the population, and identify animal-by-animal breeding recommendations.[42] The PMC website outlines its three standards for collectively managed populations: that they are maintained at the sizes necessary to meet the conservation and education missions of each species; that they retain the highest possible levels of genetic diversity; and that they do not grow beyond the zoo community's ability to care for them.[43]

The focus of the PMC on the genetics and demographics of selected zoo populations is referred to in zoo language as "the science of small population biology." PMC director Sarah Long contrasts this science with that of *large* population management:

> It's easier for [zoos] to say: "Who are your parents?—Let's trace them back to the wild." We have the software—zoos invented this software—and a lot of the science and math and algorithms behind it were developed in zoos. That's the genetic side of it. And with that, we come up with an average relatedness score. [By contrast, with] large populations you rely on . . . the pure theory that everyone's breeding randomly [and] that the genes are supposed to be flowing freely in these populations. So you can make assumptions with large populations that you can't make with small ones.[44]

Although some *in situ* animal populations have also become incredibly small—in some instances even smaller than their conspecifics in zoos—captive breeding is still fundamentally different from natural reproduction. Long explains:

> Usually [zoos] know parents, we see when the babies are born, we know infant mortality rates because we're watching them very closely. [On the other hand,] a lot of people studying . . . jaguar populations in Brazil—they don't know what the infant mortality is, they never see the litters until maybe they're much, much older. So they use zoo data to get some kind of estimate. It's wild versus zoos: . . . we might have constraints, [but] we [also] might be taking care of them better, we might be seeing everything . . . [and] we know more about [everything].[45]

This description resonates with the argument advanced throughout the book that seeing at the zoo is the foundation of knowledge and, finally, of care toward animals—and that together, these forms of governance lie at the heart of the institution of captivity. Although it is the most visible project at the zoo, the project of exhibiting animals to public view is but one aspect of the zoo's much broader scopic regime. Behind the scenes, zoo personnel see animals somewhat differently than does the public, in turn inscribing their observations into databases that then contribute to the creation of a particular body of knowledge. The here-and-now of the animal that is being watched "very closely," in Long's words, is thereby translated by programs and committees into future breeding, transfer, and contraceptive actions. In part, then, zoos justify keeping and breeding *ex situ* animals by their capacity to observe, record, and sustain these animals in ways that are often impossible with *in situ* populations.

Alongside her comparison between management models for wild and zoo animal populations, Long also draws an unusual comparison between small population biology and economic models. She begins by describing some of the difficulties of managing animal populations in terms of the ebbs and flows of supply and demand:

> You rely on supply and demand: the last time you heard, everyone wanted those kids. But the next batch of kids you had, everyone's filled up, no one wants them. . . . [So] you've got to stop breeding the parent. You might have space issues with holding the offspring. You might have social issues where they start getting aggressive, and you can't put them in a good place. So people either send them to the wrong places—bad places—or people are forced to shut down their breeding programs. If that happens, haphazardly and in an unorganized fashion, you can have these booms and busts.[46]

Long refers to the "booms and busts" in supply and demand as "delayed effects," saying that they exist in every type of managed production. There are ways to plan around these delayed effects, she suggests, comparing the zoo's population management to inventory management for the Walmart retail corporation to il-lustrate her point:

> One reason Walmart has these little up-to-the-minute electronic indicators now is that they know instantly when a shelf is empty and it helps start getting things on a truck far away. . . . It makes everything more efficient, and you can plan ahead. . . . The same goes for managing animals. . . . If we are not managing a population, you might just be looking at what's in front of you. . . . So what we try to do is plan for the space. We ask everybody at the beginning of the year, or three years ahead: . . . How much space do you have? Who wants these [animals]?[47]

Similar to Walmart, the zoo's animal management system requires production planning. In this sense, there is little difference between managing inanimate and animate things.

Yet zoo animals are more challenging to manage and supply than cans of tuna. Some captive animals are relatively easy to plan for because they breed regularly and their breeding is easily controlled. Long explains, for example, how straightforward it can be to manage many bird species: "If you have a breeding pair, and you . . . realize, 'oh, there's more demand than I thought,' this pair can then breed two clutches of kids. You have that flexibility. Or [if] there are too many babies—everyone had large clutches this year and that institution just closed—the [SSP] coordinator would say 'pull the eggs for that pair,' . . . and it's humane."[48] Indeed, short-lived animals that lay eggs, such as penguins, are effectively managed by tracking eggs, replacing real eggs with artificial copies, and incubating or destroying eggs according to the breeding plan.[49]

Other species, however, are not so easy to manipulate. Long explains, for example, that "sometimes with cotton-top tamarins . . . you want the animals to breed, [but then] you have to get the mom on contraception right after she reproduces, or while she's nursing, before she breeds again. Everything could happen very quickly."[50] Wild dogs are another example of a relatively difficult planning profile, mostly due to their variable litter size. "They can have from one to sixteen offspring, so they can do their own boom and bust in two years even with me planning as much as [I] can. [When] I recommend three pairs, I might have three offspring, or I might have thirty-six."[51] Long's narrative calls to mind similar expressions by registrar emeritus Judith Block, explored earlier in this book. When comparing zoo animals with museum artifacts, Block says, "You can think of [an animal species] kind of like a work of art. What you value about that species is in its genes and in that composition."[52] Both Long's and Block's statements highlight a unique aspect of small population management: the importance of genetics.

The genetic component of animal management makes the science of zoo management distinct and challenging in comparison with, say, managing a department store's product supply chain or a collection of art in a museum. While products in a department store are expected to be produced identically, zoo animals are reproduced for optimal genetic diversity. In addition, while art and department store products can be divided, shipped, and recombined in limitless combinations, the unique social and reproductive behaviors of animals require significant care and attention to ensure the animals' healthy survival and reproduction in combinations that are often quite limited. Long elaborates on the zoo's goal of securing population robustness through genetic diversity:

> The idea about diversity is that you make [the population] . . . as diverse as possible so it can adapt to whatever comes its way. If it has to live in a certain environment, such as zoos, for the rest of its existence, then it needs to be able to thrive there and deal with diseases or with different conditions in different areas. . . . I mean, that's the whole idea about sexually producing species—they're diverse. They . . . can constantly change, and they can adapt.

At the same time, Long explains that captive management is also about "freezing animal populations for this moment in time." For example, "If you have representatives from ten families, you want to make sure all of those get to breed equally. You don't want one family to be way better than everyone else, mostly because you have limited space. You don't want any of these lines to go extinct. *You're stopping evolution because evolution revolves around differential reproduction.*"[53] Whereas in the wild, some animals breed better than others and so their traits are passed on, at zoos "we keep everyone breeding equally, we're not selecting for anything."[54] In other words, the zoo's selection of the most diverse genes replaces natural selection of the fittest genes.

Alongside its consideration of the complexities and unknowns of the genetics and demographics of the animal, the PMC must also consider the animal's social and behavioral nature. Long says:

> [Animals] have social issues. If [you] separate an animal for a medical treatment, you have to be really careful about putting them back in because they might be a stranger by the time you reintroduce them to the group. . . . They have their delicate social balances, and so you can't just throw them together and have them be happy. You have to fission them in the proper way: take off a couple of siblings together and make a new group. . . . You can't leave one alone. So there's all these little intricacies. And those are the kind of things—the constraints and the assumptions—the nongenetic, the nondemographic factors that we have to worry about too.

Besides the scientific calculations of the animal's genetics, demographics, and social and behavioral features, another variant for successful reproduction rates are the responses to human management generated by the animal itself. Indeed, the animal's reactions can contest the scientific solidity of animal programs. Specifically, to the dismay of many zoo scientists, animals have "refused" to breed well, or to breed at all, in captivity.[55] At certain points, in other words, the animal may "kick back" at its human programmers.[56] In such instances, zoo people must invent ways to manipulate zoo animals to participate in their own conservation. In the process of complying with, or working around, the animal's agency—or, in Bruno Latour's terms, its "actancy"[57]—zoo people thus end up producing increasingly sophisticated forms of management.

Indeed, as is the case with governing humans, resistance merely engenders new forms of management. For example, animal keepers have sprayed urine containing sexual pheromones around the animal or injected hormones into its body to counter its recalcitrant reproductive behavior and to encourage breeding.[58] Some zoos in the United States also train male gorillas to allow manual sperm collection, which increases the rates of successful reproduction. As mentioned earlier, artificial reproduction techniques can improve animal welfare and conservation outcomes by simply shipping frozen gametes, rather than an entire animal that may or may not choose to comply with a breeding scheme.[59] At the same time, gorilla reproduction by natural means is preferred by zoos, and to this end the Gorilla SSP has discovered that giving females enough space to separate themselves from males improves success. Otherwise, males tend to deplete their sperm with an "unnatural frequency of mating" when the female is not in estrus.[60]

Along these lines, zoo scientists are increasingly finding that giving the captive animal the power to make reproductive choices improves reproductive outcomes. The Conservation Centers for Species Survival (C2S2) collaboration has been successful in this regard. Since 2005, five AZA institutions have come together under C2S2 to collectively manage more than twenty-five thousand acres devoted to endangered species study, management, and recovery.[61] At C2S2, zoo scientists have designed a model that allows female cheetahs to choose their mates from a selected group of males. Until then, cheetahs had been underperforming—in other words, their reproduction was under-determined because zoos had not recognized the actancy of the female cheetah. As the C2S2 zoos adjust to allow for the cheetah's involvement in the species' breeding plans, they expect an increase in successful reproduction by at least 20 percent.[62]

Data Assessment Tools

Leaving the art of animal husbandry to keepers in the field, PMC experts practice the art of small population management with databases and computer programs. Conversant in genetics, demographics, and computer programming, these experts design and use specialized data assessment tools to generate their recommendations. The two main programs used by the PMC are ZooRisk and Vortex. Vortex is an "individual-based simulation model for population viability analysis," which models the "effects of deterministic forces as well as demographic, environmental, and genetic stochastic (or random) events on the dynamics of wildlife populations."[63] The second program—ZooRisk—was developed by Lincoln Park Zoo and provides a quantitative assessment of a population's risk of extinction based on the demographic, genetic, and management processes that affect captive populations. This assessment is based on "a population's history, captive management practices, and the principles of small population biology."[64]

The ZooRisk program starts off with a studbook database containing every individual animal's genealogy, age, breeding history, and restrictions. Using this data, the program projects the future of the population at year-by-year intervals based on probabilities of death and reproduction for each individual, up to hundreds of years into the future. ZooRisk users can simulate a variety of breeding management options: they can minimize inbreeding, prohibit genetically detrimental pairs, reach a target population size, and allow imports or exports to and from the population. Management decisions are generated by running hundreds of random simulations and observing the range of likely possibilities.[65] Currently, studbook keepers prepare and deliver their databases to the PMC for analysis. However, the soon to be released "ZIMS 3" will incorporate these databases into its own global database, enabling centers like the PMC to analyze any managed population instantaneously, within one globalized software and database system.[66]

As seemingly stable and unproblematic as these programs may be to the untrained eye, a closer look at their language reveals the fragility of their assessments. From the Vortex manual: "It is important to recognize that many of the questions VORTEX asks as you construct your population model cannot be answered simply because the data do not exist. The only recourse that you will have is to enter your best guess."[67] ZooRisk's manual also highlights the importance of data quality: "For populations that are small and/or have historically been small, it is possible that demographic rates cannot be accurately determined, and you should seriously consider the appropriateness of running analyses with poor quality data."[68] AZA's task force chair Robert Wiese admits that the accuracy of software-based recommendations depends on both the quality and the quantity of the data entered into the program.[69] In other words, the results generated from population model programs are only as good as their data input. For this reason, the PMC spends significant time and resources to ensure data quality, advising regional studbook keepers on their data preparation for successful population modeling and management.[70] The results generated by these population model programs are also fragile for other reasons. From the Vortex manual: "It is possible that after you spend hours working on a VORTEX Project, the program will suddenly crash. It is also possible that you will accidentally change a very useful analysis into something that is worthless."[71]

Contracepting Animals

It doesn't take much imagination to realize that uncontrolled breeding
would lead to an overwhelming surplus of crisis proportions. As stewards
of our animals, zoo professionals are responsible for providing the highest
standards of care—a responsibility that includes ensuring we do not breed
more animals than can be properly cared for in accredited zoos.

AZA's Wildlife Contraception Center[72]

Alongside its breeding programs, the AZA also offers animal contraception
services. Situated at the Saint Louis Zoo, AZA's Wildlife Contraception Center
(WCC) "helps scientists facilitate controlled pairings—a kind of high-tech
matchmaking—while still allowing individuals to live in natural social and family groups."[73] As acknowledged on WCC's website, because one is so accustomed
to hearing about zoos' breeding projects, these services "may at first seem surprising or counter-intuitive."[74] And yet, advisers from the WCC are involved in
the everyday management of all animal programs. For example, a contraception
adviser attends the Gorilla SSP's Breeding and Transfer Plan meetings.

As in so many other contexts identified in this book, the WCC assumes a connection between captive and wild animal populations. Its website states that "the
contraceptive research carried out in zoos and aquariums is directly applicable
to the management of wild populations in parks and reserves around the
world."[75] According to the WCC, then, learning how to prevent animals from
breeding in captivity translates into the ability to prevent populations in the wild
from breeding beyond the limits that ecologists prescribe for them.

The animals reproduced in today's zoos are mostly evaluated according to
the logic of genetic management. Breeding plans are conceived and carefully
by a network of zoo professionals who share one aim: to increase the genetic
diversity of zoo populations (again, defined as its diversity in relation to the
founding population of the species in zoos). On the opposite side of the coin is
AZA's assumption that if an animal is genetically redundant, it will take up valuable space without contributing to the diversity of the population.[76] To minimize
such occurrences, certain zoo animals are "bred for extinction."[77] For example,
the crossbred "generic tiger" is no longer permitted to breed in AZA institutions,
as it arguably takes up space needed to breed "pure-origin" tiger subspecies. As
of 2010, fifty-two of ninety-seven generic tigers in AZA institutions were already
spayed or neutered.[78] The project of "breeding to extinction"—and extinction

models at large—are essential to the work of animal programs and are highly dependent on contraceptive technologies.

According to WCC director Cheryl Asa, the project of caring for animals—indeed, "the highest standards of care"[79]—requires zoos to limit breeding to no more animals than can be cared for within the zoo itself. Contraception is thus depicted as not only unavoidable but also as the most humane method for population control. Asa lays out the history of contraception management in North American zoos. She explains that "zoos have been breeding animals for some one hundred years" and that "most animals actually breed quite well."[80] Although the need to control reproduction is not new, she continues, the techniques used by zoos have changed: from separating females and males to killing or selling surplus animals and, finally, to AZA's current philosophy of proactively limiting reproduction through pharmaceutical contraception.

The current contraception system is not without its challenges. According to Asa, "human medicine is extremely expensive, too expensive." To bypass the more stringent processes required for the approval of human drugs and the different interests that affect the approval and sale of non-zoo animal drugs, the AZA has negotiated with the Food and Drug Administration (FDA) to create a special path for the speedy approval of animal drugs for the zoo industry. In effect, the FDA has approved "red" (semi-approved) drugs for the exclusive use of the AZA. Asa explains that this was possible "because we have a process in place to do the proper monitoring."[81] Still, she admits, "no product is 100 percent safe and reversible."[82] As an example, Asa tells me about a contraceptive that was broadly used by zoos based on WCC recommendations and that was later found to have serious side effects on the uterine lining of large cats.

The use of contraception in zoo animals is an important factor in shaping the recommendations of many animal programs. For example, the 2011 western lowland gorilla's SSP Population Analysis & Breeding and Transfer Plan states the following:

> All animals that are not recommended to breed should be contracepted using reversible methods unless otherwise recommended. Institutions may not choose to refrain from contracepting females by offering to "take responsibility" for resulting (non-recommended) offspring as all available spaces are to be used to further SSP goals. Females housed with males should be contracepted using low estrogen combination birth-control pills starting at the age of 5½ years. Nursing moms should be given progestin-only birth-control pills or Depo-Provera® . . . NO PERMANENT CONTRACEPTION SHOULD BE

UNDERTAKEN WITHOUT THE REVIEW AND ENDORSEMENT OF THE MANAGEMENT GROUP.[83]

Although relatively straightforward in the context of North American zoos, the use of contraception has recently become a controversial topic among zoos worldwide. Certain zoos in northern Europe have insisted, for example, that reproduction is an animal's basic natural right, and that it is better to let animals reproduce and then cull (euthanize) their offspring than to artificially prevent them from reproducing altogether. In a letter concerning culling policies at the Helsinki Zoo, the director of the World Association of Zoos and Aquariums (WAZA) states: "Recognizing that contraception may have negative impacts on the health of female animals during their reproductive age, the good functioning of social groups, the long term maintenance of viable ex situ population etc. many zoos use contraception rather selectively and choose a breed-and-cull policy instead."[84]

Furthermore, WAZA's Code of Ethics explicitly allows for the culling of animals for management reasons, requiring, however, that other options first be investigated and ruled out. In its 11th Draft of Euthanasia statement from March 2011, the European Association of Zoos and Aquaria (EAZA) poses the question, "So why breed and then cull?" stating in response that

> the application of a considered culling policy is appropriate on welfare grounds, at an individual and group level, and helps to mirror species specific population structures. While this may at first appear to be somewhat contradictory, we are ethically obliged to strike an informed balance between the life of an individual and maintaining the long term viability of a managed population. . . . Limiting the opportunity to breed, by definition, reduces an individual animal's opportunity to express one of the most important and complex set of behaviours and will thus lead to a decrease in welfare. Where local legislation allows, the culled animal can also provide enrichment for the institution's carnivores by being fed to them and increasing their welfare.[85]

EAZA was recently put on the defensive for this policy in a German court, where three staff members of Zoo Magdeburg and the zoo's director were convicted for euthanizing tiger cubs.[86] Genetic analysis after breeding had indicated that the sire was not a pure Amur tiger, but in fact showed evidence of generic tiger genes (crossbreeding). In the name of the "genetic integrity" of the Amur tiger program, deemed an "important conservation resource," the EAZA found that the cubs' euthanasia in support of the Amur tiger management was "to the highest scientific, conservation and welfare standards."[87] The

German court found differently, however, ordering the suspension of the zoo's director and three employees.[88]

The choice between breeding and culling, on the one hand, and limiting reproduction with contraception, on the other, highlights two important changes to the broad operation of the institution of captivity. First, it exemplifies the complex ethical considerations that contemporary zoos face when managing captive populations. Not so long ago, animals moved relatively easily between the domains of the wild, zoo, and pet industries. By contrast, contemporary zoos mostly manage their animals within an insular ecosystem, with limited entries and exits. Consequently, zoos today must deal with a range of ethical dilemmas that were mostly unheard of in the past.

Second, the dilemma presented here highlights the centrality of care and stewardship in the project of managing captive populations by zoos. Whereas North American zoos have taken the stance that contraception provides the highest level of care for their animals, some European zoos insist that reproduction is better for the animal's welfare. This dilemma illustrates Michel Foucault's "paradox of pastoral power": the need to constantly choose between the care of individuals and the care of the flock. And in this context, while the breeding and culling policy of some European zoos is oriented toward the individual animal and its perceived welfare, the use of contraception by North American zoos seems to be more oriented toward the project of governing the flock through controlled reproduction.

The Zoo's Reproductive Model: Critical Perspectives

Since their inception, the collective captive breeding programs of North American zoos have been criticized, sometimes even by zoo professionals themselves. Some have named these programs "a topical treatment for an epidemic," arguing that reintroduction into any sort of natural habitat may be impossible and that "intensely managed 'species parks' or 'megazoos' may be the only option for a long time to come."[89] Others have pointed out that captive breeding programs are only appropriate for a small subset of endangered species, that they are costly, and that they do not provide adequate solutions to deal with the much wider problem of habitat loss.[90] Still others have argued that these programs are "a harmful delusion," and that major resources should be channeled directly to wild population and ecosystem preservation efforts, instead of into "ill-conceived recovery captive breeding."[91] As mentioned earlier, critics have also commented that zoos have failed to develop clear and consistent criteria for species selection, suggesting that current practices should be replaced with an array of rational criteria for this purpose.[92]

Another criticism of the zoo's reproductive project is that it excludes many important animals from its scope. Indeed, some have suggested that captive breeding efforts favor species that appeal to human aesthetics and emotions, rather than those that are most vulnerable. Specifically, critics suggest that it is a species' attractiveness, physical size, the degree to which it is considered a higher form of life, and its resemblance to humans that increase support for efforts to exhibit that species at the zoo.[93] Certain studies also argue along these lines that breeding choices reflect long-standing biases: "By continuing traditional ad hoc biases toward large mammals and birds and ignoring the suitability of species for reintroduction, present priorities in effect concentrate resources on species that breed relatively poorly and that are expensive to keep and difficult to return to the wild," say zoologists Andrew Balmford and others.[94] Lee Ehmke of Minnesota Zoo suggests, similarly, that "when you get into the smaller [animals] or the more common species of mammals, they tend to not be in programs."[95] He notes that the higher form of management for the larger, more charismatic, species is "partly based on what are the animals that are considered important for zoo collections. You need these [big] animals in order to attract people."[96] Ehmke believes that zoos should exhibit smaller, less popular, and more common animals. He explains that this is the only way to educate the public about the importance of habitat, about their local environment, and about animal taxonomies and variation. Indeed, while some institutions—such as the ZooAmerica North American Wildlife Park in Pennsylvania, the Monterey Bay Aquarium, and the Arizona-Sonora Desert Museum—focus exclusively on local animals, the vast majority of zoos still focus on iconic and exotic animals.

William Conway, one of the founders of AZA's collective management system, critiques species selection in zoos from another perspective:

> If we're going to fulfill our function, we have to be able to sustain animals in zoos in the long term, stop removing them from nature, or, when we do remove them from nature, see that we can sustain them. We have too many animals in zoos taking space that probably don't need the propagation help, because there are plenty of them. So while zoos should not only be a place for endangered or threatened species, they should definitely have a focus on them. It is necessary.[97]

The positions represented here by Ehmke and Conway—both key figures in the world of contemporary North American zoos—reflect a deep-seated debate within the zoo community: while some believe that the central mission of zoos should be to educate the public, others emphasize the zoos' critical role as a breeding ground for endangered wild animals. AZA's preamble to its accreditation policies stresses both purposes, leaving the resolution of the tension between them for other venues.[98]

Animal protection organizations have offered even more sweeping critiques of AZA's breeding programs. For example, Rob Laidlaw of Zoocheck Canada questions the scientific claims behind AZA's animal breeding programs and, by extension, the overall value of these programs:

> Breeding programs are inherently flawed because you have no natural selection, so what you are getting is animals that are inbred. A lot of the SSP populations are starting with fewer than one hundred members, and a lot of those aren't viable breeders, so the endangered species breeding programs are already starting with a huge genetic strike against the program being successful. . . . They're [also] finding that changes at the genetic level—and this was never thought possible before—can occur in first-generation captive born.[99]

Naomi Rose, marine mammal scientist of the Humane Society International, remarks, similarly, that although zoos are deliberately seeking to keep their animal populations diverse in a random way, "The unfortunate truth is that you've also short-circuited natural selection. Any animal at a zoo is no longer subject to natural selection, and that's a problem."[100] The problem with zoos, according to Laidlaw and Rose, is that as hard as they might try to imitate nature, they will never succeed in artificially creating such a nature in a state of captivity. In the *ex situ* system of collaborating zoos, competition for survival and reproduction is impossible, which makes natural evolution impossible as well. Some scientists further suggest that in the insular zoo system, populations will become vulnerable because of their evolution from a small set of founders and from the loss of genetic diversity through "genetic drift."[101] These criticisms imply that although the SSP breeding and transfer plans can maximize retention of genetic diversity within the *ex situ* population, without gene flow between *ex situ* and *in situ* populations zoo animals will become something different from their wild counterparts, thereby forfeiting the justification for their captivity in zoos.

Finally, and as mentioned earlier, the AZA was also criticized widely for its strict membership requirements, which used to exclude owners of genetically important captive animals because those owners lacked proper accreditation by the AZA. This administrative critique was one of the central reasons that prompted AZA's 2010 task force to recommend a redefinition of priorities by the zoo industry.

Action Plan for the Future of AZA's SSPs

> If zoo populations are not sustainable, neither are zoos themselves. Too few populations are currently satisfying the conditions for sustainability. There is scope for revitalizing the Ark, but it requires renewed commitment and new investment.
>
> C. M. Lees and J. Wilcken, "Sustaining the Ark"[102]

Adopted by AZA's board of directors in the fall of 2010, the Action Plan for the Future of AZA's SSPs (referred to here as "the plan") focuses on creating sustainable *ex situ* populations. AZA's task force—led by Robert Wiese—is currently drafting a second, complementary action plan, which will include an assessment of *in situ* conservation programs performed by AZA-accredited zoos.[103] Although the plan will take full effect only in the fall of 2012, its repercussions are already evident in the collective management of zoo animals in North America.

The plan classifies all animal programs into three categories based on their sustainability within zoos: green, yellow, and red. In 2011, there were 30 green animal programs, 278 yellow, and 240 red.[104] "Green SSP Programs are currently sustainable for the long term," reads the plan. This means that the population is presently sustainable demographically for one hundred years or more and that it is able to retain a high amount of gene diversity (measured as larger than 90 percent in relation to the basic or founding population at zoos) over this time. There are precious few green programs, says Sara Hallager of the Smithsonian's National Zoo, because "there's a loss of gene diversity across the board and an incredibly limited amount of space."[105]

The Gorilla SSP is a good example of a green program. In 2011, the population size was 342 individuals, distributed among fifty-two AZA institutions. The SSP had then decided to grow the total population to 360 individuals over a period of two years. Gene diversity in the population was high, at 98.9 percent.[106] Another example of a green program, this time from the bird world, is the Greater Flamingo SSP. Due to its high numbers in AZA zoos, this bird population—which was initially not even assigned to an SSP by the Ciconiiformes and Phoenicopteriformes TAG—was redefined as a green SSP in 2011 and thus prioritized for collective management. The current population of greater flamingos is 572 animals divided among twelve AZA institutions. Based on the studbook, gene diversity in this population is approximately 99 percent and is expected to be slightly more than 90 percent one hundred years from now.[107]

Yellow SSP programs are *potentially* sustainable for the long term, which means that the population requires additional attention and effort to make it fully sustainable. The vast majority of animal programs are yellow. An example of a yellow program, again from the bird world, is the Laughing Kookaburra SSP. Although the Coraciiformes Taxon Advisory Group had not originally assigned this species to an SSP, in the new color-coded system it qualifies as a yellow SSP due to its numbers and gene diversity rate. In 2011, the kookaburra population's gene diversity was estimated at 94 percent and was projected to decline to 82 percent within one hundred years.[108] Another example for a yellow program is the Addax SSP. With a 2011 population size of 158 specimens held by eighteen AZA institutions and a gene diversity of 87.44 percent descended from thirteen founders, this species is projected to have only a 75.63 percent diversity rate in one hundred years, resulting in a yellow designation.[109]

Finally, red is the plan's color code for populations that have "fewer than 50 individuals."[110] The Diana monkey, for example, is an SSP-managed primate that under the new system qualifies as a red program. In 2011, this population included thirty-nine specimens in twelve institutions and two non-AZA institutions. Its gene diversity at that time was 93 percent and was expected to decline to about 76 percent over the next one hundred years.[111] The brown kiwi is another example of a red program. This "very endangered" bird[112] was designated as an SSP by the Ratite TAG in its 2010 Regional Collection Plan and was recommended for a target population size of twenty-five in AZA institutions. As a red program, the managed kiwi population consists of both AZA and EAZA populations, which together reach a population size of forty-one birds in ten institutions, five AZA and five EAZA. The plan's managers believe that cooperation and exchange between Europe and North America will be beneficial to the demographic and genetic status of both subpopulations. In 2011, the population's gene diversity was 84 percent and it was projected to retain 69 percent gene diversity in one hundred years.[113]

Sustainability is a key determinant in this newly constructed animal hierarchy: green programs are prioritized above yellow, yellow above red. The language of the plan is not clear, however, on the implications of such prioritization. Task

Figure 13. Buffalo Zoo's veterinary technician feeding the addax calf Xadda (addax spelled backward), which was hand reared by zoo staff since its mother rejected it. The addax, an endangered species, was recently designated as a yellow SSP and is one of AZA's forty-three endangered species reintroduction programs. Courtesy of Eric Lee / Buffalo Zoo.

force chair Robert Wiese explains that the new priorities are intended to instruct two different groups. First are the PMC scientists who produce the recommendations for each species and who will now be required to prioritize their limited resources by planning for the most sustainable populations first. Second are the zoos themselves, which will now have effective means for considering sustainability when deciding which animal species to include in their collections.

The plan has already triggered numerous debates within the zoo community, mainly regarding the practical implications of deeming a program red.[114] "The AZA is saying that these programs are flagged as red because those populations are important," says Sara Hallager, "but at the same time they say that they will not put the resources of the PMC into them until they become yellow. It's confusing."[115] Despite her important role in AZA's collaborative animal program enterprise, PMC director Long clarifies that she holds a different set of priorities from those expressed by the plan's drafters. Rather than ignoring red-coded species, Long informs me, she will in fact continue to prioritize these animals, at least when they are also threatened or endangered in the wild. "Even though we're not supposed to, I don't want to say [to zoos with red animals] 'we will never help you.' We can try to figure something out."[116] She further states about the PMC's priorities that "sheer number is not really a good way to prioritize. There are populations under fifty that are really important to zoos and are important maybe as an endangered species—so we want to work with them. But some of the populations are not either. They're just someone's pet project."[117]

Although the distinction between green and yellow programs—with their terminology of sustainability—may read as exclusively scientific, it is also a strategic tool to avoid AZA's strict participation requirements at the level of green programs. Specifically, the plan prioritizes both green and yellow programs for collective management, with a crucial difference: whereas participants in green SSP programs must be approved by the WCMC and are typically restricted to AZA-accredited institutions, participation in yellow SSP programs is voluntary and non-AZA member partners do not need to be approved by the WCMC.[118] Hence, a species may be designated as a yellow program so as to allow cooperation with non-AZA institutions. The color-coded managerial model thus helps to address some of the administrative problems of the previous SSP model and to institutionalize what used to be an informal practice of circumventing the rigid and uniform SSP designations and requirements. Although the red programs are given the industry's lowest priority, they are also subject to the fewest regulations, making it easier for interested zoos to cooperate with various non-AZA facilities to improve the population's sustainability. Wiese stresses that the plan's color designations are dynamic. He indicates, for example, that once individual zoos increase the viability of red animal populations to yellow or green levels, these species will be managed collectively, and vice versa.[119]

Although its drafters portray it as unproblematic, this plan exposes the underlying tensions between the sustainability of *ex situ* populations and the conservation of *in situ* populations—tensions that lie at the heart of the zoo's institutional mission and thereby of its power of care. Indeed, many of the red coded species are not only underrepresented in zoos (*ex situ*) but are also endangered in the wild (*in situ*).[120] The task force has reasoned, accordingly, that with little hope of sustainability, red species should no longer be collaboratively managed. If a zoo insists on working with a red species, it should do so on its own, without the support of AZA's administration. In other words, what were previously SSP programs are now designated red and will be phased out of the collective management system. In effect, AZA's new priorities for *ex situ* conservation are the opposite of the aims of *in situ* conservation, where the most vulnerable and threatened species are given highest priority. Under this new plan, sustainability and conservation collide.

Conclusion: Comparing Captive and Domestic Breeding

The science of small population management through selective breeding and contraception is fundamental to the institution of captivity. Obviously, this practice is not unique to zoos or to zoo animals. Much of it has been adopted from the agriculture and pet industries.[121] As with these other industries, zoos trace genetic traits and diversity through pedigrees in studbooks. Moreover, the reproductive control of captive and domestic animals shares a common history, uses similar technologies, and, as of recently, strongly relies on genetics and global management systems.[122]

But the reproductive management of captive and domestic animals also differ in many respects, four of which are described here. The first difference lies in the purposes of these projects. For the most part, the breeding of domestic animals has been an aesthetic and economic pursuit.[123] Conversely, zoos breed captive animals for the major purpose of *in situ* and *ex situ* conservation. Other purposes, such as making a profit and surviving as institutions, are portrayed by zoo professionals as relatively marginal in comparison to the protection of wildlife,[124] although in practice the survival of zoos is clearly dependent upon the survival of their animals.[125]

Second, whereas domestic animals are "bred for perfection"[126]—for creating super-animals, so to speak[127]—zoo animals are bred for the almost opposite purpose: enhanced genetic diversity. Hence, while domestic breeders value pedigrees with desirable traits—a winning thoroughbred racehorse, for example— zoo breeders value pedigrees with unique founders and few known relatives, such as a gorilla brought in from the wild. The zoo's shift in preference from the phenotype to the genotype and its emphasis on genetic diversity thus denotes a new form of small-population management that is distinct from the private breeding of domestic animals.[128] By this logic, if an animal is genetically redundant it takes up valuable zoo space without contributing to the diversity of the population.[129] Consequently, certain zoo animals—the generic tiger being one current example—are "bred for extinction"[130] or purposefully not bred. According to AZA's Tiger SSP, the current populations of 136 Amur tigers, 71 Sumatran tigers, and 56 Malayan tigers will be bred separately, while generic tigers will be phased out through a breeding moratorium.[131] In the more extreme example from the European Association of Zoos and Aquaria discussed in this chapter, a litter of tiger cubs was euthanized shortly after birth, once it became known that their sire had some generic tiger genes in his lineage.[132]

This brings me to the third distinction between zoo and domestic breeding: zoo practices of breeding for extinction and the extinction software models used by zoos are largely absent from the domestic animal context. Whereas domestic breeders are far more likely to cull, or euthanize, animals that are not slated for future reproduction, zoos are more likely to contracept or sterilize individuals identified as genetic surplus.[133] The tendency of certain Northern European zoos to cull rather than contracept has thus sparked much controversy within the zoo community.

Fourth and finally, domestic breeding is typically managed by individual and private breeders, who practice little to no centralized control other than the maintenance of registries and studbooks, and who are subject to relatively few regulatory and administrative impositions. Conversely, the zoo industry's collaborative breeding project operates within an elaborate administrative and bureaucratic structure orchestrated by the AZA and is subject to myriad regulatory regimes.

Conclusion

> If zoos didn't exist and somebody came along and said, "Well, we want you
> to have several hundred species in a captive situation, and all the exhibits
> have to be beautiful and suggest their wild habitat, and these exhibits have
> to be available to two or three million people a year so they can come see
> them, and all the animals have to be in perfect health, and, by the way . . .
> you can't take them from the wild . . . you have to breed your own," I think
> most people would say, "That's impossible, nobody could do that." . . . After
> 37 years in the zoo world, my overwhelming impression is that it's sort of a
> miracle.
>
> Dan Wharton, formerly Central Park Zoo director[1]

> Thus the 21st-century zoo must be redesigned as a buffer against biotic
> impoverishment, a powerful time machine buying continuance for
> faltering wildlife populations, a corridor of care between parks and
> reserves, and, more than ever, humanity's primary introduction to wildlife,
> a promoter of environmental literacy and a recruitment centre for
> conservationists; in fact, a conservation park.
>
> William Conway, "The Role of Zoos"[2]

The modern zoo's project of governing zoo animals effectively encloses these
animals within carefully constructed, insular, and collectively administered ecosystems. The Association of Zoos and Aquariums (AZA) orchestrates the collaboration among its 225 member institutions, most in North America. It operates
through a network of committees, plans, and programs that abide by a detailed self-
regulating regime to manage the diverse animal populations dispersed, monitored,
and shepherded within multiple zoos. Inspired by this North American model,
many world zoos are currently negotiating similar administrative structures to
collectively manage certain zoo animals on regional and even global scales.

This book has identified seven interrelated technologies of animal governance: naturalizing, classifying, seeing, naming, registering, regulating, and—what I propose is the most intense form of zoo governance—collectively reproducing zoo animals. Each chapter has reflected on one of these technologies, highlighting the processes and networks that underlie its functions within the institution of captivity.

First, I have depicted the material and spatial foundation of zoo governance: nature. Traditionally located in urban settings, North American zoos use nature as a model for designing, and as a way of justifying, captivity. The zoo's process of naturalizing its space and its animals—the work of making them seem unquestionably connected to wildlife "out there" and then of rendering this work invisible—reinforces ideas of "first nature": a pristine and distant realm that remains separate from humans. Interrelated with this process of naturalization, zoos also classify their animals. The zoo's classification system distinguishes animals from humans and categorizes such animals as domesticated or wild. The zoo animal—the vast majority of zoo professionals and animal protection activists assume—is wild. This assumption of wildness is fundamental to zoos as institutions of captivity. Indeed, captivity would make little sense, nor would it raise many objections, if not for its juxtaposition with wildness.

Zoos also govern animals through seeing and sight. Under the zoo's scopic regime, the zoo animal is displayed to the public in particular ways that both associate it with, and disassociate it from, wild nature. These two modes of display operate simultaneously to afford the public multiple views into the animal's life, thereby instituting overlapping panoptic and synoptic (or exhibitionary) regimes. When observing how zoogoers look at animals, one witnesses the bidirectional nature of the gaze: Janus-like, it operates not only on the animal subject but, even more so, on the public that gazes. Such a focus on seeing is both intensified and personalized through the project of naming animals. Animal naming encourages caretakers and the public to more intimately associate with, and thus to more directly care about, the named zoo animal. As part of naming, a series of related tasks—mainly identifying, recording, and tracking—enables the inscription of the three-dimensional body of the animal into a range of two-dimensional formats. The animal's characteristics, along with its every move, are thereby translated into virtual flows of digitized information.

As the zoo's central bureaucrat, the registrar systematically administers this increasingly sophisticated documentation regimen, encoding the relevant information about each animal into its proper place and negotiating the myriad agreements that pertain to it. The registrars are also instrumental for the project of regulating zoos and zoo animals. In this context, a plethora of official laws oscillate in their focus between animals and humans to govern the peculiar space of the zoo and the hybrid identity of its animals. Additionally, relatively adaptable industry standards and guidelines enacted by the AZA compensate for the lack of zoo-specific legislation. The interrelations between official and industry laws—in fact, the very essence of these laws—reflect and even embody the tensions between the two groups that claim to be the sole expert authorities on the captive animal's well being: zoo people and animal protection activists.

Finally, the pinnacle of modern zoo governance is the collaborative project of reproducing and contracepting captive animals. Here, the focus of animal programs on maintaining high gene diversity translates into calculated acts of breeding animals from viable captive populations and phasing out animals with redundant genotypes or from nonviable populations.

Through the discussion of these animal governance projects, a genealogy of North American zoos emerges that highlights the dramatic transformation that these zoos have undertaken in the last five decades. Geared toward care, conservation, and stewardship, the zoo's managerial model has been referred to throughout this book as a form of pastoral power—the power of care.

Concluding Notes on Pastoral Power

Until now, the study of pastoral power has been restricted to the human realm. This book moves away from this traditional outlook to assert the relevance of studying pastoral power in the hybrid human-animal setting of the zoo. The zoo's institutional exercise of pastoral power demonstrates the intricate balance and interdependency between power and care, illuminating both the complexity of governing captive animals and the ethics of care by which zoos operate. In what follows, I once again selectively characterize Michel Foucault's pastoral power concept,[3] distinguish it from other modalities of power such as sovereign power, and demonstrate its manifestations in contemporary zoos and through the story of Timmy the gorilla.

Figure 14. Caring for Maji Maji, Zoo Miami's greater kudu stud, includes a periodical hoof trimming and a routine physical exam, blood work, and fecal collection— performed and recorded here by the zoo's staff. Care for kudus also includes their collaborative management under AZA's yellow SSP program. The kudu's *ex situ* population, established in 1922, includes 222 animals distributed among thirty-four AZA and five non-AZA institutions. Courtesy of Armando-Raul Rodriguez.

First and foremost, pastoral power is a power of care. Foucault's depiction of the shepherd as someone who must arrange for his sheep's "mating in order to produce the most vigorous and fertile sheep that produce the best lambs"[4] is translatable to the modern zoo's focus on breeding. Since the 1970s, North American zoos have gradually transformed their focal mission from public entertainment to animal conservation and care. Care through conservation is practiced both directly, through raising money for *in situ* populations, and indirectly, through educating the public about their cause in the wild. Although animal husbandry has been around for centuries, the framing of reproductive control as an ecological enterprise, and thus as a form of public-interest stewardship and care, is a relatively new phenomenon. Underlying this redefinition is a novel genetic enterprise: the pursuit of diversity rather than desirable phenotypes.

The North American zoo project of managing animals to care and conserve has also become the gold standard for zoos worldwide, setting the stage for parallel projects of animal management by zoos on other continents and for a similar global administration of several dozen species.[5] Under the international umbrella of the World Association of Zoos and Aquariums, for example, Global Species Management Plans consult with international studbook keepers in the same manner that Species Survival Plans rely on regional studbooks.[6] More broadly even, the North American model is gaining prominence for governing what is still considered wild nature but is increasingly becoming enclosed, monitored, and controlled for its own protection.[7]

Foucault also emphasizes that pastoral power is aterritorial by nature. Unlike sovereign power, he suggests, this form of power is not exercised over a territory but rather over a population, and thus over a multiplicity of movements.[8] In contemporary zoos, the physical location of animals is far less important than it once was. In fact, what lies at the core of modern animal governance by North American zoos is the fluidity of animal bodies, which enables their simultaneous configuration into multiple—both physical and abstract—assemblages. The central metaphor that comes to mind when considering the aterritorial nature of modern zoos is Noah's Ark. The ark image conveys three important points: that zoos are of one body, that this body is constantly in motion, and that it sustains animals far from what are deemed their native habitats. Keenly aware of the ark metaphor, Donna Fernandes of the Buffalo Zoo suggests that Noah "only had to worry about keeping two of everything alive for a few months and didn't seem the least bit concerned about inbreeding, depression or mean kinship. We have to try to keep several hundred specimens from each managed species around for 100 plus years, which is a lot harder to do."[9] Ultimately, conserving *ex situ* and *in situ* animal populations through frequent transfers not only enables the survival of animals but also ensures the survival of zoos themselves.

In addition to its aterritorial nature, pastoral power is an individualizing power. The shepherd "does everything for the totality of his sheep, but he does everything also for each sheep in the flock."[10] Similarly, zoos make detailed decisions about the minutia of each individual animal's life: from its conception, through its naming and everyday care, to its death. At the same time, they must also care for the totality of the animals—for the flock.[11] We thus arrive at the essential paradox of pastoral power: the inherent tension between caring for the individual and caring for the flock. The last section of this book deals with this tension in the context of Timmy the gorilla.

Foucault also argues that the pastoral theme, especially in its later historical manifestations in the Church, gave rise to "a dense, complicated, and closely woven institutional network." He frames this notion as "the institutionalization of the pastorate."[12] Although Foucault is specifically referring to the Christian pastorate in Europe, his observations are also acute in the context of contemporary zoos, which similarly rely on sophisticated networks of human committees, programs, and protocols to execute their vision. Specifically, administrative bodies such as TAGs, SSPs, the WCMC, and the PMC collaborate with each other and with individual zoos to govern the everyday routines of zooland. The North American zoo is thus a remarkable example of how self-governing networks function in concert to achieve collective administrative goals.

Finally, Foucault suggests that "the essential objective of pastoral power is the salvation (*salut*) of the flock."[13] The French term *salut* can also translate into "safety," thereby avoiding the religious connotations of "salvation," but such a translation undermines some of Foucault's deeper observations. Although the interpretation of conservation as a religious enterprise might irritate some zoo people, it is of central importance to others. For example, George Rabb and Carol Saunders, both prominent zoo professionals, have written of conservation as the "universal religion of the future," suggesting that zoos should "consider how to utilize our institutions as churches or temples for the biota, how best to spread the ecological gospel . . . and how to celebrate the miracle of all life so as to secure caring for all life in the natural world."[14] Every day, zoos care for individual zoo animals, for the collective *ex situ* population, and for animals in their wild, *in situ*, state. Many zoo people would probably argue that through these acts of everyday care for animals, zoos also express care about all of humanity and, in fact, all life. These two expressions of care—care for animals and care for humans— are deeply intertwined. Although framed in scientific terms, the zoo's implicit pledge for the salvation of all animate beings can be presented as an ideological— even spiritual—mission, thus resonating with Foucault's *salut*.

The zoo's integration of the individual and collective management of animals also provides an occasion for a new examination of disciplinary modalities within the study of pastoral power. In particular, this book has extended surveillance theory beyond its more traditional focus on humans to include the surveillance of nonhumans. Exploring surveillance through the lens of zoo animals reveals how it can be seen as an expression of the power to care, in addition to its traditional interpretation as a means of authoritarian control. At the same time, this fresh perspective highlights how seemingly benign surveillance technologies (for example, electronic identification of individual fish in a tank) can easily be applied in more problematic ways (monitoring the movements of children in an amusement park). The zoo's governance project, in other words, is intimately related to the project of governing humans. Through exploring the various similarities and differences between human, animal, and inter-animal surveillance, I have contended that the project of governing animals has significant implications for humanity and deserves a much more thorough exploration than it has received thus far.

Timmy the Gorilla: Epilogue

As I was preparing my notes for this conclusion, I went back to read the story of Timmy the gorilla from the beginning. It occurred to me to contact the Louisville Zoo and see if they could provide me with an updated photo of Timmy and perhaps some supporting materials to accompany the text. After sounding a bit distant at first, the registrar eventually promised that she would try to help me if I called at another time. When I called again a couple of days later, she said: "Frankly, today we're making the decision to put him down." She explained that Timmy had been very ill, that he could not walk or eat, and that he was suffering. Hence, she said, "the zoo decided to euthanize him."[15]

"Did you know anything about this decision?" I asked Cleveland Metroparks Zoo director Steve Taylor later that day (this zoo had been Timmy's owner since 1966). "Of course," he replied. "They called us, they explained the situation, and I told them that we fully trust their decision." When I asked how he felt about this decision, Taylor replied: "It's a very sad day for the zoo. A friend of ours is going to be put to sleep. Whether it's a pet or a gorilla or your own Aunt Mabel—although we knew this day was coming, you're never quite prepared." Shortly after his death, local newspapers and television came out with the following headlines and lead-ins: "Timmy the Gorilla Dies at 52 in the Louisville Zoo: The Louisville Zoo has lost an iconic figure Tuesday morning when Timmy, a 52-year-old Silverback gorilla, was euthanized because of multiple health issues";[16] and "The Epic Life of an Iconic Gorilla: 'Timmy' Remembered (1959–

2011): Most of us thought of Timmy as a celebrity and ultimately an ambassador for lowland gorillas worldwide. He will be missed."[17]

This book has presented Timmy's life as an illustration of the transitions that have occurred in North American zoo management in the last several decades. Since Timmy entered the zoo world in 1960, his life was the subject of ever-increasing levels of investigation, documentation, management, and care. When he was alone, the zoo found company for Timmy. When he responded adequately to this companionship, the Gorilla SSP decided that it was time for Timmy to reproduce and moved him to another zoo for this purpose. And when zoo administrators believed that he had reproduced enough and was feeling overwhelmed by his large harem, they recommended moving him to one of the finest geriatric gorilla facilities in the United States.

Human keepers, administrators, and bureaucrats in zoos cared for and controlled Timmy throughout his life. They continued to do so after his death. In his life as in his death, humans served as Timmy's spokespersons, deciding what would be best for him and when. The zoo's power of care, however, extends beyond this individual animal. Steve Wing, general curator at the Louisville Zoo, explains, "When we lost Timmy, it tore up the staff. It's not easy, and you never get over it. But his keepers can't take time and grieve. They have to take care of ten living gorillas, four patas monkeys, and two pygmy hippos. They depend on them, too."[18] Beyond their responsibility to care for the individual animal, then, zoos must also care for the rest of the animals in their flock. Furthermore, zoos see themselves as caring for the entire animal kingdom. In Timmy's case, the Louisville Zoo obtained advanced permission from Timmy's official owner, Cleveland Metroparks Zoo, to perform a special necropsy in order to map his internal muscles to advance scientific knowledge that may then be applied to both *ex situ* and *in situ* gorilla populations. Although they can no longer care for Timmy, zoo professionals stress that a detailed inspection of Timmy's body will further the care of both captive gorillas and gorillas in the wild.[19]

The story of Timmy's death also illustrates some of the tensions underlying pastoral power as it is practiced in the zoo context. At the zoo, Foucault's pastoral paradox between individual and collective care translates into a three-way set of conflicts between the individual captive animal, the entire zoo population, and the wild population. One manifestation of this conflict is AZA's prioritization of green and yellow zoo programs and its phasing out of red populations. In this context, endangered animals in the wild are arguably sacrificed in the name of caring for the *ex situ* flock. Such stark empirical manifestations of the tension between the individual and the collective highlight the inherent paradox of pastoral power.

Finally, Timmy's story has also illustrated the radical transformations that have reshaped the structure and operations of accredited North American zoos since the 1970s. In the words of the former director of Lincoln Park Zoo, "Zoos are not independent islands anymore. We all cooperate with one another. We like to think that what we have is a part of the country's animal collection."[20] Alongside Timmy's transformative story, this book has also recorded many other stories by a range of zoo personnel from across North America. These stories provide a grounded account of how the power of care shapes the zoo's contemporary system of governance.

I would like to end by capturing the zoo's transformation through the eyes of Timmy the gorilla, as expressed by his zoo spokesperson, curator Steve Wing:

> I think Timmy has seen it. He has seen how zoos shifted from being two-by-two stamp collection institutions, sort of like menageries. We were then starting to build our social exhibits for gorillas, better health care, vet care, and more naturalistic exhibits. Timmy saw that. And this rarely happens nowadays. He was part of this transition. For a while, we would get gorillas from the wild. Timmy sure saw that. Then, revolution happened again: more training and public education. And each of these animals matter in the messages that we are telling our visitors. . . . Training demos show our visitors how passionate keepers are with animals and how much they care. We're not like Pepsi or Coke. We're all in it for the sake of the animals. And when we know something—we share.[21]

Notes

Introduction

1. Deets Pickett, interview by Dan Price, July 3, 1964, in CBC Digital Archives, http://archives.cbc.ca/science_technology/natural_science/clips/16618/.

2. Quoted in Ira Henry Freeman, "5 Little Gorillas End Rough Safari; Babies from Africa Arrive Ill and Heartbroken—Respond to Veterinary," *New York Times,* December 23, 1960.

3. Ibid.

4. Ibid.

5. Ibid.

6. Tad K. Schoffner (assistant animal care manager, Cleveland Metroparks Zoo), interview by author, telephone, July 29, 2011.

7. Ibid.

8. William F. Miller, "Equal Justice for All, with a '90s Twist," *Cleveland Plain Dealer,* October 2, 1991, http://global.factiva.com.

9. Michael Sangiacomo, "Timmy Sent to Bronx with Judge's OK," *Cleveland Plain Dealer,* November 1, 1991, http://global.factiva.com.

10. Kribe-Kate had a blocked fallopian tube. David Cantor, "Items of Property," in *The Great Ape Project: Equality Beyond Humanity,* ed. Paola Cavalieri and Peter Singer (New York: St. Martin's Griffin, 1996), 287.

11. Roby Elsner, "The Care and Management of Geriatric Gorillas in Captivity and the Role of Louisville Zoo's Husbandry Program," *Animal Keepers' Forum* 36, no. 4/5 (2009): 177–86.

12. Michael Sangiacomo, "Timmy Arrives at New Home in Bronx Zoo," *Cleveland Plain Dealer,* November 2, 1991, http://global.factiva.com.

13. Michael Sangiacomo, "Expert Says Zoos May Be Animals' Only Future Hope," *Cleveland Plain Dealer,* November 1, 1991, http://global.factiva.com.

14. Schoffner, interview.

15. Miller, "Equal Justice."

16. Lisa Couturier, *The Hopes of Snakes, and Other Tales from the Urban Landscape* (Boston: Beacon Press, 2005).

17. *In Defense of Animals v. Cleveland Metroparks Zoo*, 785 F.Supp.100 (Ohio 1991).

18. Sangiacomo, "Timmy Sent."

19. Sangiacomo, "Timmy Arrives."

20. Sangiacomo, "Timmy Sent."

21. Elsner, "Care and Management."

22. Thomas Wilms and Undine Bender, *International Studbook for the Western Lowland Gorilla: Gorilla g. gorilla 2010* (Frankfurt am Main, Germany: Frankfurt Zoo, 2011), http://library.sandiegozoo.org/studbooks/primates/gorilla2010.pdf.

23. Dan Wharton (director of Central Park Zoo, 1994–2007; chairman, Gorilla SSP, 1992–2006; North American regional studbook keeper, 1987–2011), interviews by author, telephone, April 6 and May 19, 2011; e-mail messages to author, August 2011–March 2012.

24. Ibid.

25. Ibid.

26. Louisville Zoo, *Male Gorilla Timmy at Louisville 22 May 2004 to 22 June 2004,* in specimen report for LOUISVILL/102476 (Louisville, KY: Louisville Zoological Garden, 2004), database report on file with author.

27. Elsner, "Care and Management."

28. Kara Bussabarger, "Louisville Zoo Welcomes New Female Gorilla," Louisville Zoo Media Advisory, May 5, 2008, http://www.louisvillezoo.org/news/press/MR/2008/MR%2008-06-30_gorilla.htm.

29. Kara Bussabarger, "Timmy Turns 50!" Louisville Zoo Media Advisory, January 8, 2009, http://www.louisvillezoo.org/news/press/MR/2009/MR%2009-01-08_timmy.htm.

30. Ibid. In 2008, ECO-CELL, North America's premier cell-phone recycling program, recognized the Louisville Zoo as the top zoo in North America for cell-phone recycling efforts. Kara Bussabarger, "A Day in the Life of the Gorilla Forest Staff," Louisville Zoo, www.louisvillezoo.org/collection/exhibits/gforest/art_GorillaStaff.pdf.

31. Kara Bussabarger, "Happy Birthday, Timmy!" Louisville Zoo Media Advisory, January 17, 2009, http://www.louisvillezoo.org/news/press/MR/2009/MR%2009-01-17_timmy.htm.

32. Although the majority of interviews and observations for this book were performed at zoos, my use of the term "zoo" throughout this book usually encompasses aquariums as well.

33. This specific phrase is from Susan Chin (vice president of planning and design, and chief architect, Exhibition and Graphic Arts Department, Bronx Zoo), interview by author, on-site, Bronx, NY, July 17, 2009.

34. "AZA Annual Conference," AZA, http://www.aza.org/annualconference/.

35. Donna Haraway, *Primate Visions: Gender, Race, and Nature in the World of Modern Science* (New York: Routledge, 1989), 9.

36. As discussed in this book, not all zoo animals are managed collectively. Of six thousand or so species kept in AZA-affiliated zoos and aquariums, as of September 2011 only 537 are managed by AZA's collaborative management system. See "Zoo and Aquarium Statistics," AZA, updated September 21, 2011, http://www.aza.org/zoo-aquarium-statistics/.

37. Jim Breheny (senior vice president of living institutions, Wildlife Conservation Society; director, Bronx Zoo), interview by author, on-site, Bronx, NY, July 15, 2009.

38. Chin, interview.

39. Immersion founder Jon Coe explains some of the challenges of immersion design: "We (immersion founders) argued [that] immersion subliminally predisposed people to see animals and landscape as inseparable, and thus the necessity of saving gorilla habitat as well as gorillas. The ironic counter version is that perhaps people seeing such seemingly beautiful and appropriate artificial habitats in zoos may think wild habitats are no longer important because we can save gorillas in amazing artificial zoo habitats." Jon Coe (landscape architect, Jon Coe Design), interviews by author, on-site, Buffalo, NY, February 10–11, 2012; Skype interview, February 19, 2012; e-mail messages, February–April 2012.

40. Pat Thomas (general curator, Bronx Zoo), interview by author, on-site, Bronx, NY, July 14, 2009.

41. Ibid.

42. Louisville's four-acre Gorilla Forest won the 2003 AZA Exhibit Award for immersion design. See Louisville Zoo, "Gorilla Forest," http://www.louisvillezoo.org/collection/exhibits/gforest/.

43. Ibid.

44. Arne Judd, "Storyline: The Heart and Soul of a Zoological Project," *Central Kentucky Architect*, June 2002, http://www.ajrcarchitecture.com/ckc-newsletter-june-2002.

45. Jon Coe, e-mail message.

46. Elsner, interview.

47. But see Lévi-Strauss's very different explanation of the same phenomenon: Claude Lévi-Strauss, *The Savage Mind (Nature of Human Society)* (Chicago: University of Chicago Press, 1966), 205.

48. Dan Wharton and Sarah Long, *North American Studbook for the Western Lowland Gorilla (Gorilla gorilla gorilla)* (Brookfield, IL: Chicago Zoological Society Brookfield Zoo, 2010).

49. "Gorilla Facts," Louisville Zoo, http://www.louisvillezoo.org/collection/exhibits/gforest/gf-facts.htm.

50. Louisville Zoo, "Male Gorilla Timmy." Notation such as the "1.2" here is common in the zoo industry, referring to the number of males and females in a group, with males

listed first. In this instance, 1.2 means one male and two females. Three females, for example, would be noted as 0.3.

51. Louisville Zoo, "Clinical Notes—Individual Specimen Report," Acc. #: 102476, MedARKS Database (on file with author).

52. 537 of approximately six thousand species held in zoos are managed by AZA's collaborative management system. See "Zoo and Aquarium Statistics."

53. "Event" includes capture, birth, transfer, and death, and "Rearing" indicates whether the gorilla was raised by a gorilla parent or by human hand. Wharton and Long, *North American Studbook*, 21.

54. Wilms and Bender, *International Studbook*.

55. Wildlife Conservation Society, Breeding Loan Agreement Between Wildlife Conservation Society and Cleveland Metroparks Zoo and Louisville Zoological Garden, March 16, 2004 (on file with author).

56. International Air Transport Association, *Live Animal Regulations* (Montreal: IATA, 2009), 36th ed., 34 (container requirement).

57. AZA Ape TAG, "Standardized Animal Care Guidelines for Gorillas (*Gorilla gorilla*)" (Silver Spring, MD, 2008), 23. Unpublished draft, on file with author.

58. Steve H. Taylor (director, Cleveland Metroparks Zoo), interview by author, telephone, August 2, 2011.

59. Wharton, interview.

60. Taylor, interview.

61. Tara Stoinski and Grace Fuller, "About the Ape TAG," Ape TAG, http://www .clemetzoo.com/apetag/aboutTAG.html.

62. Wharton, e-mail message. Also see Nancy Roe Pimm, *Colo's Story: The Life of One Grand Gorilla* (Colombus, OH: Columbus Zoo and Aquarium, 2011). Pimm describes the life of the first captive gorilla at the Columbus Zoo from birth, through childhood, into adult life as a mother, teacher, and now the oldest living gorilla in captivity. The gorilla, named Colo, is appreciated for teaching "generations of zookeepers and veterinarians what's best for all gorillas in captivity." Summary available at http://columbuszoobooks .com/wordpress/?category_name=colos-story.

63. Kristen Lukas et al., *Population Analysis and Breeding and Transfer Plan: Western Lowland Gorilla* (Gorilla gorilla gorilla) *AZA Species Survival Plan® Green Program* (Chicago: Lincoln Park Zoo Population Management Center, 2011), 1.

64. Lisa Faust et al., *Zoo Risk: A Risk Assessment Tool; Version 3.8 User's Manual* (Chicago: Lincoln Park Zoo, 2008), http://www.lpzoo.org/sites/default/files/pdf/cs/ZooRisk _Manual_3_80.pdf, 76.

65. Wharton, interview.

66. Ibid.

67. Buffalo Zoo director Donna Fernandes explains: "In the past, particularly when zoos operated through city or county parks departments, animal keepers were classified

as laborers or maintenance workers. They entered the field with very little experience and most of the animal husbandry training was done on the job since few college programs existed for zoo keeping careers. Nowadays, entry-level keepers have considerable training in animal husbandry, handling and restraint, zoo nutrition, etc. Animal curators generally hold advanced degrees and have more specialized knowledge in areas such as small population management, animal behavior, endocrinology, water quality and chemistry." Donna Fernandes (president and CEO, Buffalo Zoo), interviews by author, on-site, Buffalo Zoo, Buffalo, NY, May 8, 2009, and September 30, 2010; direct observation during four zoo tours conducted between May 2009 and November 2010, Buffalo Zoo; e-mail messages to author, 2010–12.

68. Lukas et al., *Population Analysis*, 4.

69. Wharton, interview.

70. The breeding of zoo animals is prioritized by a number indicating mean kinship (MK), which represents the degree to which, in this case, the gorilla is related to all other captive gorillas. A wild gorilla like Timmy started out with an MK of 0, but as he produced more offspring, his MK increased to 0.012. Gorillas with the fewest kin and lowest MK are bred first in order to conserve their genes. In 2011, all the gorillas chosen to breed had an MK of 0.011 or less.

71. Lukas et al., *Population Analysis*, 1.

72. Even among zoo personnel, some have criticized the common use of this term by zoos. "But what about gorillas, etc as 'cash cows' to keep zoo running?" asks designer Jon Coe (e-mail message). Former executive director of the Arizona-Sonora Desert Museum complains more broadly that "very few zoos exhibit their animals in ways that seriously really care about the health of the animals. . . . Ninety percent of zoos do a terrible job." Rick Brusca (executive director, Arizona-Sonora Desert Museum, 2001–2011), interview by author, on-site, Tucson, AZ, March 17, 2012; e-mail messages March-April 2012.

73. Quoted in Dan Klepal, "Timmy the Gorilla etc.," *Louisville Courier-journal.com* (Louisville, KY), August 2, 2011, http://www.courier-journal.com/apps/pbcs.dll/article ?AID=2011308020078.

74. Elsner, "Care and Management," 186.

75. Ibid., 178.

76. "Animal Care Manuals," AZA, http://www.aza.org/animal-care-manuals/.

77. Ibid.

78. AZA Ape TAG, *Standardized Animal Care.*

79. AZA, *The Accreditation Standards and Related Policies: 2011 Edition* (Silver Spring, MD: Association of Zoos and Aquariums, 2011), http://www.aza.org/uploadedFiles /Accreditation/AccreditationStandards.pdf. Some zoo professionals argue to the contrary that "very few zoos have serious conservation programs, most of it is just bologna, it's just fluff. . . . But, they really work hard with their public relations [department] to convince their visitors that they are serious about conservation" (Brusca, interview).

80. "Zoo and Aquarium Statistics."

81. John Walczak and Monika Fiby, "Louisville Zoological Garden—Gorilla Forest," *Zoolex: Your Free Access to International Zoo Design*, 2003, http://www.zoolex.org/zoolexcgi /view.py?id=658.

82. G. B. Rabb and C. D. Saunders, "The Future of Zoos and Aquariums: Conservation and Caring," *International Zoo Yearbook* 39: 1–26, 2 (emphasis and capitalization in original).

83. Ibid., 15.

84. AZA, *Species Survival Plan® Program Handbook* (Silver Spring, MD: Association of Zoos and Aquariums, 2011), http://www.aza.org/uploadedfiles/animal_care_and _management/tags,_ssps,_pmps,_studbooks,_sags/azaspeciessurvivalplanhandbook _2011.pdf.

85. Kristen E. Lukas (Gorilla SSP coordinator; curator of conservation and science, Cleveland Metroparks Zoo), interview by author, on-site in Chattanooga, TN, and telephone, March 30, 2011; e-mail messages to author, August 2011–April 2012.

86. "Animal Rights Uncompromised: Zoos," PETA, http://www.peta.org/about/why -peta/zoos.aspx.

87. Rowland-Homolak, quoted in Miller, "Equal Justice."

88. Wharton, interview.

89. Nikolas Rose, "Government, Authority and Expertise in Advanced Liberalism," *Economy and Society* 22, no. 3 (1993): 283–99.

90. Similar to Thomas Hobbes's use of the term "sovereign" in *The Leviathan* to indicate someone who is authorized by contract to talk on behalf of the people, Bruno Latour uses the term "spokeperson" to reflect the condensed interactions developed by a host of actors, or as a way by which a macro-actor can be subsituted for a heterogenous mass of micro-actors. Bruno Latour, *Science in Action: How to Follow Scientists and Engineers through Society* (Cambridge, MA: Harvard University Press, 1987), 71; Patrice Flichy, *Understanding Technological Innovation: A Socio-Technical Approach* (Cheltenham, UK: Edward Elgar Publishing, 2007), 54.

91. I use the term "technology" in the Foucauldian sense to mean an art, skill, trade, or applied science, also referred to as a "technique." The Greeks understood *techne* to be the primary human activity referring to a physical or mental act of constructing reality. Moreover, as Martin Heidegger has pointed out, *techne*, like *episteme*, is a form of truth making. Thus, when Michel Foucault talks about technologies of power, he recognizes that for every technology deployed, there is a simultaneously constituted domain of knowledge, or truth, that explains the inseparability of Power/Knowledge. See Foucault-L mail-list, post from June 19, 1999, http://foucault.info/Foucault-L/archive/msg05689 .shtml; Michel Foucault, *Security, Territory, Population: Lectures at the Collège de France, 1977–78*, ed. Michel Senellart et al., trans. Graham Burchell (New York: Picador / Palgrave Macmillan, 2009), 8–11.

92. Foucault, *Discipline and Punish*; Michel Foucault, *The Order of Things: An Archaeology of the Human Sciences* (London: Routledge, 2005 [1966]); Foucault, *Security, Territory, Population*.

93. Foucault, *Discipline and Punish*.

94. Ibid., 195.

95. Michel Foucault argues that between the seventeenth and eighteenth centuries, a new, more subtle form of power emerged that differed from its predecessor, sovereign power. Sovereign power relied on the exercise of a brutal display of force through torture and execution. According to Foucault, the new form of power, discipline, "is a type of power, a modality for its exercise, comprising a whole set of instruments, techniques, procedures, application, [and] targets. . . . And it may be taken over . . . by 'specialized' institutions, such as the prison." Michel Foucault, *Discipline and Punish: The Birth of the Prison*, 1st American U.S. ed. (New York: Pantheon Books, 1977), 215. As discussed here and in Chapter 3, panoptic design is an effective means of establishing discipline.

96. AZA Ape TAG, *Standardized Animal Care*. Jon Coe clarifies that at the zoo, "training is reward-based. No punishment or correction (negative reinforcement) is ever used." Coe, e-mail message.

97. The term "spectacular" is used through this book to refer to something that is founded on, or driven by, seeing (spectation), rather than the term's more common meaning as striking or sensational.

98. Jeremy Bentham, "Panopticon (Preface)," in *The Panopticon Writings*, ed. Miran Bozovic (London: Verso, 1995), 29–95.

99. Jacques-Alain Miller, "Jeremy Bentham's Panoptic Device," trans. Richard Miller, *October* 41 (1987): 3–29, 8.

100. Christopher Gad and Peter Lauritsen, "Situated Surveillance: An Ethnographic Study of Fisheries Inspection in Denmark," *Surveillance and Society* 7, no. 11 (2009): 49–57, 55; Annemarie Mol, Ingunn Moser, and J. Pols, eds., *Care in Practice: On Tinkering in Clinics, Homes and Farms* (Bielefeld, Germany: Transcript, 2010).

101. Paul Boyle (AZA senior vice president for conservation and education), interview by author, telephone, October 2, 2009.

102. See, for example, Janet Finch and Dulcie Groves, eds., *A Labour of Love: Women, Work, and Caring* (Boston: Routledge & Kegan Paul, 1983); Carol Gilligan, *In a Different Voice: A Psychological Theory and Women's Development* (Cambridge, MA: Harvard University Press, 1982); Nel Noddings, *Caring: A Feminine Approach to Ethics and Moral Education* (Berkeley and Los Angeles: University of California Press, 1984); Mary Daly and Jane Lewis, "The Concept of Social Care and the Analysis of Contemporary Welfare States," *British Journal of Sociology* 51, no. 2 (2000): 281–98; Kari Wærness, "Caring as Women's Work in the Welfare State," in *Patriarchy in a Welfare Society*, ed. Harriet Holter (Oslo: Universitetsforlaget, 1984), 67–87.

103. Foucault, *Security, Territory, Population*, 117.

104. Ibid., 165; Ben Golder, "Foucault and the Genealogy of Pastoral Power," *Radical Philosophy Review* 10, no. 2 (2007): 157–76, 166.

105. Foucault, *Security, Territory, Population*, 127.

106. Ibid., 143.

107. Ibid., 127.

108. Ibid.

109. "The pastorate is connected to salvation, since its essential, fundamental, objective is leading individuals, or, at any rate, allowing individuals to advance and progress on the part of salvation." Ibid., 166–7. The element of salvation is also discussed in the conclusion of this book.

110. Ibid., 126. In contrast, sovereign power—which involves obedience to the law of the king or central authority figure—is exercised over a territory.

111. Ibid., 128.

112. Sara Hallager (biologist, Smithsonian Institution, National Zoological Park; Ratite TAG chair; SSP Kori Bustard coordinator; SSP Red-Legged Seriema coordinator; SSP Roadrunner coordinator; and chair of Avian Scientific Advisory Group), interview by author, telephone, December 16, 2011.

113. Foucault, *Security, Territory, Population*, 149.

114. After Timmy's departure, Kate was paired with another sterile male gorilla, Oscar, but the two did not get along. Kate was then transferred to Fort Worth in November 1992 and died there in December 1996. From *North American Studbook* and "Four gorilla bachelors get new pad at zoo" August 5, 1994, Cleveland.com, http://www.cleveland.com/whateverhappened/index.ssf/1994/08/four_gorilla_bachelors_get_new.html.

115. Sangiacomo, "Timmy Arrives"; Couturier, *Hopes of Snakes*.

116. Patrick Biernacki and Dan Waldorf, "Snowball Sampling: Problems and Techniques of Chain Referral Sampling," *Sociological Methods and Research* 10, no. 2 (1981): 141–63.

117. For an in-depth discussion of my methodology see Irus Braverman, "Who's Afraid of Engaged Legal Geography? Advocating a Methodical Turn in Law and Geography," in *The Expanding Spaces of Law: A Timely Legal Geography*, ed. Irus Braverman et al. (under review).

118. But see Susan Davis, *Spectacular Nature: Corporate Culture and the Sea Word Experience* (Berkeley and Los Angeles: University of California Press, 1997); Carrie Friese, "Models of Cloning, Models for the Zoo: Rethinking the Sociological Significance of Cloned Animals," *BioSocieties* 4 (2010b): 367–90; Charis Thompson, "Confessions of a Bioterrorist: Subject Position and Reproductive Technologies," in *Playing Dolly: Technocultural Formations, Fantasies, and Fictions of Assisted Reproduction*, ed. E. Ann Kaplan and Susan Squier (Piscataway, NJ: Rutgers University Press, 1999), 189–219; Susan Willis, "Looking at the Zoo," *South Atlantic Quarterly* 98, no. 4 (1999): 669–87.

119. Irus Braverman, *Planted Flags: Trees, Land, and Law in Israel/Palestine* (Cambridge: Cambridge University Press, 2009).

Chapter One

1. David Hancocks, *A Different Nature: The Paradoxical World of Zoos and Their Uncertain Future* (Berkeley and Los Angeles: University of California Press, 2001), xix.

2. More precisely, in September 2011 the AZA accredited "225 AZA-accredited zoos and aquariums in 7 countries: USA: 214 in 48 states; Canada: 5; Mexico: 2; Argentina: 1; Bahamas: 1; Bermuda: 1; Hong Kong: 1." The accredited institutions are of several different types: "142 zoos; 37 aquariums; 9 both zoo and aquariums; 19 safari and theme parks; 15 science and nature centers; 2 aviaries; 1 butterfly house." "Zoo and Aquarium Statistics."

3. Scott Montgomery, "The Zoo: Theatre of the Animals," *Science as Culture* 4, no. 4 (1995): 565–600, 573.

4. "Zoo and Aquarium Statistics."

5. Vernon Kisling, *Zoo and Aquarium History: Ancient Animal Collections to Zoological Gardens* (Boca Raton, FL: CRC Press, 2000).

6. Catherine Bell, ed., *Encyclopedia of the World's Zoos*, vol. 3, *R–Z* (Chicago: Fitzroy Dearborn Publishers, 2001), 1434.

7. Paul Harpley (manager, interpretation, culture and design, Toronto Zoo), interview by author, on-site, Toronto, June 17, 2009; Kisling, *Zoo and Aquarium History*.

8. Robert Mullan and Garry Marvin, *Zoo Culture* (Urbana: University of Illinois Press, 1998), xiii.

9. Eric Baratay and Elizabeth Hardouin-Fugier, *A History of Zoological Gardens in the West* (London: Reaktion Books, 2002), 263.

10. "Hagenbeck Tierpark und Tropen-Aquarium," *Zoo and Aquarium Visitor*, 2007, http://www.zandavisitor.com/forumtopicdetail-411-Hagenbeck_Tierpark_und_Tropen -Aquarium-Zoos. Zoo designer Jon Coe qualifies this statement, noting that old photos show that many cages with iron bars still existed in Hagenbeck's zoos and were incorporated into artificial rockwork (Coe, e-mail message).

11. Baratay and Hardouin-Fugier, *History of Zoological Gardens*, 2.

12. Robert Shibley and Lynda H. Schneekloth, *The Olmsted City: The Buffalo Olmsted Park System: Plan for the 21st Century* (Buffalo, NY: Buffalo Olmsted Park Conservancy, 2008), 11, http://bfloparks.org/images/uploads/masterplan.pdf.

13. Elizabeth Hanson, *Animal Attractions: Nature on Display in American Zoos* (Princeton, NJ: Princeton University Press, 2002).

14. Ibid.

15. Ibid., 24.

16. Ibid.

17. Kisling, *Zoo and Aquarium History*.

18. "About AZA," AZA, http://www.aza.org/about-aza/.

19. Irus Braverman, "Looking at Zoos," *Cultural Studies* 25, no. 6 (2011b): 809–42.

20. Roderick Nash, *Wilderness and the American Mind* (New Haven, CT: Yale University Press, 1982), 44.

21. Kay Anderson, "Culture and Nature at the Adelaide Zoo: At the Frontiers of 'Human' Geography," *Transactions of the Institute of British Geographers* 20, no. 3 (1995): 275–94, 279. Many of my interviewees have agreed that the American zoo is largely an urban phenomenon. However, I was unable to obtain particular statistics on this matter from the AZA.

22. Thomas Birch, "The Incarceration of Wildness: Wilderness Areas as Prisons," *Environmental Ethics* 12, no. 1 (1990): 3–26; Chris Philo, "Animals, Geography, and the City: Note on Inclusions and Exclusions," *Environment and Planning D: Society and Space* 13, no. 6 (1995): 655–81.

23. Raymond Williams, *The Country and the City* (Oxford: Oxford University Press, 1973).

24. John Berger, *About Looking* (New York: Pantheon, 1980); Kate Soper, *What Is Nature? Culture, Politics and the Non-Human* (Oxford: Blackwell, 1995).

25. Anderson, "Culture and Nature."

26. Baratay and Hardouin-Fugier, *History of Zoological Gardens*, 224.

27. Desmond Morris, *The Human Zoo: A Zoologist's Study of the Urban Animal* (New York: McGraw-Hill, 1969).

28. Birch, "Incarceration of Wildness," 4.

29. Birch, "Incarceration of Wildness." See also Richard Grove, *Green Imperialism: Colonial Expansion, Tropical Island Edens and the Origins of Environmentalism, 1600–1860* (Cambridge: Cambridge University Press, 1996).

30. Birch, "Incarceration of Wildness," 4.

31. Bert Castro (president & CEO, Phoenix Zoo), interview by author, Phoenix, AZ, March 19, 2012.

32. Davis, *Spectacular Nature*, 8.

33. Soper, *What Is Nature?*; Williams, *Country and the City*.

34. Neil Smith, *Uneven Development: Nature, Capital, and the Production of Space* (New York: Blackwell, 1984), 33; see also David Pepper, *Eco-Socialism: From Deep Ecology to Social Justice* (London: Routledge, 1993); Noel Castree, "Socializing Theory: Theory, Practice and Politics," in *Social Nature: Theory, Practice and Politics*, ed. Noel Castree and Bruce Braun (Oxford: Blackwell, 2001), 1–36.

35. Breheny, interview.

36. Chin, interview.

37. Harpley, interview.

38. Hanson, *Animal Attractions*; Leo Marx, *The Machine in the Garden* (New York: Oxford University Press, 1964).

39. Davis, *Spectacular Nature*, 103.

40. Fernandes, interview.

41. The Arizona-Sonora Desert Museum is one of the few exceptions to this tendency of zoos toward exhibiting exotic animals. According to this zoo's former executive director: "Very few zoos focus on the region that they are embedded in. . . . The Desert Museum was conceived by a guy who came from New York and wanted to interpret the Sonoran desert for the local residents" (Brusca, interview). The exhibition of local nature is not without its problems, however. Current director Craig Ivanyi recounts: "We are immersed in the Sonoran desert and [so], to some degree, we are actually immersed in the environment we represent. And that is a beauty and a curse: because you have a fourteen mile drive to town and, for some people, this distance is a challenge. Along with the animals, we are rural. [Also,] on the outside of our perimeter fence we have lions, bobcats, all the animals that we have inside, and one of the challenges is making sure they stay on *that* side of the fence. A perimeter fence like that does not keep snakes out. Rattlesnakes, desert tortoises—all of those things that occur around here occur on our premises as well, so there are unique challenges and opportunities. . . . My point is that conservation is just as relevant in your own backyard as it is in Africa and we are ignoring it. I am not suggesting [that other zoos] become something different, I am asking them to embrace their own." Craig Ivanyi (executive director, Arizona-Sonora Desert Museum), interview by author, on-site, Tucson, AZ, March 14, 2012; e-mail messages March-April 2012 (emphasis added).

42. Chin, interview. Designer Jon Coe adds: "Many immersion exhibits are themed as a pseudo-safari, including many of my designs. . . . This, to make [visitors] believe in *in situ* sanctuaries" (Coe, e-mail message).

43. Alexander Wilson, *The Culture of Nature: North American Landscape from Disney to the Exxon Valdez* (Toronto: Between the Lines, 1991).

44. Anderson, "Culture and Nature," 282; Montgomery, " Zoo."

45. James Brown and Mark Lomolino, *Biogeography*, 2nd ed. (Sunderland, MA: Sinauer Associates, 1998); Harpley, interview.

46. Hagenbeck had already invented the concept of zoogeography in 1908 (Coe, e-mail message).

47. Harpley, interview.

48. Irus Braverman, "Zootopia: Utopia and Dystopia in the Zoological Garden," in *Earth Perfect? Nature, Utopia, and the Garden*, ed. Annette Giesecke and Naomi Jacobs (London: Black Dog Publishing, 2012); Davis, *Spectacular Nature*, 95.

49. Montgomery, "Zoo," 589.

50. Davis, *Spectacular Nature*; Willis, "Looking at the Zoo."

51. Brusca, interview.

52. From "Touring the Zoo," North Carolina Zoo, http://www.nczoo.org/visit/touring thezoo.html.

53. Willis, "Looking at the Zoo," 677.

54. "COST Advertisement," in *Connect* magazine (Silver Spring, MD: Association of Zoos and Aquariums), May 2011, 16.

55. Chin, interview.

56. Jon Coe, "One Hundred Years of Evolution in Great Ape Facilities in American Zoos," in *Proceedings of the AZA 1995 Western Regional Conference* (Bethesda, MD: American Zoo and Aquarium Association, 1996). Jon Coe clarifies that the term, theory, and practice of "landscape immersion" was invented jointly by Grant Jones, Dennis Paulson, David Hancocks, and himself as part of the Long Range Plan for Woodland Park Zoo, 1976 (e-mail message).

57. Coe, interview.

58. Ibid.

59. "COST Advertisement."

60. Breheny, interview.

61. "What Is an Immersion Exhibit?" Saint Louis Zoo, http://www.stlzoo.org/yourvisit /thingstoseeanddo/riversedge/immersion.htm.

62. Breheny, interview.

63. Chin, interview.

64. Gwen Howard (architect for the Buffalo Zoo, Foit Albert Associates), interview by author, interviewee's residence, July 24, 2009; on-site tour, Buffalo Zoo, Buffalo, NY, July 31, 2009.

65. Gregg Mitman, *Reel Nature: American Romance with Wildlife on Film* (Cambridge, MA: Harvard University Press, 1999), 13.

66. Breheny, interview.

67. Cindy Lee (curator of fishes, Toronto Zoo), interview by author, on-site, Toronto, June 17, 2009.

68. Paul Shepard, *Thinking Animals: Animals and the Development of Human Intelligence* (Athens: University of Georgia Press, 1998), 248.

69. Lee Ehmke (director and CEO, Minnesota Zoo; president of the World Association of Zoos and Aquariums Council; former director of planning and design, Bronx Zoo), interview by author, telephone, July 21, 2009.

70. RodentPro.com®, website, http://www.rodentpro.com/.

71. *Connect Magazine.*

72. E. G. Ludwig, "People at Zoos: A Sociological Approach," *International Journal for the Study of Animal Problems* 2, no. 6 (1981): 310–16, 316.

73. Brusca, e-mail message. Current director of the desert museum Craig Ivanyi adds: "Offering live foods is definitely the exception and this is almost always done out of public view. However, when considering public sensitivity about animals being offered dead

prey during visitor hours, we have worried that we can risk sanitizing nature to such a degree that even 'wild' animals no longer appear to do anything wild. So, with lower vertebrates and invertebrates, we don't worry about whether the visiting public witnesses an animal eating a dead prey animal (such as a snake eating a mouse or a rat). We prefer to go this route and use these times as interpretive opportunities. It is true that we are in a rural area and the southwestern U.S. to boot. Perhaps this means people are more accepting of this [here]" (Ivanyi, e-mail message).

74. Breheny, interview.

75. Another aspect of the distinction between humans and nature is the definition of native versus exotic animals. At the Arizona-Sonora Desert Museum, the rule is that animals must be native to be exhibited. This zoo's former director says about the definition of native: "If it lives here naturally it is native. . . . If humans had anything to do with it being here then it is not native. It is an exotic. And the Sonoran desert's biggest environmental challenge is actually invasive exotic species. That is our most serious conservation issue" (Brusca, interview).

76. Braverman, "Looking at Zoos."

77. Vicki Croke, *The Modern Ark: The Story of Zoos: Past, Present, and Future* (New York: Scribner, 1997), 81. By contrast, exhibit designer Jon Coe suggests that the hotdogs are sold at the zoo "just [like] popcorn or soft drinks are sold in lobby of theatre between performances. Is this wrong?" (Coe, e-mail message).

78. Ehmke, interview.

79. Ibid.

80. Mullan and Marvin, *Zoo Culture*, 54.

81. Ibid., 52.

82. Willis, "Looking at the Zoo."

83. Coe, e-mail message.

84. Smith, *Uneven Development*.

85. Coe responds: "You and others seem to imply that 'objectification' is a bad thing. Yet it is a time-honored tradition in religion, for example, where respect, love and fear are common themes. Why not also apply these to nature as well?" (Coe, e-mail message).

86. AZA, "AZA Five-Year Strategic Plan: 2011–2015," http://www.aza.org/uploaded Files/About_Us/AZA%20Strategic%20Plan.pdf.

87. Fernandes, interview.

88. Hanson, *Animal Attractions*; Nigel Rothfels, *Savages and Beasts: The Birth of the Modern Zoo* (Baltimore: Johns Hopkins University Press, 2002).

89. Friese, "Models of Cloning," 372.

90. Ibid.

91. Ehmke, interview.

92. Breheny, interview.

93. Carmi Penny (chair, Wild Pig, Peccary, and Hippo TAG; director of collections husbandry science; curator of mammals, San Diego Zoo Global), interview by author, on-site, AZA 2011 midyear meeting, Chattanooga, TN, March 21, 2011.

94. *Oxford Dictionaries*, April 2010 (Oxford University Press), s.v. "care," http://oxford dictionaries.com/definition/care. As mentioned in the introduction, care is also a central concept in feminist literature.

95. P. W. Schultz, "Inclusion with Nature: The Psychology of Human-Nature Relations," in *Psychology of Sustainable Development*, ed. P. Schmuck and P. W. Schultz (Boston: Kluwer Academic Publishers, 2002), 61–78

96. Rabb and Saunders, "Future of Zoos and Aquariums," 14.

97. Indeed, even when exercised by an inferior—for example, when a subordinate animal grooms its superior—the practice of care still asserts itself as a technology of power.

98. Vicky Singleton, "Good Farming Control or Care?" in Mol, Moser, and Pols, *Care in Practice*.

99. Ibid., 241.

100. Gad and Lauritsen, "Situated Surveillance," 55.

101. Randi Meyerson (Polar Bear SSP coordinator; veterinarian, Toledo Zoo), interview by author, telephone, January 31, 2011.

102. Fernandes, interview.

103. Stacey Johnson, *Regional Collection Plan for Bears in North America 2010* (Bear TAG, 2010), 6.

104. Meyerson, interview.

105. Tara Stoinski (Ape TAG chair; manager of conservation partnerships, Zoo Atlanta), interview by author, telephone, January 10, 2011.

106. Stoinski, interview. Also see the debate about Cheetah's identity, "Cheetah Dead: Chimpanzee Sidekick from 1930s Tarzan Flicks Dies at 80," *Huffington Post*, December 28, 2011, http://www.huffingtonpost.com/2011/12/28/cheetah-the-chimpanzee-obituary _n_1172283.html; Kim Severson, "Death of a Chimpanzee Revives Doubts About Its Film Résumé," *New York Times*, December 31, 2011.

107. William Conway, "Buying Time for Wild Animals with Zoos," *Zoo Biology* 29 (2010): 1–8.

108. Fernandes, interview.

109. Elsewhere, Swaziland elephants were bought for $100,000 each, and the giant pandas' standard loan terms include a fee of up to $1,000,000 per year; http://www.cbc .ca/news/canada/calgary/story/2010/11/01/toronto-pandas.html. Journalist Thomas French describes the full story of these elephants and other charismatic animals at Tampa's Lowry Park Zoo. Thomas French, *Zoo Story: Life in the Garden of Captives* (New York: Hyperion, 2010). By contrast, the bulk wholesale cost of frozen feeder rodents that are used to feed many of the zoo's larger carnivores ranges from 12 cents for

X-Small pinkies to $10 for the XXX-Large rabbits. See "Frozen feeder price list," http://www.rodentpro.com/rp_pricelist.pdf. The different value figures placed on different animals at the zoo recall the statement in *Animal Farm* that although all animals are equal, some are more equal than others. George Orwell, *Animal Farm* (New York: Penguin Group USA, 1996), 133.

110. Breheny, interview.

111. Fernandes, e-mail message.

112. And increasingly so due to design and construction costs. For example, remodeling the polar bear exhibit is expected to cost the Buffalo Zoo over $14.5 million. Still, zoos continue to remodel their facilities. A quick scan of the May 2011 issue of AZA's monthly magazine *Connect* reveals a variety of routine zoo expenditures. Companies that offer their services to zoos include Aqualogic, building titanium water chillers and heat pumps; RodentPro.Com specializing "in the production and distribution of mice, rats, rabbits, guinea pigs, chicks, and quail"; Prairie States Insurance Inc., "20 years insuring all types of animals, including exotic & domestic"; LGL Animal Care Products Inc., specializing in restraint cages and lift tables; NETS Unlimited Inc., designing "alterNETives"; COST, specializing in exhibit fabrication; and WDM architects, who "eat sleep live think make nature." *Connect Magazine.*

113. In the United States, only four companies compete over the zoo gift shop market. This explains the strikingly similar gift shop items found in almost every zoo in the country. T-shirts, mugs, stuffed animals, and numerous other animal gadgets are standard products in this non-exhibit display of animals (Fernandes, interview).

114. Dave Ireland (curator of conservation, Toronto Zoo), interview by author, onsite, Toronto, June 17, 2009.

115. Fernandes, e-mail message.

116. Ibid.

117. Davis, *Spectacular Nature.*

118. Ibid.

119. Steve Burnes, "Zoo Boise's New Mission," *Connect*, January 2012, 19 (emphasis added).

120. "Zoo and Aquarium Statistics."

121. Braverman, "Looking at Zoos."

122. Mike Carpenter (senior biologist, Permit Division, U.S. Fish and Wildlife Service), interview by author, telephone, August 20, 2009.

123. For a discussion of the latter, see Margaret Crawford, "The World in a Shopping Mall," in *Variations on a Theme Park: The New American City and the End of Public Space*, ed. Michael Sorkin (New York: Hill & Wang, 1992), 3–30.

124. Davis, *Spectacular Nature.*

125. Paraphrasing Bill Martin and Eric Carle, *Panda Bear, Panda Bear, What Do You See?* (New York: Henry Holt and Co., 2003).

126. Personal observation, February 2010.

127. Jennifer Price, "Looking for Nature at the Mall: A Field Guide to the Nature Company," in *Uncommon Ground: Rethinking the Human Place in Nature*, ed. William Cronon (New York: W. W. Norton, 1996): 186–203.

128. Rob Laidlaw (founder and director, Zoocheck Canada), interview by author, telephone, January 28, 2011.

129. Coe, e-mail message.

Chapter Two

1. Quoted in Foucault, *Order of Things*, xvi.

2. Plato, *Statesman*, trans. Benjamin Jowett (Teddington, England: Echo Library, 2006), 37.

3. Geoffrey Bowker and Susan Leigh Star, *Sorting Things Out: Classification and Its Consequences* (Cambridge, MA: MIT Press, 1999), 17.

4. Modern taxonomy now includes the rank of phylum between kingdom and class and the rank of family between order and genus that were not present in Linnaeus's original system (Fernandes, e-mail message).

5. Haraway, *Primate Visions*, 9.

6. Ibid., 10.

7. Ibid., 9.

8. "About the ICZN," International Commission on Zoological Nomenclature, http://iczn.org/content/about-iczn.

9. Jean Miller (registrar, Buffalo Zoo), interview by author, on-site, Buffalo Zoo, Buffalo, NY, June 13 and 15, 2009.

10. Ibid.

11. Foucault, *Order of Things*, 154.

12. William Bogard, *The Simulation of Surveillance: Hypercontrol in Telematic Societies* (Cambridge: Cambridge University Press, 1996); Kevin Haggerty and Richard Ericson, "The Surveillant Assemblage," *British Journal of Sociology* 51, no. 4 (2000): 605–22.

13. Robert Wilson, ed., *Species: New Interdisciplinary Essays* (Cambridge, MA: MIT Press, 1999); Anna George and Richard Mayden, "Species Concepts and the Endangered Species Act: How a Valid Biological Definition of Species Enhances the Legal Protection of Biodiversity," *Natural Resources Journal* 45 (2005): 377; Carrie Friese, "Classification Conundrums: Categorizing Chimeras and Enacting Species Preservation," *Theory and Society* 39, no. 2 (2010a): 145–72.

14. R. S. Chundawat et al., "*Panthera tigris*," in *IUCN Red List of Threatened Species, Version 2011.2* (IUCN: 2011), http://www.iucnredlist.org.

15. "Generic Tiger SSP," Tiger SSP, http://www.mnzoo.org/tigerSSP/genericSSP.html.

16. "Animal Welfare Act Regulations," 50 CFR §17.21 (2010).

17. As discussed in detail in Chapter 7. See EAZA's "Statement on Behalf of the European Association of Zoos and Aquaria (EAZA) and the EAZA Conservation Breeding Programme for Tigers (the Tiger EEP) in Reference to the Recent Conviction of Staff of Zoo Magdeburg for the Management Euthanasia of Three Hybrid Tigers," June 22, 2010 (EAZA Executive Office: 2010), http://www.waza.org/files/webcontent/public_site/5.conservation/code_of_ethics_and_animal_welfare/EAZA_EEP%20Tiger%20Statement%20_2010.pdf.

18. Chundawat et al., "*Panthera tigris.*"

19. The U.S. Fish and Wildlife Service maintains lists of both domestic and foreign endangered species protected under the Endangered Species Act. The list of species is available at http://www.fws.gov/endangered/species/. CITES is a treaty that restricts international trade of endangered and threatened species. CITES I species are listed in Appendix I of the treaty as critically endangered. CITES II species are listed in Appendix II, and although not critically endangered, these species are threatened and require international trade restrictions for survival. CITES species are listed at http://www.cites.org/eng/app/appendices.php (for further discussion, see Chapter 6).

20. PMPs are AZA's Population Management Plan programs that do not require AZA accreditation from their members. As of 2011, these programs are being phased out by the AZA (see Chapter 7).

21. William Conway (president, Wildlife Conservation Society; director, Bronx Zoo, 1966–99), interview by author, on-site, Bronx, NY, July 14, 2009.

22. Stoinski, interview.

23. Meyerson, interview.

24. "Gorilla Range," Gorilla SSP, http://www.clemetzoo.com/gorillassp/GorillaRange.html; Walsh et al., "*Gorilla gorilla,*" in *IUCN Red List of Threatened Species. Version 2011.2* (IUCN: 2008), http://www.iucnredlist.org.

25. See "Gorilla Range." Interestingly, while the Gorilla SSP notes *ex situ* and *in situ* populations together on the gorilla range page, the International Union for Conservation of Nature (IUCN) makes no mention of *ex situ* gorilla populations in its description of gorilla ranges, as if the captive gorillas do not exist or contribute to the conservation of the species.

26. Hanson, *Animal Attractions.*

27. Willis, "Looking at the Zoo," 674.

28. Ibid.

29. Croke, *Modern Ark,* 199.

30. Randy Malamud, *Reading Zoos: Representations of Animals and Captivity* (New York: New York University Press, 1998), 32.

31. Ibid.

32. David Hancocks (former director, Woodland Park Zoo, Seattle, WA; director, Open Range Zoo, Werribee, Australia), e-mail message to author, February 2, 2011.

33. Laidlaw, interview.

34. Ron Kagan (director, Detroit Zoo), interview by author, telephone, February 2, 2011.

35. Ibid.

36. Meyerson, interview.

37. Other unnatural behaviors, such as gorillas watching *Oprah* on television (as described in Chapter 3), are considered benign and even framed as behavioral enrichment.

38. Stoinski, interview.

39. Naomi Rose (senior scientist, Humane Society International), interview by author, telephone, February 7, 2011.

40. Rose, interview (emphasis added).

41. Rose, interview.

42. C. Andrainarivo et al., "*Hapalemur alaotrensis*," in *IUCN Red List of Threatened Species, Version 2011.2* (IUCN: 2008), http://www.iucnredlist.org.

43. S. Schliebe et al., "*Ursus maritimus*," in *IUCN Red List of Threatened Species, Version 2011.2* (IUCN: 2008), http://www.iucnredlist.org.

44. Walsh et al., "*Gorilla gorilla*"; M. Robbins and L. Williamson, "*Gorilla beringei*," in *IUCN Red List of Threatened Species, Version 2011.2* (IUCN: 2008), http://www.iucnredlist.org.

45. Stuart Wells (Director of conservation and science, Phoenix Zoo), interview by author, on-site, Phoenix, AZ, March 19, 2012. See also IUCN SSC Antelope Specialist Group, "*Oryx leucoryx*," in *IUCN Red List of Threatened Species, Version 2011.2* (IUCN: 2011), http://www.iucnredlist.org.

46. Breheny, interview.

47. Wharton, interview.

48. Stoinski, interview.

49. Ibid.

50. Meyerson, interview.

51. Wharton, interview.

52. "African Elephant," San Diego Safari Park, http://www.sdzsafaripark.org/park-wildlife/african_elephant.html.

53. Laidlaw, interview.

54. See "Exotic Pet Trade," ASPCA, http://www.aspca.org/Fight-Animal-Cruelty/exotic-pet-faq.aspx; Bryan Christy, *The Lizard King: The True Crimes and Passions of the World's Greatest Reptile Smugglers* (New York: Twelve, 2008).

55. "Summary of State Laws Relating to Private Possession of Exotic Animals," *Born Free USA*, http://www.bornfreeusa.org/b4a2_exotic_animals_summary.php.

56. Holly Richards, "Zoo Diligently Monitoring Exotic Animals," *Zanesville (OH) Times Recorder*, November 1, 2011, http://www.zanesvilletimesrecorder.com/.

57. Associated Press, "Reports Detail the Chase for Freed Exotic Animals," *New York Times*, November 5, 2011, http://www.nytimes.com/2011/11/06/us/reports-detail-chase -for-freed-exotic-animals-in-ohio.html?_r=1&scp=2&sq=zanesville&st=cse.

58. "Dangerous Animals," Ohio Department of Natural Resources, http://www .ohiodnr.com/dangerouswildanimals/tabid/23387/default.aspx. The zoo's legal stance on this issue is further discussed in Chapter 6.

59. Wharton, interview.

60. Laidlaw, interview.

61. Ibid.

62. "Children's Zoo," Philadelphia Zoo, http://www.philadelphiazoo.org/zoo/Zoo -Habitats/Children-s-Zoo.htm.

63. "Present," Buffalo Zoo, http://www.buffalozoo.org/present.html.

64. "Children's Zoo," Philadelphia Zoo.

65. "Animals & Exhibits," Lincoln Children's Zoo, http://www.lincolnzoo.org/animals /exhibits.

66. Fernandes, interview; see also Irus Braverman, "Animal Immobilities: A Study of Animals, Law, and the American City," *Law and Social Inquiry* (under review).

67. "Activities," San Diego Zoo, http://www.sandiegozoo.org/zoo/plan_your_trip /activities.

68. "Children's Zoo," Wildlife Conservation Society, http://www.bronxzoo.com /animals-and-exhibits/exhibits/childrens-zoo.aspx.

69. "Visit Daily Activities," Phoenix Zoo, http://www.phoenixzoo.org/visit/daily _activities.aspx.

70. Rabb and Saunders, "Future of Zoos and Aquariums," 15.

71. Although listed in the context of the petting experience, the animals in the Toronto Zoo's Kids Zoo (goats, llama) are not included in the zoo's general directory of animals. See "Animals," Toronto Zoo, http://www.torontozoo.com/ExploretheZoo /Animals.asp?pg=20 and "Zellers Discovery Zone," Toronto Zoo, http://www.torontozoo .com/ExploretheZoo/ZellersDiscoveryZone.asp.

72. Fernandes, e-mail message.

73. On the latter, see Peter Sandøe et al., "Staying Good While Playing God: The Ethics of Breeding Farm Animals," *Animal Welfare* 8, no. 4 (1999): 313–28.

74. Judith Block (registrar emeritus, Smithsonian Institution, National Zoological Park), interview by author, telephone, September 4, 2009; Willis, "Looking at the Zoo."

75. Kevin Hetherington, "The Unsightly: Touching the Parthenon Frieze," *Theory, Culture, Society* 19, no. 5/6 (2002): 187–205, 189.

76. Ibid., 193.

Chapter Three

1. Henri Lefebvre, *The Production of Space*, trans. Donald Nicholson-Smith (Malden, MA: Blackwell, 1991), 76.

2. Braverman, "Looking at Zoos"; Davis, *Spectacular Nature*; Willis, "Looking at the Zoo."

3. Anderson, "Culture and Nature"; Berger, *About Looking*; Rebecca Bishop, "Journeys to the Urban Exotic: Embodiment and the Zoo-Going Gaze," *Humanities Research* 11, no. 1 (2004): 106–24; Braverman, "Looking at Zoos"; Randy Malamud, *Reading Zoos*.

4. Hetherington, "Unsightly," 198.

5. Martin Jay, "Scopic Regimes of Modernity," in *Vision and Visuality*, ed. Hal Foster (Seattle: Bay Press, 1998), 3–23; Martin Jay, *Downcast Eyes: The Denigration of Vision in Twentieth-Century French Thought* (Berkeley and Los Angeles: University of California Press, 1994).

6. Hetherington, "Unsightly," 199. However, several zoos are experimenting with exhibit features that offer involvement experiences, whereby a visitor can sense signals or circumstances in the environment in a way that is similar to what an animal may experience. See Rabb and Saunders, "Future of Zoos and Aquariums," 11. For example, at the Arizona-Sonora Desert Museum visitors are invited to wear artificially designed bat ears to experience the sensitivities of bat hearing (personal observation, March 18, 2012).

7. Willis, "Looking at the Zoo," 675.

8. Howard, interview.

9. Ibid.

10. Ibid.

11. Kevin Hetherington, "Museums and the Visually Impaired: The Spatial Politics of Access," *Sociological Review* 48, no. 3 (2000): 444–63.

12. Mullan and Marvin, *Zoo Culture*, 32.

13. Rothfels, *Savages and Beasts*.

14. "The Human Zoo: Science's Dirty Secret," in *Race: Science's Last Taboo* (Channel 4, 2009), http://raceandscience.channel4.com/media/pdfs/Context-HumanZoo.pdf.

15. Harvey Blume, "Ota Benga and the Barnum Perplex," in *Africans on Stage: Studies in Ethnological Show Business*, ed. B. Lindfors (Bloomington: Indiana University Press, 1999), 188–202.

16. Jerry Bergman, "Ota Benga: The Pygmy Put on Display in a Zoo," *Journal of Creation* 14, no. 1 (2000): 81–90.

17. Phillips Bradford and Harvey Blume, *Ota Benga: The Pygmy in the Zoo* (New York: St. Martin's Press, 1992), 304.

18. Mullan and Marvin, *Zoo Culture*.

19. Tony Bennett, "The Exhibitionary Complex," *New Formations* 4 (Spring 1988): 73–83, 92.

20. Ibid., 95. See also Anderson, "Culture and Nature"; Haraway, *Primate Visions*.

21. Smith, *Uneven Development*.

22. Ehmke, interview. Ehmke was also director of planning and design at the Bronx Zoo (1998–2000).

23. For a different design approach see Jon Coe, "Third Generation Conservation," *2009 ARAZPA Conference Proceedings*, Australia, www.joncoedesign.com/pub/PDFs /ThirdGenerationConservation.pdf.

24. Disney's® Animal Kingdom in Orlando is another example of exhibiting indigenous humans outside of the formal animal exhibit. Jon Coe describes that "Disney hires African students to work in the 'Mombasa' themed area selling ice cream and other snacks from carts, thus creating the effect of being in Africa while also creating jobs and educational opportunities for African students" (Coe, e-mail message).

25. "Maasai Journey at Woodland Park Zoo," Woodland Park Zoo, archived in Internet Archive Wayback Machine, http://web.archive.org/web/20080905180123/http://www .zoo.org/maasai_journey/index.html. In 2011, the Woodland Park Zoo still held special storytelling events with "Maasai interpreters." The zoo's website reads accordingly, "Share an unforgettable experience of African culture through the dramatic storytelling of real-life wildlife encounters by a Maasai interpreter": announced in an April 6, 2011, press release at http://www.zoo.org/page.aspx?pid=1606. The Woodland Park Zoo has also partnered with the Maasai Association near Tarangire National Park to restore natural water holes. See "Waterhole Restoration Project," Woodland Park Zoo, http://www .zoo.org/page.aspx?pid=904.

26. Manuel Valdes, "A Misguided Use of Zoo Guides?" *Seattle Times*, August 8, 2007, http://seattletimes.nwsource.com/html/localnews/ 2003826534_maasai08m.html.

27. Ibid.

28. A similar separation also occurs in wildlife and safari parks, where humans are rarely allowed to coexist with animals. For example, upstream of Ruaha National Park, Tanzania farmers and pastoralists have been removed from the Ihefu wetlands, which sustain the Great Ruaha River and wildlife in the park. A major exception to this separation is the Ngorongoro Conservation Area, which includes Maasai pastoralists and is contested precisely for this reason. I would like to thank my research assistant Joseph Holler for this comment.

29. Harpley, interview.

30. Chin, interview.

31. Tom Mason (curator of birds and invertebrates, Toronto Zoo), interview by author, on-site, Toronto, June 17, 2009.

32. Mullan and Marvin, *Zoo Culture*.

33. Chin, interview.

34. Davis, *Spectacular Nature*, 97.

35. Ibid.

36. Quoted in Mullan and Marvin, *Zoo Culture*, 65.

37. Croke, *Modern Ark*, 79.

38. Judd, "Storyline," 3–4.

39. Breheny, interview.

40. Willis, "Looking at the Zoo," 679. Jon Coe disagrees. Using his design of Louisville's Gorilla Forest as an example, he argues that it is the gorillas who are in fact surrounding and overlooking the visitors, "truly turning the dominance tables in favor of the gorillas" (Coe, e-mail message).

41. Ibid., 682

42. "Vanishing™ Coil Mesh," A thru Z Consulting and Distributing Inc., http://www.athruzcages.com/vanishing.html.

43. Howard, interview.

44. Chin, interview.

45. Ibid.

46. Cyndi Griffin (gorilla keeper, Buffalo Zoo), e-mail message to author, August 26, 2009.

47. Willis, "Looking at the Zoo," 678. Apparently, orangutans also like to look back at zoo visitors. See "Orang-utans 'like looking back at zoo visitors,'" *Telegraph* (UK), June 7, 2010, http://www.telegraph.co.uk/science/science-news/7808406/Orang-utans-like-looking-back-at-zoo-visitors.html. And rumors have it that a beluga whale is also into looking back. See http://www.youtube.com/watch?v=EP6Y_0FpSUk.

48. Berger, *About Looking*, 26. See also John Berger, *Ways of Seeing* (London: Penguin, 2008), 5.

49. Many zoo professionals would disagree with this statement. See, for example, Jon Coe, "Increasing Affiliative Behavior between Zoo Animals and Zoo Visitors," in *1999 AZA Convention Proceedings* (American Zoo and Aquarium Association, Silver Spring, MD), 216–220, http://www.joncoedesign.com/pub/technical.htm.

50. Eldon Smith (director of wildlife care, Toronto Zoo), interview by author, Toronto, June 16, 2009.

51. Ibid.

52. "The San Diego Zoo and Wild Animal Park Live Cams," San Diego Zoo, http://www.sandiegozoo.org/livecams/.

53. Mullan and Marvin, *Zoo Culture*, 76.

54. Berger, *About Looking*, 14.

55. Mitman, *Reel Nature*, 13; Brett Mills, "Television Wildlife Documentaries and Animals' Right to Privacy," *Continuum* 24, no. 2 (2010): 193–202.

56. Mills, "Television Wildlife Documentaries," 199.

57. Stoinski, interview.

58. Ehmke, interview.

59. Mason, interview.

60. Croke, *Modern Ark.*

61. Ehmke, interview.

62. Ibid.

63. Quoted in Baratay and Hardouin-Fugier, *History of Zoological Gardens*, 221.

64. Coe, e-mail message.

65. Ehmke, interview.

66. Ibid. Designer Coe adds: "Tame animals are individually conditioned through long familiarity . . . to be comfortable with the few humans they trust, but are fearful and may be dangerous to humans they don't know. . . . Thus there is a behavioural spectrum with totally wild at one end and totally domesticated and tamed animals at the other reflecting both genetic manipulation of species and breeds and 'socialization' and conditioning of individuals" (e-mail message). See also Heini Hediger. *Wild Animals in Captivity* (New York: Dover Publications, 1964).

67. Howard, interview.

68. Elsner, interview. Timmy's exhibit in Cleveland had no outdoor space. Elsner explains that "back in the day, we didn't know as much as we do today about gorillas' natural history, and a high priority was placed on cleaning and disinfection" (e-mail message).

69. Tour of the Buffalo Zoo, April 2010.

70. Griffin, e-mail message.

71. Howard, interview.

72. Fernandes, interview

73. Ibid.

74. Breheny, e-mail message. .

75. William Rapley (executive director, conservation, education, and research, Toronto Zoo), e-mail message to author, August 18, 2009.

76. Ralph R. Acampora, "Zoos and Eyes: Contesting Captivity and Seeking Successor Practices," *Society & Animals* 13, no. 1 (2005): 68–88, at 75.

77. Ralph R. Acampora, "Extinction by Exhibition: Looking at and in the Zoo," *Human Ecology Review* 5, no. 1, 1998: 1–4, at 1.

78. Bentham, "Panopticon (Preface)."

79. Foucault, *Discipline and Punish*, 201–2.

80. Mullan and Marvin, *Zoo Culture*, 43.

81. Acampora, "Zoos and Eyes," 79. Designer Coe remarks that the acculturation of animals to the human gaze is "not a goal, but a side effect. The goal is public engagement, education, and support for animals" (e-mail message).

82. According to Foucault, discipline's success depends on the combination of three elements: hierarchical observation, normalizing judgment, and examination. See Foucault, *Discipline and Punish*, "Part Three: The Means of Correct Training," 170–94. These elements have been explored by most Foucauldian scholars in the human context only.

However, as I have argued in the introduction, there is no real reason to stop there. Although the subject of the gaze at the zoo is a nonhuman animal, it may still be disciplined: its body and actions can be observed, normalized, and examined to fit ideas about correct and proper conduct.

83. Acampora, "Zoos and Eyes," 79.

84. Bennett, "Exhibitionary Complex," 74.

85. Ibid., 85–86.

86. Thomas Mathiesen, "The Viewer Society: Michel Foucault's 'Panopticon' Revisited," *Theoretical Criminology* 1, no. 2 (1997): 215–34.

87. "Zoo and Aquarium Statistics."

88. Bentham, "Panopticon (Preface)."

89. Jacques-Alain Miller, "Jeremy Bentham's Panoptic Device," trans. Richard Miller, *October* 41 (1987): 3–29, at 8.

90. Ibid., 9.

91. Hancocks, *Different Nature*, xviii.

92. John H. Falk et al., *Why Zoos and Aquariums Matter: Assessing the Impact of a Visit to a Zoo or Aquarium* (Silver Spring, MD: Association of Zoos and Aquariums, 2007). Over a three-year period, more than 5,500 visitors participated in the studies. "We drew on various quantitative and qualitative methods, including written questionnaires, interviews, tracking studies, and Personal Meaning Mapping (PMM), which identified individual changes in visitors' thinking by allowing them to respond to a series of questions prior to and after their visit" (p. 4).

93. But see rebuttal study, Lori Marino et al., "Do Zoos and Aquariums Promote Attitude Change in Visitors? A Critical Evaluation of the American Zoo and Aquarium Study," *Society and Animals* 18 (2010): 126–38.

94. Lukas, interview. Since watching television is also "seeing with one's own eyes," what Lukas's son seems to be implying is an even more subtle distinction between merely seeing an animal and actually being present with this animal in a shared space and time.

95. Thomas, interview.

Chapter Four

1. Foucault, *Order of Things*, 146.

2. 1769 King James Version. Incidentally, the biblical description has triggered sophisticated calculations to prove that this naming task could indeed be accomplished within one working day, apparently requiring Adam to name an animal every six seconds. Henry Morris, *KJV New Defenders Study Bible* (Nashville, TN: Thomas Nelson, 2006).

3. Foucault, *Security, Territory, Population*, 146.

4. "Zoo and Aquarium Statistics."

5. "About ZIMS," ISIS, http://www2.isis.org/products/.

6. For an explanation about my use of this term in the context of zoos, see Irus Braverman, "Foucault Goes to the Zoo: Zooveillance in North America," *Surveillance & Society* (forthcoming, 2012).

7. Bogard, *Simulation of Surveillance*, 3.

8. Latour, *Science in Action*, 215–57.

9. Roger Clarke, "Information Technology and Dataveillance," *Communications of the ACM* 31, no. 5 (1988): 498–512; Kevin Haggerty and Richard Ericson, eds., *The New Politics of Surveillance and Visibility* (Toronto: University of Toronto Press, 2006), 3.

10. James Scott, *Seeing Like a State* (New Haven, CT: Yale University Press, 1998).

11. Ibid.

12. Lévi-Strauss, *Savage Mind*, 215.

13. Mary T. Phillips, "Proper Names and the Social Construction of Biography: The Negative Case of Laboratoty Animals," *Qualitative Sociology* 17, no. 2 (1994): 119–42, at 123.

14. Ibid., 121.

15. Haggerty and Ericson, *New Politics*.

16. Vicki Hearne, *Adam's Task: Calling Animals by Name* (New York: Skyhorse Publishing, 2007).

17. See *The American Stud Book: Principal Rules and Requirements* (New York: Jockey Club, 2008), http://www.jockeyclub.com/pdfs/rules_08_final.pdf. Also see "Guide to Racing: History of Racehorses," British Horseracing Authority, http://www.britishhorseracing.com/goracing/racing/racehorses/history.asp. To be registered as a thoroughbred, a foal must be conceived by a natural act of copulation and its genetic parentage verified by a certified laboratory.

18. See "Breed Info," Canadian Horse Breeders Association, http://www.lechevalcanadien.ca/breed.htm.

19. Miller, interview.

20. Fernandes, e-mail message.

21. Rachél Watkins Rogers (registrar, Zoo Miami), interview by author, in-person, Islamorada, FL, August 6, 2009.

22. Miller, interview.

23. Ibid.

24. Fernandes, e-mail message.

25. Erika Brason, "Controversy over 'Malia' the Baby Giraffe," Buffalo News WGRZ.com, February 6, 2009, http://www.wgrz.com/news/local/story.aspx?storyid= 63936 &catid=37.

26. "Elephant Cam," San Diego Zoo Safari Park, http://www.sdzsafaripark.org/video/elephant_cam.html.

27. Yadira Galindo, "Panda Cub Receives Name," *San Diego Zoo Giant Pandas Blog*, November 17, 2009, http://blogs.sandiegozoo.org/2009/11/17/panda-cub-receives-name/.

28. See video and story: "Toronto Zoo Gorilla Names His Son 'Nassir,'" *CityNews Toronto*, November 18, 2009, http://www.citytv.com/toronto/citynews/life/family/article /63555–toronto-zoo-gorilla-names-his-son-nassir.

29. "Penguin Named—New Way to Meet Penguins," *Tennessee Aquarium Blog*, January 7, 2011, http://tennesseeaquarium.blogspot.com/2011/01/penguin-named-new-way-to-meet-penguins.html.

30. "Name an Animal," Greater Los Angeles Zoo Association, http://www.lazoo.org /support/nameananimal/.

31. Ibid.

32. "Name a Roach," Bronx Zoo, http://www.bronxzoo.com/name-a-roach/.

33. "Zoo Octopus Gets a Name," *Washington Post*, December 19, 2011, http://www .washingtonpost.com/lifestyle/kidspost/octopus-at-zoo-gets-a-name/2011/12/15 /gIQAV2554O_story.html.

34. Phillips, "Proper Names," 121.

35. Miller, interview.

36. Fernandes, e-mail message (parenthetical clarification in original).

37. Phillips, "Proper Names," 121.

38. Miller, interview.

39. Ibid.

40. "About ISIS," ISIS, http://www2.isis.org/AboutISIS/.

41. Miller, interview.

42. Ibid.

43. Association of Zoos and Aquariums, *AZA Regional Studbook Keeper Handbook* (Silver Spring, MD: Association of Zoos and Aquariums, 2011), http://www.aza.org/upload edFiles/Animal_Care_and_Management/TAGs,_SSPs,_PMPs,_Studbooks,_SAGs/AZA RegionalStudbookKeeperHandbook_2011(2).pdf; World Association of Zoos and Aquariums, *Resource Manual for International Studbook Keepers* (Gland, Switzerland: World Association of Zoos and Aquariums, 2011), http://www.waza.org/files/webcontent/public _site/5.conservation/international_studbooks/resource_manual/ISB_Resource_Manual _14Nov2011.pdf.

44. Bruno Latour and Emilie Hermant, *Paris: Invisible City*, trans. Liz Carey-Libbrecht, http://bruno-latour.fr/virtual/.

45. Block, interview (emphasis added).

46. Miller, interview.

47. "Penguin Family Trees: Rooted in Science," *Tennessee Aquarium Blog*, April 21, 2011, http://tennesseeaquarium.blogspot.com/2011/04/penguin-family-trees-rooted-in -science.html.

48. Miller, interview.

49. "Global Animal Management, Inc.," Global Animal Management Inc., http://www.mygamonline.com/.

50. Bonnie Malkin, "Muffy the Long Lost Scruffy Puppy Found After 9 Years and 2000km," *Telegraph* (UK), July 30, 2009, http://www.telegraph.co.uk/news/worldnews/australiaandthepacific/australia/5939696/Muffy-the-long-lost-scruffy-puppy-found-after-9-years-and-2000km.html.

51. "ZIMS FAQ," ISIS, http://www2.isis.org/products/Pages/FAQ.aspx.

52. Katina Michael and Amelia Masters, "Applications of Human Transponder Implants in Mobile Commerce," in *The Eighth World Multiconference on Systemics, Cybernetics and Informatics*, 1st ed., ed. N. Callaos et al. (Orlando, FL: International Institute of Informatics and Systemics, 2005), 505–12, http://works.bepress.com/kmichael/35.

53. Hugo Martin, "Microchip Wristband Becomes a Theme Park Essential," *Los Angeles Times*, May 2, 2009, http://articles.latimes.com/2009/may/02/business/fi-wrist2.

54. Rob Stein, "Implantable Medical ID Approved by FDA," *Washington Post*, October 14, 2004, http://www.washingtonpost.com/wp-dyn/articles/A29954-2004Oct13.html.

55. Barnaby Feder, "Report of Cancer Hurts Maker of Chip Implants," *New York Times*, September 11, 2007, http://www.nytimes.com/2007/09/11/technology/11micro.html.

56. "PositiveID Corporation Successfully Completes Development of Its Continuous Glucose Sensor to Accurately Measure Glucose Levels in Human Blood," PositiveID Corp. press releases and media, July 14, 2011, http://investors.positiveidcorp.com/redesign/releasedetail.cfm?ReleaseID=591423.

57. Irus Braverman, "Civilized Borders: A Study of Israel's New Border Regime," *Antipode: A Radical Journal of Geography* 43, no. 2 (2011a) 264–95; Braverman, "Governing with Clean Hands: Automated Public Toilets and Sanitary Surveillance," *Surveillance & Society* 8, no. 1 (2010) 1–27.

58. Marx, *Machine in the Garden*.

59. Haggerty and Ericson, "Surveillant Assemblage," 609.

60. Miller, interview

61. Ibid.

62. Ibid.

63. Claire Swedberg, "RFID Chips Tell Fish Tales at Aquarium," *RFID Journal*, July 13, 2011, http://www.rfidjournal.com/article/view/8592.

64. Bowker and Star, *Sorting Things Out*, 5.

65. Bogard, *Simulation of Surveillance*, 16.

66. Michelle Peters, "The Global Conservation Community Is Going Online: 18 Zoos Are Leading the Way," ISIS Newsroom, April 5, 2010, archived in *Zoo News Digest*, http://zoonewsdigest.blogspot.com/2010/04/monumental-change-in-professional.html.

67. "About ZIMS."

68. Miller, interview.

69. Sue Dubois, Kevin Johnson, and Brandie Smith, "The ZIMS Project: Building Better Zoological Information Systems for Zoos and Aquariums," *International Animal Data Information Systems Reports*, http://www.iadisc.org/reports/building_better_info _systems.htm.

70. "Products and Services," ISIS, 2011, http://www2.isis.org/membership/Pages/ISIS -Services.aspx.

71. Ibid. (emphasis added).

72. "About ZIMS."

73. Dubois, Johnson, and Smith, "ZIMS Project" (emphasis added).

74. Rogers, interview.

75. Ibid.

76. Miller, interview.

77. Ibid.

78. Boyle, interview.

79. Ibid.

80. Ibid.

81. Ibid. See also Chapter 7.

82. Clarke, "Information Technology."

83. Haggerty and Ericson, *New Politics*, 16.

84. Joann M. Earnhardt, Steven D. Thompson, and Ginny Turner-Erfort, eds., *Standards for Data Entry and Maintenance of North American Zoo and Aquarium Animal Records Databases* (Chicago: Lincoln Park Zoo, 1998), http://www.lpzoo.org/sites/default /files/data_entry_standards.pdf. In the same document, this question is raised: Are wild-caught bird eggs hatched in captivity wild or captive-bred? Actually, they are both, but the computer system does not allow such an entry (ibid, 14).

85. Phillips, "Proper Names," 138.

86. Miller, interview.

Chapter Five

1. Gad and Lauritsen, "Situated Surveillance," 52.

2. Rogers, interview.

3. Gail Anderson, ed., *Reinventing the Museum: Historical and Contemporary Perspectives on the Paradigm Shift* (Lanham, MD: AltaMira Press, 2004); Mary Case, ed., *Registrars on Records: Essays on Museum Collection Management* (Washington, DC: Registrars Committee of the American Museums, 1988); John Simmons, *Things Great and Small: Collection Management Policies* (Washington, DC: American Association of Museums, 2006); Stephen Weil, *Rethinking the Museum and Other Meditations* (Washington, DC: Smithsonian Institution Press, 1990); Stephen Weil, *Making Museums Matter* (Washington, DC: Smithsonian Institution Press, 2002).

4. See, for example, Baratay and Hardouin-Fugier, *History of Zoological Gardens*; Jesse Donahue and Eric Trump, *The Politics of Zoos: Exotic Animals and Their Protectors* (DeKalb: Northern Illinois University Press, 2006); Mullan and Marvin, *Zoo Culture*; Colin Tudge, *Last Animals at the Zoo: How Mass Extinction Can Be Stopped* (Washington, DC: Island Press, 1992).

5. Berger, *About Looking*; Braverman, "Looking at Zoos"; Davies, *Spectacular Nature*.

6. Bruno Latour, *Reassembling the Social: An Introduction to Actor-Network-Theory* (Oxford: Oxford University Press, 2005).

7. Donahue and Trump, *Politics of Zoos*.

8. Andrea Drost (curatorial assistant, Toronto Zoo), interview by author, on-site, Toronto, June 16, 2009.

9. Block, interview.

10. Ibid.

11. This problem went beyond snakes and reptiles: see Joanne M. Earnhardt, Steven D. Thompson, and Kevin Will, "ISIS Database: An Evaluation of Records Essential for Captive Management," *Zoo Biology* 14, no. 6 (1995): 493–508.

12. Ibid. (emphasis added).

13. Ibid.

14. Ibid. Incidentally, the registrar's role is not as clearly defined in the zoo's institutional structure outside of North American and European zoos. In Jerusalem's Biblical Zoo, for example, this role is considered a marginal administrative chore that rotates between the zoo's various staff. Shmulik Yedvab (general curator, Biblical Zoo), interview by author, on-site, Jerusalem, Israel, June 6, 2011.

15. Ibid. (emphasis added).

16. Ibid.

17. Rogers, interview.

18. Ibid.

19. Ibid.

20. Ibid.

21. Ibid.

22. Ibid. (emphasis added).

23. Miller, interview.

24. Lynn McDuffie (assistant curator of records, Disney's Animal Kingdom), interview with author, telephone, January 8, 2010.

25. Ibid.

26. Ibid.

27. Faust et al., *Zoo Risk*.

28. McDuffie, interview.

29. Rogers, interview.

30. Specimen report for LOUISVILL/102476, June 17, 2004.

31. Miller, interview.

32. Rogers, interview.

33. Ibid.

34. Miller, interview.

35. Haggerty and Ericson, *New Politics*, 611.

36. Bogard, *Simulation of Surveillance*; David Lyon, *Surveillance Society: Monitoring Everyday Life* (Philadelphia: Open University Press, 2001).

37. Swedberg, "RFID Chips Tell Fish Tales."

38. Block, interview.

39. McDuffie, interview; Rogers, interview.

40. McDuffie, interview.

41. Foucault, *Security, Territory, Population*, 122–23.

42. Nilda Ferrer (curator of registrar, animal management services, Bronx Zoo), interview by author, on-site, Bronx, NY, July 1, 2009.

43. Miller, interview.

44. Ibid.

45. Drost, interview

46. Miller, interview (emphasis added).

47. See also Geordie Duckler, "Towards a More Appropriate Jurisprudence Regarding the Legal Status of Zoos and Zoo Animals," *Journal of Animal Law* 3 (1997): 189–200.

48. International Air Transport Association, *Live Animal Regulations*.

49. Ferrer, interview.

50. Drost, interview.

51. Ferrer, interview.

52. Ibid.

53. Block, interview. Museum registrars are described similarly as continually encountering "potential disorder, which they hold in check by strict allegiance to procedure." Case, *Registrars on Records*, 27.

54. Ibid.

55. Ibid.

56. Willis, "Looking at the Zoo."

57. Case, *Registrars on Records*, 33.

58. Block, interview; Case, *Registrars on Records*; Simmons, *Things Great and Small*.

59. Hetherington, "Museums and the Visually Impaired"; Hetherington, "Unsightly."

60. Block, interview.

61. Ibid.

62. Ibid.

63. Case, *Registrars on Records*, 133.

64. Ibid.

65. Case, *Registrars on Records*, 141.

Chapter Six

1. William Conway, "The Role of Zoos in the 21st Century," *International Zoo Yearbook* 38, no. 1 (2003): 7–13, at 11.

2. The use of the term "official" with regard to laws is not without its problems. AZA standards and guidelines are no less official than traditional laws (for this reason the term "formal" would not have been more suitable here). Alternatively, using the term "state" laws would run into a problem of scale: in the American legal system, state laws refer to the norms enacted by the state, rather than federal or local governments, and would thus exclude the latter. One could also refer to official laws as "public" and to industry laws as "private"—but this would introduce yet another set of complications. So, for lack of a better term, I have settled on "official laws."

3. Kristin Vehrs (executive director, Association of Zoos and Aquariums), interview by author, telephone, November 9, 2009.

4. For example, the United Kingdom's Zoo Licensing Act 1981, http://www.legislation .gov.uk/ukpga/1981/37, and European Union Council Directive 1999/22/EC of March 29, 1999, relating to the keeping of wild animals in zoos, http://eur-lex.europa.eu/LexUriServ /LexUriServ.do?uri=CELEX:31999L0022:EN:HTML.

5. Hancocks, e-mail message.

6. Here I am drawing on Giorgio Agamben's characterization of the "state of exception" as distinguished from the "state of emergency" based on the sovereign's ability to transcend the rule of law in the name of the public good. See Giorgio Agamben, *State of Exception* (Chicago: University of Chicago Press, 2005). Although an analysis of states of exception and the biopolitical framework within which they operate could provide valuable insights into the institution of captivity, they are beyond the scope of this book.

7. The administration of the AWA includes mandatory annual inspections of certain licensed exhibitors by APHIS, as well as inspections in response to citizen complaints. Tracy Coppola, program associate, Born Free USA, e-mail message to author, December 16, 2011.

8. Gary Francione, *Animals, Property, and the Law* (Philadelphia: Temple University Press, 1995).

9. "Animal Welfare: AWA Inspection Information," USDA—APHIS, 2010, http:// www.aphis.usda.gov/animal_welfare/inspections.shtml.

10. Since 1998 the AWA has regulated pet stores selling certain species, such as "pocket pets." See "Regulation of Pocket Pets," *Animal Welfare Information Center Bulletin* 9, no. 1–2 (1998), http://www.nal.usda.gov/awic/newsletters/v9n1/9n1aphis.htm#toc1.

11. As part of their entertainment, fairs often have pig races, petting zoos, performing tiger acts, tiger cub photo ops, monkey acts, etc. Such exhibitors are regulated by the AWA. Animal Welfare Act, 7 U.S.C. §2132(h) (2011).

12. Animal Welfare Act, 7 U.S.C. §2132(h) (2011).

13. Animal Welfare Act Regulations, 9 C.F.R. §1.1 (2007).

14. Animal Welfare Act, 7 U.S.C. §2143(a)(2)(A) (2009).

15. Kristin L. Vehrs, "United States Wildlife Regulations," in *Wild Mammals in Captivity: Principles and Techniques*, ed. Devra Kleiman et al. (Chicago: University of Chicago Press, 1996), 593–99, 594.

16. Animal Welfare Act, 7 USC §2132(g) (2011). This situation may soon change, as the USDA is in the process of finalizing standards to regulate birds used in exhibition. See "USDA Seeks Comments on the Regulation of Birds, Rats and Mice," APHIS press release, June 4, 2004, http://www.aphis.usda.gov/lpa/news/2004/06/ac_birdratmice.html. See also "How Birds Came Under the Animal Welfare Act—a Brief History," National Avian Welfare Alliance, http://nawabirds.com/history.htm.

17. Nicole Paquette, formerly of Born Free USA, "The Status of Captive Wild Animals in the U.S.: An Overview of the Problems and the Laws," http://www.bornfreeusa.org.

18. Chris Philo and Chris Wilbert, eds., *Animal Spaces, Beastly Spaces: New Geographies of Human-Animal Relations* (London: Routledge, 2000), 7.

19. Owain Jones, "(Un)Ethical Geographies of Human–Non-human Relations: Encounters, Collectives and Spaces," in *Animal Spaces, Beastly Spaces: New Geographies of Human-Animal Relations*, ed. Chris Philo and Chris Wilbert (London: Routledge, 2000), 267–90.

20. Orwell, *Animal Farm*, 133.

21. Vehrs, interview.

22. Chris Draper (senior scientific researcher, Born Free Foundation, UK), e-mail message to author, December 16, 2011.

23. Katherine Meyer (founding partner, Meyer, Glitzenstein and Crystal, Washington, DC), interview by author, telephone, March 15, 2011.

24. Office of Inspector General Rep. No. 33002-3-SF, *Audit Report APHIS Animal Care Program Inspection and Enforcement Activities* (Department of Agriculture, 2005), http://www.usda.gov/oig/webdocs/33002-03-SF.pdf.

25. Ibid., i–iii.

26. Coppola, e-mail message. Coppola also notes that "unlike other acts involving wildlife, such as the ESA, the AWA does not generally allow private individuals to file suit based on animal welfare concerns because it lacks a citizen suit provision."

27. "Summary of Listed Species: Listed Populations and Recovery Plans," U.S. Fish and Wildlife Service, updated January 16, 2012, http://ecos.fws.gov/tess_public/pub/Box score.do.

28. Endangered Species Act, 16 U.S.C. §15323 (2009).

29. Ibid.

30. Lawrence Liebesman and Rafe Petersen, *Endangered Species Deskbook* (Washington, DC: Island Press, 2003).

31. *Babbitt v. Sweet Home Chapter of Communities for a Great Oregon*, 515 U.S. 687 (1995).

32. Endangered Species Act, 16 U.S.C. §3(2), §1516(16) (1973).

33. John Wiens and Maria Servedio, "Species Delimitation in Systematics: Inferring Diagnostic Differences Between Species," *Proceedings of the Royal Society of London Series B* 267, no. 1444 (2000): 631–36, at 632; Jack Sites Jr. and Jonathon Marshall, "Delimiting Species: A Renaissance Issue in Systematic Biology," *Trends Ecology & Evolution* 18, no. 9 (2003): 462–70, at 462; Marla Conley, "Caring for Dolphins, Otters, and Octopuses: Speciesism in the Regulation of Zoos and Aquariums," *Animal Law* 15 (2009): 237–64.

34. Endangered Species Act, 16 U.S.C. §1533(b)(1)(A) (1973).

35. George and Mayden, "Species Concepts and the Endangered Species Act."

36. Ibid.

37. Nicole Paquette, "The Status of Captive Wild Animals in the U.S.: An Overview of the Problem and the Laws," Born Free USA, http://www.bornfreeusa.org; Animal Welfare Act, 50 C.F.R. §17 (2010).

38. U.S. Fish and Wildlife Service, "Captive-bred Wildlife Registration under the U.S. Endangered Species Act" (2012), http://www.fws.gov/international/pdf/reg.pdf.

39. Animal Welfare Act Regulations, 50 C.F.R. §17.3 (2004).

40. Endangered Species Act, 16 U.S.C. §1539(a)(1)(A) (2011).

41. According to Tracy Coppola of Born Free USA, "One has to question the impact this exemption has on conservation of species in the wild. Import permits issued under the CBW system seem to encourage captivity by allowing trades and loans of animals between zoos in the United States and abroad" (e-mail message).

42. Endangered Species Act, 16 U.S.C. §1539(a)(1) (1973).

43. Quoted in James Carroll, "Lawmakers Push to Allow Zoos to Keep Rescuing Polar Bears," *Louisville Courier-Journal*, November 13, 2011, http://www.ongo.com/v/2315934/-1/FEF7BB5BC8DDDD38/lawmakers-push-to-allow-zoos-to-keep-rescuing-polar-bears.

44. Ibid.

45. Lacey Act, 16 U.S.C. §3372(e)(2)(A) (1990).

46. Kali Grech, "Detailed Regulation of the Laws Affecting Zoos," Animal Legal and Historical Center (East Lansing: Michigan State University College of Law, 2004), http://www.animallaw.info/articles/dduszoos.htm.

47. Marine Animal Protection Act, 16 U.S.C. §1361(5)(b) (1972).

48. African Elephant Conservation Act, 16 U.S.C. §§4201–4245 (1988).

49. Great Ape Conservation Act, 15 U.S.C. §1543 (2000).

50. Wild Bird Conservation Act, 16 U.S.C. §4901 (1992).

51. Marine Animal Protection Act.

52. Public Health Services Act, 42 U.S.C. §264 (1959).

53. Gail Galland et al., "Taking Animals Across International Borders," in *CDC Health Information for International Travel* (New York: Oxford University Press, 2012), http://wwwnc.cdc.gov/travel/yellowbook/2012/chapter-6-conveyance-and-transportation -issues/taking-animals-and-animal-products-across-international-borders.htm.

54. On the key importance of ideas about pollution, disease, and contamination to the construction of every society, see Mary Douglas, *Purity and Danger: An Analysis of Concepts of Pollution and Taboo* (New York: Routledge, 1966).

55. Breheny, interview.

56. The Public Health and Welfare Act, 42 U.S.C. §§264-272 (2009).

57. Convention on International Trade in Endangered Species (CITES), 27 U.S.T. §1087 (1973).

58. Ibid., Art. 3 (2); "The CITES Species," CITES, last updated November 21, 2011, http://www.cites.org/eng/disc/species.php.

59. Ibid.

60. Adam Roberts (executive vice president, Born Free USA), interview by author, telephone, March 1, 2011; see also *Born Free USA v. Norton*, 278 F. Supp. 2d 5 (D.D.C., 2003), in which plaintiffs filed suit to challenge the U.S. Fish and Wildlife Service's decision to issue permits to San Diego Zoo and Lowry Park Zoo that allow the importation of eleven African elephants from Swaziland, arguing that the officials did not follow proper CITES import protocol. The court held in favor of the zoos, concluding that the advocates failed to show a likelihood of success and an overall detriment to the species to warrant preliminary injunctive relief.

61. Draper, e-mail message. Draper writes, "Prohibiting cruelty is of course a long way off promoting good animal welfare, as would be required under the legislation of many other countries." He adds that England and Wales provide a good example for this, as their Animal Welfare Act of 2006 (http://www.legislation.gov.uk/ukpga/2006/45/contents) legislates against unnecessary suffering (§4) and introduces what has been termed a "duty of care" to ensure that the needs of an animal are met (§9). Similar legislation exists in Scotland and Northern Ireland. Other examples of zoo-specific legislation from countries outside the United States include the Indian Wildlife Protection Act, ch. 4 (1972), http://cza.nic.in/wild.html, and New Zealand's specific code of welfare for animals in zoos under their Animal Welfare Act (1999), http://www.biosecurity.govt.nz/animal-welfare /req/codes/zoo.

62. Born Free USA, Summary of State Laws Relating to Exhibiting Exotic Animals, http://bornfreeusa.org/b4a2_exhibiting.php.

63. Rogers, interview.

64. *Gooding v. Chutes Co.*, 155 P. 620 (Cal. 1909).

65. Duckler, "Legal Status of Zoos."

66. Ibid., 191.

67. *Animal Protection, Education, and Information Foundation v. Friends of the Zoo for Springfield, Missouri, Inc.*, 891 S.W.2d 177 (Mo. Ct. App. 1995); see also *State v. Bartee*, 374 F.3d 906 (10th Cir. 2004).

68. Duckler, "Legal Status of Zoos," 190.

69. Taylor, interview. The National Zoo's website provides more details about this unusual decision: "On 31 December 1991, six of the seven institutions that owned the majority of the captive *Leontopithecus rosalia* population agreed to transfer ownership of their animals to the Brazilian government. Monkey Jungle, Inc., in Miami, Florida, retained ownership of their animals for financial reasons, but still participates fully in the program and remains a signatory of the respective Cooperative Research and Management Agreement. As a result, the Brazilian government is the owner of all but a handful of the 489 existing specimens of captive golden lion tamarins. This may be the first example of a species in which the ownership (but not possession) of all but a very few captive animals by multiple international zoos was returned to the jurisdiction of the native country." See also "History of the Golden Lion Tamarin Captive Breeding Program," National Zoo, http://nationalzoo.si.edu/SCBI/EndangeredSpecies/GLTProgram/ZooLife /History.cfm.

70. Wilms and Bender, *International Studbook*.

71. Ibid.

72. Taylor, interview.

73. Lukas, e-mail message.

74. *Sea World Parks & Entertainment LLC v. Marineland of Canada Inc.* (2011) O.J. No.4265 (Can. Ont. C.A.).

75. U.S. Fish and Wildlife Service, 63 Fed. Reg. 52,824 (October 1, 1998).

76. Ibid.

77. Gail Davies, "Virtual Animals in Electronic Zoos: The Changing Geographies of Animal Capture and Display," in Philo and Wilbert, *Animal Spaces*, 243–66, at 252.

78. Anderson, *Reinventing the Museum*; S. M. P. Benbow, "Zoos: Public Places to View Private Lives," *Journal of Popular Culture* 33, no. 4 (2000): 13–24.

79. According to the AZA, 54 percent of zoos are nonprofit, 35 percent are public, and 11 percent are for-profit. See "Zoo and Aquarium Statistics," AZA.

80. Some background about the Buffalo Zoo: the Buffalo Zoo is a midsize zoo that generates an annual income of approximately $7 million. Fernandes provides the financial breakdown for this amount: "Our public funding from the city and county has remained pretty level for the last twenty years. . . . Right now it's $136,000 from the city. New York State gives us around $200,000 . . . and Erie County has sort of been fairly consistent at $1.5 million for the last ten years. But the bulk of the money we make through ticket sales and gift shop and food and rides and parking and membership and special events. We earn roughly $1.5 million from ticket sales, a little over $500,000 from

food, and around $500,000 from gifts. . . . The carousel makes about $40,000 a year, [and] the train made $27,000 last year. Parking is $130,000. Then membership is like $1.1 million. Then 'Adopt an Animal'—which is, people give money—is about $150,000. Then we get about $28,000 for facility rentals. And the annual fund where we just have people give us money at the end of the year is around $335,000." According to Fernandes, her zoo's hybrid public/nonprofit organization reflects the situation of many North American zoos. "We're a nonprofit society—the Zoological Society of Buffalo—that manages the zoo on behalf of the City of Buffalo. The City of Buffalo owns the zoo and its buildings. . . . [And] even though the society has been the one raising the money and rebuilding, it all belongs to the city. The society owns the animals. [So] if there ever would be an issue and they were going to close the zoo, we could [prevent] some city manager from selling them at an auction and guarantee the integrity of where the animals would be placed." Since 2001, the Buffalo Zoo has experienced a steady growth in visitor numbers and in its overall revenue. In 2010, the zoo had approximately 450,000 visitors, more than all other public institutions in Buffalo combined (Fernandes, interview).

81. National Park Service, "National Registry of Historic Places Inventory—Nomination Form: Olmsted Parks and Parkways Thematic Resources," 1982, http://pdfhost.focus.nps .gov/docs/NRHP/Text/64000580.pdf.

82. Buffalo, NY, Pres. Code art.1, §337 (2011); Shibley and Schneekloth, *The Olmsted City*.

83. Fernandes, interview.

84. Howard, interview.

85. Fernandes, interview.

86. Breheny, interview.

87. Kevin Bell (president and CEO, Lincoln Park Zoo, Chicago; former chair, 2009, board of directors, the Association of Zoos and Aquariums), interview by author, telephone, July 23, 2009.

88. Mullan and Marvin, *Zoo Culture*, 52.

89. Evelyn Junge and William McKeown (lawyers, General Counsel Department, Bronx Zoo), interview by author, telephone, July 28, 2009.

90. Howard, interview.

91. Michel Callon, "Some Elements of a Sociology of Translation: Domestication of the Scallops and the Fishermen of St. Brieuc Bay," in *Power, Action and Belief: A New Sociology of Knowledge*, ed. John Law (London: Routledge & Kegan Paul, 1986), 196–233; Davies, "Virtual Animals," 251.

92. Davies, "Virtual Animals," 253.

93. Sarah Whatmore, *Hybrid Geographies: Natures Cultures Spaces* (Thousand Oaks, CA: Sage Publications, 2002).

94. David Delaney, *Law and Nature* (Cambridge: Cambridge University Press, 2003).

95. For example, in March 2012, a 24-year-old silverback gorilla from the Buffalo Zoo took advantage of an unlocked door in his living quarters and slipped into the space behind it, used by zoo personnel but closed to the public. The keeper took refuge inside the holding area of a female gorilla and her newborn baby. Meanwhile, police sent in a SWAT team to secure the area while a veterinarian used a handheld blowgun to sedate the escaped gorilla through a porthole. This was the zoo's first animal escape (Fernandes, tour of the Buffalo Zoo, March 22, 2012).

96. Howard, interview.

97. Ibid.

98. New York State Building Code, ch. 3, §312 (2007). Group U includes aircraft hangars, bathhouse facilities, carports, greenhouses, private garages, sheds, tanks, and toilet facilities.

99. Howard, interview.

100. Zoo director Donna Fernandes explains that "we were already installing two watering systems to the animal area—an extensive irrigation system . . . to support the plant life, and a huge overhead misting system to maintain the appropriate humidity for the animal inhabitants. Without the "U" classification, we would have had to also install a sprinkler system, which was redundant with the overhead misting system, which can also function as a fire deterrent" (e-mail message).

101. Howard, interview.

102. Sarah Whatmore, "Rethinking the Human in Human Geography," in *Human Geography Today*, ed. John Allen, Doreen Massey, and Phil Sarre (Oxford: Polity Press, 1999), 22–40; Bruce Braun, "Environmental Issues: Writing a More-Than-Human Urban Geography," *Progress in Human Geography* 29, no. 5 (2005): 635–50; Jody Emel, Chris Wilbert, and Jennifer Wolch, "Animal Geographies," *Society and Animals* 10, no. 4 (2002): 407–12.

103. Americans with Disabilities Act, 42 U.S.C. §12101 (1990).

104. Ibid., 42 U.S.C. §12102(1)(A) (1990).

105. Howard, interview.

106. Ibid.

107. Hetherington, "Museums and the Visually Impaired," and "Unsightly."

108. Occupational Safety and Health Act of 1970, Pub. L. No. 91-596, §5(a)(1) (1970).

109. Ibid.

110. OSHA to SeaWorld of Florida LLC, "Citation and Notification of Penalty," August 23, 2010, http://www.osha.gov/dep/citations/seaworld-citation-notification-of-penalty .pdf, 5; "US Labor Department's OSHA Cites SeaWorld of Florida Following Animal Trainer's Death," US Department of Labor, August 23, 2010, http://www.osha.gov/pls /oshaweb/owadisp.show_document?p_table=NEWS_RELEASES&p_id=18207.

111. Ibid. A Department of Labor press release quotes Les Grove, an OSHA director in Florida: "All employers are obligated to assess potential risks to the safety and health of their employees and take actions to mitigate those risks. . . . In facilities that house wild animals, employers need to assess the animals under their care and to minimize human-animal interaction if there is no safe way to reliably predict animal behavior under all conditions."

112. OSHA, "US Labor Department's OSHA Cites SeaWorld."

113. OSHA, "Citation and Notification of Penalty."

114. For example, People for the Ethical Treatment of Animals (PETA) petitioned OSHA to ban all direct contact between elephants and zoo or circus employees. Ashley Gonzales, "PETA Petitions OSHA to Bar Direct Contact with Elephants to Prevent Worker Injuries," PETA news release, March 24, 2011, http://www.peta.org/mediacenter /news-releases/PETA-Petitions-OSHA-to-Bar-Direct-Contact-with-Elephants-.aspx.

115. In Defense of Animals (IDA) describes this tool as "a steel-tipped weapon resembling a fireplace poker" that controls elephants "through the threat of painful punishment." See "In Defense of Animals Applauds Dramatic Policy Shift That Ends Most Cruel Training of Elephants in Zoos," In Defense of Animals, August 22, 2011, http://www .idanews.org/ida-breaking-news/elephants/in-defense-of-animals-applauds-dramatic -policy-shift-that-ends-most-cruel-training-of-elephants-in-zoos/.

116. Andrew Smith to Dr. Jeffry P. Bonner, chair of AZA board of directors, letter, Elephant Managers Association, Lake Elsinore, CA, September 1, 2011, https://elephant managers.com/uploads/EMA_Response_to_AZA_Final.pdf.

117. Vehrs, interview.

118. See, for example, "Uncompromising Stands on Animal Rights," PETA, http:// www.peta.org/about/why-peta/.

119. Vehrs, interview.

120. Donahue and Trump, *Politics of Zoos.*

121. Ibid., 13.

122. Ibid., 37.

123. Senator J. James Exon, 140 *Cong. Rec.* S5492-95 (daily ed. March 24, 1994).

124. AZA, *Accreditation Standards.*

125. Association of Zoos and Aquariums (senior official speaking on condition of anonymity), interview by author, telephone, January 25, 2010.

126. Ibid. AZA executive director Kristin Vehrs provides a different perspective: ideally, she would actually prefer to see a unified official code that would apply to zoos across the board and that would be both regulated and enforced by the United States government. She believes, however, that such government regulation would be impractical because of the highly territorial nature of state agencies. Vehrs attributes the current eclectic and complicated state of official zoo laws to the historical influence of animal protection groups. In her view, animal protection groups have been operating according

to the assumption that "if you can't close zoos, then make them as difficult and complicated to operate as possible." According to Vehrs, then, the relative power of animal protection groups is what has caused the fragmented state of official zoo laws, rather than the relative strength of the AZA to fend off such law (interview).

127. "Statement on Ohio Animal Escapes," AZA, press release, October 19, 2011 (emphasis added), http://www.aza.org/PressRoom/detail.aspx?id=21841.

128. "Rescued Zanesville Animals Being Taken by Thompson Family," Columbus Zoo, press release, October 27, 2011, http://www.colszoo.org/news_room/press_releases /rescued_zanesville_animals_being_taken_by_thompson_family.aspx.

129. "Born Free USA Says Wild Animal Incident in Ohio Spotlights the Tragedy and Danger of Keeping Wild Animals in Captivity," Born Free USA, press release, October 19, 2011, http://www.bornfreeusa.org/press.php?p=2998&more=1.

130. Despite these standards, Born Free USA tracked 277 reported incidents in AZA zoos for the period between 1990 and 2011. See http://www.bornfreeusa.org/database/exo _incidents.php?facility=AZA.

131. Chris Draper of the Born Free Foundation disagrees: "The relationship between exhibiting animals and conservation or education is not as clear cut as zoos might have us believe. There is little solid evidence that zoos have a significant role to play in *in situ* conservation, for example, and the educational claims are generally untested" (e-mail message).

132. AZA, *Accreditation Standards*, 62–66.

133. Ibid., 62.

134. Ibid.

135. Ibid., 64.

136. Ibid.

137. Grech, "Detailed Regulation."

138. AZA, *Guide to Accreditation of Zoological Parks and Aquariums (and Accreditation Standards): 2006 Edition* (Silver Spring, MD: Association of Zoos and Aquariums, 2006), http://www.wolfconsulting.us/files/AZA%202006%20Accreditation%20Standards .pdf, 10.

139. Grech, "Detailed Regulation."

140. Anonymous AZA senior official, interview.

141. "List of Accredited Zoos and Aquariums," AZA, September 2011, http://www.aza .org/current-accreditation-list/.

142. AZA, *Accreditation Standards*.

143. Ibid., 4.

144. Conway, interview.

145. AZA, *Guide to Accreditation*, 7.

146. Thomas, interview.

147. Ibid.

148. Fernandes, interview.

149. "AZA, Animal Care Manuals."

150. "AZA, *Taxon Advisory Group (TAG) Handbook* (Silver Spring, MD: Association of Zoos and Aquariums, 2011), http://www.aza.org/uploadedFiles/Animal_Care_and_Man agement/TAGs,_SSPs,_PMPs,_Studbooks,_SAGs/AZATAGHandbook_2011.pdf., 30.

151. AZA Ape TAG, *Standardized Animal Care.*

152. Ibid., 2.

153. Ibid., 4.

154. As mentioned earlier in this chapter, official regulations have not yet been enacted in support of the federal legislation.

155. AZA Ape TAG, *Standardized Animal Care*, 78–79.

156. Draper, e-mail message.

Chapter Seven

1. C. M. Lees and J. Wilcken, "Sustaining the Ark: The Challenges Faced by Zoos in Maintaining Viable Populations," *International Zoo Yearbook* 43, no. 1 (2009): 6–18, at 9.

2. Stoinski, interview.

3. Hearne, *Adam's Task.*

4. As mentioned earlier, in September 2011, approximately 550 species were managed by either mandatory SSPs or voluntary studbooks, out of approximately 6,000 unique species in AZA institutions. See "Zoo and Aquarium Statistics," AZA.

5. Michael Soulé et al., "The Millennium Ark: How Long a Voyage, How Many Staterooms, How Many Passengers?" *Zoo Biology* 5, no. 2 (1986): 101–13.

6. Sarah Burnett, "Rare Cats Born Through Amazing Science at Audubon Center for Research of Endangered Species," Audubon Nature Institute press release, March 10, 2011, http://www.auduboninstitute.org/media/audubonheadlines/rare-cats-born-through -amazing-science.

7. "Frozen Zoo," Audubon Nature Institute, http://www.auduboninstitute.org/frozen -zoo.

8. Soulé et al., "Millennium Ark."

9. Boyle, interview. See also "Animal Programs," AZA, http://www.aza.org/animal -programs/.

10. "Animal Programs."

11. Breheny, interview.

12. Miller, interview.

13. Smith, interview.

14. Fernandes, interview.

15. Lee, interview.

16. Taxa are grouped across different layers of the classification system and are not confined to genus, class, order, or otherwise. Accordingly, TAGs group together everything from a specific family (Ape TAG) to a class (Amphibian TAG), suborder (Snake TAG), and even a combination of multiple taxa in one TAG (Marine Mammal TAG, Antelope and Giraffe TAG). The definition of TAGs is thus fluid, demonstrating that a taxon could be a group as defined by any taxonomy.

17. AZA, *Taxon Advisory Group*, 5.

18. Ibid.

19. AZA, *Species Survival Plan* Program Handbook* (Silver Spring, MD: Association of Zoos and Aquariums, 2011), http://www.aza.org/uploadedFiles/Animal_Care_and _Management/TAGs,_SSPs,_PMPs,_Studbooks,_SAGs/AZASpeciesSurvivalPlanHand book_2011.pdf.

20. Observations by author at AZA's midyear meeting, Chattanooga, TN, March 23, 2011. Also see AZA, http://www.aza.org/Proceedings/.

21. "TAG-SSP," Avian Scientific Advisory Group, http://aviansag.org/tags.html.

22. AZA, *Taxon Advisory Group*, 22.

23. AZA, *Regional Collection Plan (RCP) Handbook* (Silver Spring, MD: Association of Zoos and Aquariums, 2011), http://www.aza.org/uploadedFiles/Animal_Care_and _Management/TAGs,_SSPs,_PMPs,_Studbooks,_SAGs/AZARCPHandbook_2011.pdf.

24. Robert Wiese (chair, Task Force on the Sustainability of Zoo-based Populations; chief life sciences officer, San Diego Zoo Global), interview by author, telephone, November 9, 2010.

25. See "Zoo and Aquarium Statistics" and "Animal Programs Database" in AZA webpage.

26. AZA, *Accreditation Standards*, 53–54.

27. This number, as well as other numbers that pertain to animal programs, should be considered with a grain of salt. The shuffling of priorities that has been taking place within the AZA since 2011 has put many of its animal programs—especially SSPs—in a state of flux. So, for example, in response to my simple question, "How many bird SSPs are there?" Sara Hallager replies, "See, that is all different now, because of the way AZA restructured everything. I could not even begin to tell you a number because so many TAGs have not even evaluated their programs—yeah, because all of these changes just happened within the last year. So some programs that may have been SSPs are no longer SSPs. Some programs that were not SSPs now are SSPs. It's really confusing." Hallager, interview.

28. Hallager, interview.

29. See searchable database of SSPs and studbooks at "Animal Programs Database," AZA, http://www.aza.org/animal-programs-database/, as well as summary statistics at "Zoo and Aquarium Statistics."

30. "Studbooks," AZA, http://www.aza.org/studbooks/.

31. AZA, *Species Survival Plan*, 34.

32. Lukas et al., *Population Analysis*, 1.

33. AZA, *Accreditation Standards*, 53–54; See also Lukas et al., *Population Analysis*, 13–14.

34. AZA, *Species Survival Plan*, 17–18.

35. Ibid., 53–54; Lukas, e-mail message.

36. Thomas, interview.

37. Ibid.

38. Miller, interview.

39. Indeed, Fernandes of the Buffalo Zoo suggests that the AZA has "fixed this loophole." In her words, "We wanted to ensure the well-being of SSP animals from cradle to grave so animals could no longer be sent to nonmember institutions. Of course, a consequence of the new policy is that SSPs were no longer allowed to work with some of the really successful private breeders (aviculturists) or universities holding genetically valuable animals (e.g. Duke Primate Center)." Fernandes, e-mail message. This fixing of loopholes created a tighter, more stringent SSP administration, which in turn provided incentive for the subsequent changes in the SSP program structure (as discussed herein).

40. Sarah Long (PMC director, Saint Louis Zoo), interview by author, in-person, Chattanooga, TN, AZA 2011 midyear meeting, March 22, 2011.

41. Wiese, interview.

42. AZA, *Species Survival Plan*.

43. "Population Management Center," Lincoln Park Zoo, http://www.lpzoo.org/conservation-science/science-centers/population-management-center.

44. Long, interview.

45. Ibid.

46. Ibid.

47. Ibid.

48. Ibid.

49. Tennessee Aquarium Blog, "Penguin Family Trees."

50. Long, interview.

51. Ibid.

52. Block, interview.

53. Long, interview (emphasis added).

54. Ibid.

55. Andrew Balmford, Georgina Mace, and N. Leader-Williams, "Designing the Ark: Setting Priorities for Captive Breeding," *Conservative Biology* 10, no. 3 (1996): 719–27.

56. Whatmore, *Hybrid Geographies*.

57. "I propose to call whoever and whatever is represented *actant.*" Latour, *Science in Action*, 84 (emphasis in original).

58. Gabriela Mastromonaco (curator of reproductive programs, Toronto Zoo), interview by author, telephone, July 6, 2009.

59. Lukas, e-mail message.

60. AZA Ape TAG, *Standardized Animal Care*, 61–62.

61. C2S2 website, http://www.conservationcenters.org/.

62. Boyle, interview.

63. Phillip Miller and Robert Lacy, *VORTEX: A Stochastic Simulation of the Extinction Process Version 9.21 User's Manual* (Apple Valley, CA: Conservation Breeding Specialist Group [SSC/IUCN], 2003), http://www.life.illinois.edu/ib/451/v921manual.pdf.

64. Faust et al., *Zoo Risk*, 4.

65. Ibid.

66. "About ZIMS."

67. Miller and Lacy, *VORTEX*, 1 (capitalization and italics in original).

68. Faust et al., *Zoo Risk*, 9.

69. Wiese, interview.

70. "Population Management Center."

71. Miller and Lacy, *VORTEX*, 9.

72. "The Need for a Wildlife Contraception Center," Saint Louis Zoo, http://www.stlzoo.org/animals/scienceresearch/contraceptioncenter/whycontraception.htm.

73. Ibid.

74. Ibid.

75. Ibid.

76. Friese, "Models of Cloning," 378.

77. Boyle, interview.

78. Tara Harris, "Generic Tiger SSP," *Tiger SSP*, 2010, retrieved on August 3, 2011, http://www.mnzoo.org/tigerssp/genericSSP.html.

79. Cheryl Asa (director of research, Saint Louis Zoo; director, AZA Contraception Center), interview by author, telephone, February 2, 2011.

80. Ibid.

81. Ibid.

82. Ibid.

83. Lukas et al., *Population Analysis*, 6 (italics and capitals in original).

84. Peter Dollinger, "WAZA Director Replies to Claims on Animal Culling in Helsinki Zoo," letter on file with author, October 12, 2004; see also WAZA, *Building a Future for Wildlife—The World Zoo and Aquarium Conservation Strategy* (Bern, Switzerland: WAZA Executive Office, 2005), 62.

85. EAZA, "Euthanasia Statement," September 26, 2011, http://www.eaza.net/about/ Documents/EAZA%20Euthanasia%20statement.pdf.

86. EAZA, "Statement on Behalf."

87. Ibid.

88. "Though none of the zoo workers will actually serve any time, should there be a new offence the zoo director must pay an €8,100 fine, the court said. The employees defended their decision as a practical measure, saying the mongrel tigers were worthless, could not be used for breeding and would have taken up valuable space at the Magdeburg Zoo from pure-blooded animals. They said they had no other alternative because other zoos were not interested in taking on the tiger cubs. But the judge at the district court found the four guilty, saying there were 'no sufficient reasons to kill less valuable, but totally healthy animals.'" "Court convicts Magdeburg Zoo workers for killing tiger cubs," *Local, Germany's News in English*, June 17, 2010, http://www.thelocal.de/society/20100617 -27927.html.

89. Conway, "Role of Zoos," 11.

90. Balmford et al., "Designing the Ark."

91. Snyder et al., "Limitations of Captive Breeding: Reply to Gippoliti and Carpaneto," *Conservation Biology* 11, no. 3 (1997): 808–10.

92. See Balmford et al., "Designing the Ark," where the authors suggest choosing animals based upon (1) their ability to breed well in captivity, and (2) the potential for their reintroduction into nature.

93. Michael Hutchins, Kevin Willis, and Robert J. Wiese, "Strategic Collection Planning: Theory and Practice," *Zoo Biology* 14, no. 1 (1995): 5–25.

94. Balmford et al., "Designing the Ark," 725.

95. Ehmke, interview.

96. Ibid.

97. Conway, interview.

98. AZA, *Accreditation Standards*, 4.

99. Laidlaw, interview. For example, experiments with the silver fox have shown that wild animals can be bred for domestication after just a few generations; see Lyudmila N. Trut, "Early Canid Domestication: The Farm-Fox Experiment," *American Scientist* 87, no. 2 (1999): 160–69.

100. Rose, interview.

101. Genetic drift is the change in the frequency of a gene variant in a population due to chance. Also see Robert Lacy, "The Importance of Genetic Variation to the Viability of Mammalian Populations," *Journal of Mammology* 78, no. 2 (1997): 320–35.

102. Lees and Wilcken, "Sustaining the Ark," 14.

103. Wiese, interview.

104. Statistics based on searches of animal program designations, December 2011, from "Animal Programs Database," AZA, http://www.aza.org/animal-programs-database/.

105. Hallager, interview.

106. Kristen Lukas et al., *Population Analysis*.

107. Hallager, interview.

108. Ibid.

109. Population Analysis & Breeding and Transfer Plan, Addax (*Addax nasomaculatus*), AZA Species Survival Plan Yellow Program, April 21, 2011. From the plan's acknowledgment: "As I reflect on the new direction that AZA has charted for sustainability of its programs, I am compelled to recognize the special contribution that Fossil Rim Wildlife Center has made to the sustainability of addax in the SSP. Without their long-term institutional commitment to addax, including a long stretch as a non-AZA member participant, I have little doubt in my mind that this would be a Red Program, not an SSP" (ibid., 3). This quote illustrates both the institutional advantages of the new SSP structure and the dynamic nature of its designations.

110. Paul Boyle et al., "A Report by the AZA Task Force on the Sustainability of Zoo-Based Populations: Phase 1," *Connect*, January 2010, 9–12 (Silver Spring, MD: Association of Zoos and Aquariums), http://www.aza.org/Membership/detail.aspx?id=16616.

111. Population Analysis & Breeding and Transfer Plan, Diana Monkey (*Cercopithecus diana diana*), AZA Red Program, AZA Studbook, draft, October 25, 2011.

112. Hallager, interview.

113. Ibid. See also Population Analysis & Breeding and Transfer Plan: Northern Island Brown Kiwi (*Apteryx australis mantelli*), AZA Red Program, April 12, 2011.

114. AZA's midyear meeting, March 21–23, 2011 (participatory observations).

115. Hallager, interview.

116. Long, interview.

117. Ibid.

118. AZA, *Regional Collection Plan*, 6.

119. Wiese, interview; AZA, *Species Survival Plan*.

120. "Many ungulate species in our care suffer a double whammy—they are declining in zoos and they are declining in the wild. Without the safety net that an assurance population in AZA zoos provides, some of these species will vanish not just from our zoos but from our planet." Martha Fisher, "Thundering Herds or Fading Hoofbeats: The Future of AZA's Ungulates is in Our Hands," *Connect* (March 2012): 16–21

121. Friese, "Models of Cloning," 378.

122. Margaret Derry, *Bred for Perfection: Shorthorn Cattle, Collies, and Arabian Horses Since 1800* (Baltimore: Johns Hopkins University Press, 2003); Sarah Franklin, *Dolly Mixtures: The Remaking of Genealogy* (Durham, NC: Duke University Press, 2007); Donna Haraway, "Cloning Mutts, Saving Tigers: Ethical Emergents in Technocultural Dog Worlds," in *Remaking Life & Death: Toward an Anthropology of the Biosciences*, ed. Sarah Franklin and Margaret Lock (Santa Fe, NM: School of American Research Press, 2003): 293–327; Harriet Ritvo, "Possessing Mother Nature: Genetic Capital in

Eighteenth-Century Britain," in *Early Modern Conceptions of Property*, ed. John Brewer and Susan Staves (London: Routledge, 1995), 413–26.

123. Haraway, "Cloning Mutts"; Ritvo, "Possessing Mother Nature."

124. Conway, interview.

125. Friese, "Models of Cloning," 384.

126. Derry, *Bred for Perfection*.

127. Haraway, "Cloning Mutts."

128. Friese, "Models of Cloning," 384.

129. Ibid., 378.

130. Boyle, interview.

131. 2011 Statistics from Tiger SSP website, http://www.mnzoo.org/tigerSSP/, accessed December 2011.

132. EAZA, "Statement on behalf."

133. Fernandes, e-mail message.

Conclusion

1. Wharton, interview.

2. Conway, "Role of Zoos," 10.

3. As mentioned in the introduction, mine is a selected list of characteristics of pastoral power. Foucault's analysis includes a few others. See Foucault, *Security, Territory, Population*, 115–30, 163–85.

4. Ibid., 143.

5. Boyle, interview.

6. "Conservation Through Zoos and Aquariums," World Association of Zoos and Aquariums, http://www.waza.org/en/site/conservation. Specifically, WAZA and ISIS have collaborated to publish 190 international studbooks as well as 1,350 regional studbooks, including those of the AZA. "ISIS/WAZA Studbook Library," World Association of Zoos and Aquariums, http://www.waza.org/en/site/conservation/international-studbooks/studbook-library. The statistics included here reflect the contents of the 2011 ISIS/WAZA Studbook Library DVD.

7. See, for example, the research collaboration between Lincoln Park Zoo and the Jane Goodall Institute in Gombe National Park, Tanzania, which uses methods developed in zoos to monitor chimpanzee health in the park. See "Project Information," Lincoln Park Zoo,http://www.lpzoo.org/conservation-science/projects/gombe-field-research/project-information.

8. Foucault, *Security, Territory, Population*, 126.

9. Fernandes, e-mail message.

10. Ibid., 128.

11. Ibid.

12. Foucault, *Security, Territory, Population*, 164.

13. Ibid., 126.

14. Rabb and Saunders, "Future of Zoos and Aquariums," 19; David Sloan Wilson, *Darwin's Cathedral: Evolution, Religion, and the Nature of Society* (Chicago: University of Chicago Press: 2002).

15. Elaine Huddleston (registrar, Louisville Zoo), communication with author, telephone, August 1, 2011.

16. Klepal, "Timmy the Gorilla."

17. Jordan Schaul, "The Epic Life of an Iconic Gorilla: 'Timmy' Remembered (1959–2011)," *National Geographic Daily News*, August 10, 2011, http://newswatch.nationalgeographic.com/ 2011/08/04/the-epic-life-of-an-iconic-gorilla-timmy-remembered-1959-2011/.

18. Steve Wing (general curator, Louisville Zoo), interview by author, telephone, August 5, 2011.

19. Ibid.

20. Quoted in Sangiacomo, "Timmy Arrives."

21. Wing, interview.

Bibliography

Interviews

Allard, Ruth. Executive vice president, conservation & visitor experiences, Phoenix Zoo. On-site, Phoenix, AZ, March 19, 2012.

Aquilina, Jerry. General curator, Buffalo Zoo. On-site, Buffalo, NY, June 13, 2009.

Asa, Cheryl. Director of research, Saint Louis Zoo; director, AZA Contraception Center. Telephone, February 2, 2011.

Association of Zoos and Aquariums (senior official speaking on condition of anonymity). Telephone, January 25, 2010.

Bell, Kevin. President and CEO, Lincoln Park Zoo, Chicago; former chair (2009), board of directors of the Association of Zoos and Aquariums. Telephone, July 23, 2009.

Belterman, Robert. Animal data and transport manager, Rotterdam Zoo, Netherlands. Telephone, September 3, 2009.

Block, Judith. Registrar emeritus, Smithsonian Institution, National Zoological Park, Washington, DC. Telephone, September 4, 2009.

Boyle, Paul. Senior vice president for conservation and education, Association of Zoos and Aquariums. Telephone, November 24, 2010.

Breheny, Jim. Senior vice president of living institutions, Wildlife Conservation Society; director, Bronx Zoo. On-site, Bronx, NY, July 15, 2009; e-mail messages, August 18, 2009.

Brusca, Rick. Former executive director (2001–2011), Arizona-Sonora Desert Museum. In person, Tucson, AZ, March 17, 2012; e-mail messages, March-April 2012.

Butler, Nancy. Registrar, Detroit Zoo. Telephone, October 2, 2009.

Carpenter, Mike. Senior biologist, Permit Division, U.S. Fish and Wildlife Service. Telephone, August 20, 2009.

Castro, Bert. President & CEO, Phoenix Zoo. On-site, Phoenix, AZ, March 19, 2012.

Chin, Susan. Vice president of planning and design and chief architect, Exhibition and Graphic Arts Department, Bronx Zoo. On-site, Bronx, NY, July 17, 2009.

Coe, Jon. Landscape architect, Jon Coe Design. On-site, Buffalo, NY, February 10–11, 2012; Skype, February 19, 2012; e-mail messages, February-April, 2012.

Colodner, Debra. Director of education, Center for Sonoran Desert Studies. On-site, Tucson, AZ, March 14, 2012.

Conway, William. President, Wildlife Conservation Society; director, Bronx Zoo, 1966–99. On-site, Bronx, NY, July 14, 2009.

Coppola, Tracy. Program associate, Born Free USA. E-mail messages, December 16, 2011.

Draper, Chris. Senior scientific researcher, Born Free Foundation, UK. E-mail messages, December 16, 2011.

Drost, Andrea. Curatorial assistant, Toronto Zoo. On-site, Toronto, Canada, June 16, 2009.

Ehmke, Lee. President, World Association of Zoos and Aquariums; director and CEO, Minnesota Zoo; director of planning and design, Bronx Zoo (1998–2000). Telephone, July 21, 2009.

Elsner, Roby. Zoo Miami manager of primates; former supervisor of gorillas, Louisville Zoo. Telephone, August 8, 2011; e-mail messages, January–April, 2012.

Fernandes, Donna. President and CEO, Buffalo Zoo. On-site, Buffalo, NY, May 8, 2009, September 30, 2010; six zoo tours conducted between May 2009 and March 2012, Buffalo Zoo; e-mail messages, 2010–12.

Ferrer, Nilda. Curator of registrar, animal management services, Bronx Zoo. On-site, Bronx, NY, July 1, 2009.

Griffin, Cyndi. Gorilla keeper, Buffalo Zoo. E-mail messages, August 26, 2009.

Hallager, Sara. Biologist, Smithsonian Institution, National Zoological Park, Washington, DC; Ratite TAG chair; SSP Kori Bustard coordinator; SSP Red-Legged Seriema coordinator; SSP Roadrunner coordinator; chair of Avian Scientific Advisory Group (ASAG). Telephone, December 16, 2011.

Hancocks, David. Former director, Woodland Park Zoo, Seattle, WA; director, Open Range Zoo, Werribee, Australia. E-mail message, February 2, 2011.

Harpley, Paul. Manager, interpretation, culture, and design, Toronto Zoo. On-site, Toronto, Canada, June 17, 2009.

Howard, Gwen. Architect for the Buffalo Zoo, Foit-Albert Associates. Interviewee's residence, Buffalo, NY, July 24, 2009; on-site tour, Buffalo Zoo, July 31, 2009.

Huddleston, Elaine. Registrar, Louisville Zoo. Telephone, August 1, 2011.

Ireland, Dave. Curator of conservation, Toronto Zoo. On-site, Toronto, Canada, June 17, 2009.

Ivanyi, Craig. Executive director, Arizona-Sonora Desert Museum. On-site, Tucson, AZ, March 14 & 16, 2012; e-mail messages, March–April 2012.

Junge, Evelyn. General Counsel Department, Bronx Zoo. Telephone, July 28, 2009.

Kagan, Ron. Director, Detroit Zoo. Telephone, February 2, 2011.

Krentz, Pam. Registrar, Cleveland Metroparks Zoo. Telephone, December 7, 2009.

Laidlaw, Rob. Founder and director, Zoocheck Canada. Telephone, January 28, 2011.

Lee, Cindy. Curator of fishes, Toronto Zoo. On-site, Toronto, Canada, June 17, 2009.

Long, Sarah. PMC director, Saint Louis Zoo. In person, AZA 2011 midyear meeting, Chattanooga, TN, March 22, 2011.

Lukas, Kristen E. Gorilla SSP coordinator; curator of conservation and science, Cleveland Metroparks Zoo. On-site in Chattanooga, TN, and telephone, March 30, 2011; e-mail messages, August 2011–April 2012.

Martin, Debby. Registrar, Toronto Zoo. On-site, Toronto, Canada, June 16, 2009.

Mason, Tom. Curator of birds and invertebrates, Toronto Zoo. On-site, Toronto, Canada, June 17, 2009.

Mastromonaco, Gabriela. Curator of reproductive programs, Toronto Zoo. Telephone, July 6, 2009.

McDuffie, Lynn. Assistant curator of records, Disney's Animal Kingdom, Orlando, FL. Telephone, January 8, 2010.

McKeown, William. General Counsel Department, Bronx Zoo, Bronx, NY. Telephone, July 28, 2009.

Meyer, Katherine. Founding partner, Meyer, Glitzenstein & Crystal, Washington, DC. Telephone, March 15, 2011.

Meyerson, Randi. Polar Bear SSP coordinator; veterinarian, Toledo Zoo, Toledo, OH. Telephone, January 31, 2011.

Miller, Jean. Registrar, Buffalo Zoo. On-site, Buffalo, NY, June 13 and 15, 2009.

Morse, Laura. Registrar, National Zoological Park, Washington, DC. Telephone, September 29, 2009.

Penny, Carmi G. Chair, Wild Pig, Peccary, and Hippo TAG; director of collections husbandry science; curator of mammals, San Diego Zoo Global. On-site, AZA 2011 midyear meeting, Chattanooga, TN, March 21, 2011.

Rapley, William. Executive director, conservation, education, and research, Toronto Zoo. On-site, Toronto, Canada, June 16, 2009.

Reininger, Ken. General curator, North Carolina Zoo. On-site, AZA 2011 midyear meeting, Chattanooga, TN, March 23, 2011.

Roberts, Adam. Executive director, Born Free USA. Telephone, March 1, 2011.

Roberts, Corinne. Registrar and front gate manager, Zoo Boise, Boise, ID. Telephone, December 11, 2009.

Rogers, Rachèl Watkins. Registrar, Zoo Miami. In person, Islamorada, FL, August 6, 2009.

Rose, Naomi. Senior scientist, Humane Society International. Telephone, February 7, 2011.

Schoffner, Tad K. Assistant animal care manager, Cleveland Metroparks Zoo. Telephone, July 29, 2011.

Smith, Eldon. Director of wildlife care, Toronto Zoo. On-site, Toronto, Canada, June 16, 2009.

Stockton, Ken. Former director of design, Arizona-Sonora Desert Museum. On-site, Tucson, AZ, March 16, 2012.

Stoinski, Tara. Ape TAG chair; manager of conservation partnerships, Zoo Atlanta. Telephone, January 10, 2011.

Taylor, Steve H. Director, Cleveland Metroparks Zoo. Telephone, August 2, 2011.

Thomas, Pat. General curator, Bronx Zoo. On-site, Bronx, NY, July 14, 2009.

Vehrs, Kristin. Executive director, Association of Zoos and Aquariums. Telephone, November 9, 2009.

Wells, Stuart. Director of conservation and science, Phoenix Zoo. On-site, Phoenix, AZ, March 19, 2012.

Wensvoort, Jaap. Nutritionist, Toronto Zoo. On-site, Toronto, Canada, June 16, 2009.

Wharton, Dan. Director of Central Park Zoo, 1994–2007; chairman, Gorilla SSP, 1992–2006; North American regional studbook keeper 1987–2011. Telephone, April 6 and May 19, 2011; e-mail messages, August 2011–March 2012.

Wiese, Robert. Chair, Task Force on the Sustainability of Zoo-Based Populations; chief life sciences officer, San Diego Zoo Global. Telephone, November 9, 2010.

Wing, Steve. General curator, Louisville Zoo. Telephone, August 5, 2011.

Yedvab, Shmulik. General curator, Biblical Zoo. On-site, Jerusalem, Israel, June 6, 2011.

Books and Articles

Acampora, Ralph R. "Zoos and Eyes: Contesting Captivity and Seeking Successor Practices." *Society & Animals* 13, no.1 (2005): 69–88.

———. "Extinction by Exhibition: Looking at and in the Zoo." *Human Ecology Review* 5, no. 1 (1998): 1–4.

Agamben, Giorgio. *State of Exception*. Chicago: University of Chicago Press, 2005.

Anderson, Gail, ed. *Reinventing the Museum: Historical and Contemporary Perspectives on the Paradigm Shift*. Lanham, MD: AltaMira Press, 2004.

Anderson, Kay. "Culture and Nature at the Adelaide Zoo: At the Frontiers of 'Human' Geography." *Transactions of the Institute of British Geographers* 20, no. 3 (1995): 275–94.

Balmford, Andrew, Georgina Mace, and N. Leader-Williams. "Designing the Ark: Setting Priorities for Captive Breeding." *Conservation Biology* 10, no. 3 (1996): 719–27.

Baratay, Eric, and Elizabeth Hardouin-Fugier. *A History of Zoological Gardens in the West*. London: Reaktion Books, 2002.

Bell, Catherine, ed. *Encyclopedia of the World's Zoos*. Vol. 3, R–Z. Chicago: Fitzroy Dearborn Publishers, 2001.

Benbow, S. M. P. "Zoos: Public Places to View Private Lives." *Journal of Popular Culture* 33, no. 4 (2000): 13–24.

Bennett, Tony. "The Exhibitionary Complex." *New Formations* 4 (Spring 1988): 73–83.

Bentham, Jeremy. "Panopticon (Preface)." In *The Panopticon Writings*, edited by Miran Bozovic, 29–95. London: Verso, 1995.

Berger, John. *Ways of Seeing*. London: Penguin, 2008.

———. *About Looking*. New York: Pantheon Books, 1980.

Bergman, Jerry. "Ota Benga: The Pygmy Put on Display in a Zoo." *Journal of Creation* 14, no. 1 (2000): 81–90.

Biernacki, Patrick, and Dan Waldorf. "Snowball Sampling: Problems and Techniques of Chain Referral Sampling." *Sociological Methods and Research* 10, no. 2 (1981): 141–63.

Birch, Thomas. "The Incarceration of Wildness: Wilderness Areas as Prisons." *Environmental Ethics* 12, no. 1 (1990): 3–26.

Bishop, Rebecca. "Journeys to the Urban Exotic: Embodiment and the Zoo-Going Gaze." *Humanities Research* 11, no. 1 (2004): 106–24.

Blume, Harvey. "Ota Benga and the Barnum Perplex." In *Africans on Stage: Studies in Ethnological Show Business*, edited by B. Lindfors, 188–202. Bloomington: Indiana University Press, 1999.

Bogard, William. *The Simulation of Surveillance: Hypercontrol in Telematic Societies*. Cambridge: Cambridge University Press, 1996.

Bowker, Geoffrey, and Susan Leigh Star. *Sorting Things Out: Classification and Its Consequences*. Cambridge, MA: MIT Press, 1999.

Bradford, Phillips, and Harvey Blume. *Ota Benga: The Pygmy in the Zoo*. New York: St. Martin's Press, 1992.

Braun, Bruce. "Environmental Issues: Writing a More-Than-Human Urban Geography." *Progress in Human Geography* 29, no. 5 (2005): 635–50.

Braverman, Irus. "Who's Afraid of Engaged Legal Geography? Advocating a Methodical Turn in Law and Geography" in *The Expanding Spaces of Law: A Timely Legal Geography*, ed. Irus Braverman et al. (under review).

———. "Animal Immobilities: A Study of Animals, Law, and the American City," *Law and Social Inquiry* (under review).

———. "Foucault Goes to the Zoo: Zooveillance in North America," *Surveillance & Society* (forthcoming, 2012).

———. "Zootopia: Utopia and Dystopia in Zoological Garden." In *Earth Perfect? Nature, Utopia, and the Garden*, edited by Annette Giesecke and Naomi Jacobs. London: Black Dog Publishing, 2012.

———. "Civilized Borders: A Study of Israel's New Border Regime." *Antipode: A Radical Journal of Geography* 43, no. 2 (2011a): 264–95.

———. "Looking at Zoos." *Cultural Studies* 25, no. 6 (2011b): 809–42.

———. "Governing with Clean Hands: Automated Public Toilets and Sanitary Surveillance." *Surveillance & Society* 8, no. 1 (2010): 1–27.

————. *Planted Flags: Trees, Land, and Law in Israel/Palestine*. Cambridge: Cambridge University Press, 2009.

Brown, James, and Mark Lomolino. *Biogeography*. 2nd ed. Sunderland, MA: Sinauer Associates, 1998.

Callon, Michel. "Some Elements of a Sociology of Translation: Domestication of the Scallops and the Fishermen of St. Brieuc Bay." In *Power, Action and Belief: A New Sociology of Knowledge*, edited by John Law, 196–233. London: Routledge & Kegan Paul, 1986.

Cantor, David. "Items of Property." In *The Great Ape Project: Equality Beyond Humanity*, edited by Paola Cavalieri and Peter Singer, 280–90. New York: St. Martin's Griffin, 1996.

Case, Mary, ed. *Registrars on Records: Essays on Museum Collection Management*. Washington, DC: Registrars Committee of the American Museums, 1988.

Castree, Noel, "Socializing Theory: Theory, Practice, and Politics." In *Social Nature: Theory, Practice, and Politics*, edited by Noel Castree and Bruce Braun, 1–36. Oxford: Blackwell, 2001.

Castree, Noel, C. Nash, N. Badmington, B. Braun, J. Murdoch, and S. Whatmore. "Mapping Posthumanism: An Exchange." *Environment and Planning A* 36, no. 8 (2004): 1341–63.

Christy, Bryan. *The Lizard King: The True Crimes and Passions of the World's Greatest Reptile Smugglers*. New York: Twelve, 2008.

Clarke, Roger. "Information Technology and Dataveillance." *Communications of the ACM* 31, no. 5 (1988): 498–512.

Conley, Marla. "Caring for Dolphins, Otters, and Octopuses: Speciesism in the Regulation of Zoos and Aquariums." *Animal Law* 15 (2009): 237–64.

Conway, William. "Buying Time for Wild Animals with Zoos." *Zoo Biology* 29 (2010): 1–8.

————. "The Role of Zoos in the 21st Century." *International Zoo Yearbook* 38, no. 1 (2003): 7–13.

Couturier, Lisa. *The Hopes of Snakes, and Other Tales from the Urban Landscape*. Boston: Beacon Press, 2005.

Crawford, Margaret. "The World in a Shopping Mall." In *Variations on a Theme Park: The New American City and the End of Public Space*, edited by Michael Sorkin, 3–30. New York: Hill & Wang, 1992.

Croke, Vicki. *The Modern Ark: The Story of Zoos: Past, Present, and Future*. New York: Scribner, 1997.

Daly, Mary, and Jane Lewis. "The Concept of Social Care and the Analysis of Contemporary Welfare States." *British Journal of Sociology*, 51, no. 2 (2000): 281–98.

Davies, Gail. "Virtual Animals in Electronic Zoos: The Changing Geographies of Animal Capture and Display." In *Animal Spaces, Beastly Spaces: New Geographies of Human-*

Animal Relations, edited by Chris Philo and Chris Wilbert, 243–66. London: Routledge, 2000.

Davis, Susan. *Spectacular Nature: Corporate Culture and the Sea World Experience.* Berkeley and Los Angeles: University of California Press, 1997.

Delaney, David. *Law and Nature.* Cambridge: University of Cambridge, 2003.

Derry, Margaret. *Bred for Perfection: Shorthorn Cattle, Collies, and Arabian Horses Since 1800.* Baltimore: John Hopkins University Press, 2003.

Donahue, Jesse, and Eric Trump. *The Politics of Zoos: Exotic Animals and Their Protectors.* DeKalb: Northern Illinois University Press, 2006.

Douglas, Mary. *Purity and Danger: An Analysis of Concepts of Pollution and Taboo.* New York: Routledge, 1966.

Duckler, Geordie. "Towards a More Appropriate Jurisprudence Regarding the Legal Status of Zoos and Zoo Animals." *Journal of Animal Law* 3 (1997): 189–200.

Earnhardt, Joanne M., Steven D. Thompson, and Kevin Will. "ISIS Database: An Evaluation of Records Essential for Captive Management." *Zoo Biology* 14, no. 6 (1995): 493–508.

Elsner, Roby. "The Care and Management of Geriatric Gorillas in Captivity and the Role of Louisville Zoo's Husbandry Program." *Animal Keepers' Forum* 36, no. 4/5 (2009): 177–86.

Emel, Jody, Chris Wilbert, and Jennifer Wolch. "Animal Geographies." *Society and Animals* 10, no. 4 (2002): 407–12.

Falk, John H., Eric M. Reinhard, Cynthia L. Vemon, Kerry Bronnenkant, Joe E. Heimlich, and Nora L. Deans. *Why Zoos and Aquariums Matter: Assessing the Impact of a Visit to a Zoo or Aquarium.* Silver Spring, MD: Association of Zoos and Aquariums, 2007.

Finch, Janet, and Dulcie Groves, eds. *A Labour of Love: Women, Work, and Caring.* Boston: Routledge & Kegan Paul, 1983.

Flichy, Patrice. *Understanding Technological Innovation: A Socio-Technical Approach.* Cheltenham, UK: Edward Elgar Publishing, 2007.

Foucault, Michel. *Security, Territory, Population: Lectures at the Collège de France, 1977–78.* Edited by Michel Senellart, Francois Ewald, Alessandro Fontana, and Arnold I. Davidson, translated by Graham Burchell. New York: Picador / Palgrave Macmillan, 2009.

———. *The Order of Things: An Archaeology of the Human Sciences.* London: Routledge, 2005 (originally published 1966).

———. *Discipline and Punish: The Birth of the Prison,* 1st U.S. ed. New York: Pantheon Books, 1977.

Francione, Gary. *Animals, Property, and the Law.* Philadelphia: Temple University Press, 1995.

Franklin, Sarah. *Dolly Mixtures: The Remaking of Genealogy.* Durham, NC: Duke University Press, 2007.

French, Thomas. *Zoo Story: Life in the Garden of Captives.* New York: Hyperion, 2010.

Friese, Carrie. "Classification Conundrums: Categorizing Chimeras and Enacting Species Preservation." *Theory and Society* 39, no. 2 (2010a): 145–72.

———. "Models of Cloning, Models for the Zoo: Rethinking the Sociological Significance of Cloned Animals." *BioSocieties* 4 (2010b): 367–90.

Gad, Christopher, and Peter Lauritsen. "Situated Surveillance: An Ethnographic Study of Fisheries Inspection in Denmark." *Surveillance and Society* 7, no. 1 (2009): 49–57.

George, Anna, and Richard Mayden. "Species Concepts and the Endangered Species Act: How a Valid Biological Definition of Species Enhances the Legal Protection of Biodiversity." *Natural Resources Journal* 45 (2005): 369–77.

Gilligan, Carol. *In a Different Voice: A Psychological Theory and Women's Development.* Cambridge, MA: Harvard University Press, 1982.

Golder, Ben. "Foucault and the Genealogy of Pastoral Power." *Radical Philosophy Review* 10, no. 2 (2007): 157–76.

Grove, Richard. *Green Imperialism: Colonial Expansion, Tropical Island Edens and the Origins of Environmentalism, 1600–1860.* Cambridge: Cambridge University Press, 1996.

Haggerty, Kevin, and Richard Ericson, eds. *The New Politics of Surveillance and Visibility.* Toronto: University of Toronto Press, 2006.

Haggerty, Kevin, and Richard Ericson. "The Surveillant Assemblage." *British Journal of Sociology* 51, no. 4 (2000): 605–22.

Hancocks, David. *A Different Nature: The Paradoxical World of Zoos and Their Uncertain Future.* Berkeley and Los Angeles: University of California Press, 2001.

Hanson, Elizabeth. *Animal Attractions: Nature on Display in American Zoos.* Princeton, NJ: Princeton University Press, 2002.

Haraway, Donna. "Cloning Mutts, Saving Tigers: Ethical Emergents in Technocultural Dog Worlds." In *Remaking Life & Death: Toward an Anthropology of the Biosciences,* edited by Sarah Franklin and Margaret Lock, 293–327. Santa Fe, NM: School of American Research Press, 2003.

———. *Primate Visions: Gender, Race, and Nature in the World of Modern Science.* New York: Routledge, 1989.

Hearne, Vicki. *Adam's Task: Calling Animals by Name.* New York: Skyhorse Publishing, 2007.

Hediger, Heini. *Wild Animals in Captivity.* New York: Dover Publications, 1964.

Hetherington, Kevin. "The Unsightly: Touching the Parthenon Frieze." *Theory, Culture, Society* 19, no. 5/6 (2002): 187–205.

———. "Museums and the Visually Impaired: The Spatial Politics of Access." *Sociological Review* 48, no. 3 (2000): 444–63.

Hutchins, Michael, Kevin Willis, and Robert J. Wiese. "Strategic Collection Planning: Theory and Practice." *Zoo Biology* 14, no. 1 (1995): 5–25.

Jay, Martin. *Downcast Eyes: The Denigration of Vision in Twentieth-Century French Thought*. Berkeley and Los Angeles: University of California Press, 1994.

———. "Scopic Regimes of Modernity." In *Vision and Visuality*, edited by Hal Foster, 3–23. Seattle, WA: Bay Press, 1988.

Jones, Owain. "(Un)Ethical Geographies of Human–Non-human Relations: Encounters, Collectives and Spaces." In *Animal Spaces, Beastly Spaces: New Geographies of Human-Animal Relations*, edited by Chris Philo and Chris Wilbert, 267–90. London: Routledge, 2000.

Kisling, Vernon. *Zoo and Aquarium History: Ancient Animal Collections to Zoological Gardens*. Boca Raton, FL: CRC Press, 2000.

Lacy, Robert. "The Importance of Genetic Variation to the Viability of Mammalian Populations." *Journal of Mammology* 78, no. 2 (1997): 320–35.

Latour, Bruno. *Reassembling the Social: An Introduction to Actor-Network-Theory*. Oxford: Oxford University Press, 2005.

———. *Science in Action*. Cambridge, MA: Harvard University Press, 1987.

Latour, Bruno, and Emilie Hermant. *Paris: Invisible City*. Translated by Liz Carey-Libbrecht. http://bruno-latour.fr/virtual/.

Lees, C. M., and J. Wilken. "Sustaining the Ark: The Challenges Faced by Zoos in Maintaining Viable Populations." *International Zoo Yearbook* 43, no. 1 (2009): 6–18.

Lefebvre, Henri. *The Production of Space*. Translated by Donald Nicholson-Smith. Malden, MA: Blackwell, 1991.

Lévi-Strauss, Claude. *The Savage Mind (Nature of Human Society)*. Chicago: University of Chicago Press, 1966.

Liebesman, Lawrence, and Rafe Petersen. *Endangered Species Deskbook*. Washington, DC: Island Press, 2003.

Ludwig, E. G. "People at Zoos: A Sociological Approach." *International Journal for the Study of Animal Problems* 2, no. 6 (1981): 310–16.

Lyon, David. *Surveillance Society: Monitoring Everyday Life*. Philadelphia: Open University Press, 2001.

Malamud, Randy. *Reading Zoos: Representations of Animals and Captivity*. New York: New York University Press, 1998.

Marino, Lori, Scott O. Lilienfeld, Randy Malamud, Nathan Nobis, and Ron Broglio. "Do Zoos and Aquariums Promote Attitude Change in Visitors? A Critical Evaluation of the American Zoo and Aquarium Study." *Society and Animals* 18 (2010): 126–38.

Martin, Bill and Eric Carle. *Panda Bear, Panda Bear, What Do You See?* New York: Henry Holt and Co., 2003.

Marx, Leo. *The Machine in the Garden*. New York: Oxford University Press, 1964.

Mathiesen, Thomas. "The Viewer Society: Michel Foucault's 'Panopticon' Revisited." *Theoretical Criminology* 1, no. 2 (1997): 215–34.

Miller, Jacques-Alain. "Jeremy Bentham's Panoptic Device." Translated by Richard Miller. *October* 41 (1987): 3–29.

Mills, Brett. "Television Wildlife Documentaries and Animals' Right to Privacy." *Continuum* 24, no. 2 (2010): 193–202.

Mitman, Gregg. *Reel Nature: American Romance with Wildlife on Film.* Cambridge, MA: Harvard University Press, 1999.

Mol, Annemarie, Ingunn Moser, and Jeannette Pols, eds. *Care in Practice: On Tinkering in Clinics, Homes and Farms.* Bielefeld, Germany: Transcript, 2010.

Montgomery, Scott. "The Zoo: Theatre of the Animals." *Science as Culture* 4, no. 4 (1995): 565–600.

Morris, Desmond. *The Human Zoo: A Zoologist's Study of the Urban Animal.* New York: McGraw-Hill, 1969.

Morris, Henry. *KJV New Defenders Study Bible.* Nashville, TN: Thomas Nelson, 2006.

Mullan, Robert, and Garry Marvin. *Zoo Culture.* Urbana: University of Illinois Press, 1998.

Nash, Roderick. *Wilderness and the American Mind.* New Haven, CT: Yale University Press, 1982.

Noddings, Nel. *Caring: A Feminine Approach to Ethics and Moral Education.* Berkeley and Los Angeles: University of California Press, 1984.

Orwell, George. *Animal Farm.* New York: Penguin Group USA, 1996 (originally published 1946).

Pepper, David. *Eco-Socialism: From Deep Ecology to Social Justice.* London: Routledge, 1993.

Phillips, Mary T. "Proper Names and the Social Construction of Biography: The Negative Case of Laboratory Animals." *Qualitative Sociology* 17, no. 2 (1994): 119–42.

Philo, Chris. "Animals, Geography, and the City: Note on Inclusions and Exclusions." *Environment and Planning D: Society and Space* 13, no. 6 (1995): 655–81.

Philo, Chris, and Chris Wilbert, eds. *Animal Spaces, Beastly Spaces: New Geographies of Human-Animal Relations.* London: Routledge, 2000.

Pimm, Nancy Roe. *Colo's Story: The Life of One Grand Gorilla.* Columbus, OH: Columbus Zoo and Aquarium, 2011.

Plato. 360 B.C.. *Statesman.* Translated by Benjamin Jowett. Teddington, England: Echo Library, 2006.

Price, Jennifer. "Looking for Nature at the Mall: A Field Guide to the Nature Company." In *Uncommon Ground: Rethinking the Human Place in Nature,* edited by William Cronon, 186–203. New York: W. W. Norton, 1996.

Rabb, G. B., and C. D. Saunders. "The Future of Zoos and Aquariums: Conservation and Caring." *International Zoo Yearbook* 39, no. 1 (2006): 1–26.

Ritvo, Harriet. "Possessing Mother Nature: Genetic Capital in Eighteenth-Century Britain." In *Early Modern Conceptions of Property*, edited by John Brewer and Susan Staves, 413–26. London: Routledge, 1995.

Rose, Nikolas. "Government, Authority and Expertise in Advanced Liberalism." *Economy and Society* 22, no. 3 (1993): 283–99.

Rothfels, Nigel. *Savages and Beasts: The Birth of the Modern Zoo.* Baltimore: Johns Hopkins University Press, 2002.

Sandøe, Peter, Birte Nielsen, Lars Christensen, and Poul Sørensen. "Staying Good While Playing God: The Ethics of Breeding Farm Animals." *Animal Welfare* 8, no. 4 (1999): 313–28.

Schultz, P. W. "Inclusion with Nature: The Psychology of Human-Nature Relations." In *Psychology of Sustainable Development*, edited by P. Schmuck and P. W. Schultz, Boston: Kluwer Academic Publishers (2002): 61–78.

Scott, James. *Seeing Like a State.* New Haven, CT: Yale University Press, 1998.

Shepard, Paul. *Thinking Animals: Animals and the Development of Human Intelligence.* Athens: University of Georgia Press, 1998.

Simmons, John. *Things Great and Small: Collection Management Policies.* Washington, DC: American Association of Museums, 2006.

Singleton, Vicky. "Good Farming: Control or Care?" In *Care in Practice: On Tinkering in Clinics, Homes and Farms*, edited by Annemarie Mol, Ingunn Moser, and Jeannette Pols, 235–56. Bielefeld, Germany: Transcript, 2010.

Sites, Jack, Jr., and Jonathon Marshall. "Delimiting Species: A Renaissance Issue in Systematic Biology." *Trends Ecology & Evolution* 18, no. 9 (2003): 462–70.

Smith, Neil. *Uneven Development: Nature, Capital, and the Production of Space.* New York: Blackwell, 1984.

Snyder, Noel, Scott Derrickson, Steven Beissinger, James Wiley, Thomas Smith, William Toone, and Brian Miller. "Limitations of Captive Breeding: Reply to Gippoliti and Carpaneto." *Conservation Biology* 11, no. 3 (1997): 808–10.

Soper, Kate. *What Is Nature? Culture, Politics and the Non-Human.* Oxford: Blackwell, 1995.

Soulé, Michael, Tom Foose, Michael Gilpin, and William Conway. "The Millennium Ark: How Long a Voyage, How Many Staterooms, How Many Passengers?" *Zoo Biology* 5, no. 2 (1986): 101–13.

Thompson, Charis. "Confessions of a Bioterrorist: Subject Position and Reproductive Technologies." In *Playing Dolly: Technocultural Formations, Fantasies, and Fictions of Assisted Reproduction*, edited by E. Ann Kaplan and Susan Squier, 189–219. Piscataway, NJ: Rutgers University Press, 1999.

Trut, Lyudmila N. "Early Canid Domestication: The Farm-Fox Experiment." *American Scientist* 87, no. 2 (1999): 160–69.

Tudge, Colin. *Last Animals at the Zoo: How Mass Extinction Can Be Stopped.* Washington, DC: Island Press, 1992.

Vehrs, Kristin L. "United States Wildlife Regulations." In *Wild Mammals in Captivity: Principles and Techniques*, edited by Devra Kleiman, S. Lumpkin, M. E. Allen, and K. V. Thompson, 593–99. Chicago: University of Chicago Press, 1996.

Wareness, Kari. "Caring as Women's Work in the Welfare State." In *Patriarchy in a Welfare Society*, edited by Harriet Holter, 67–87. Oslo, Norway: Universitetsforlaget, 1984.

Weil, Stephen. *Making Museums Matter*. Washington, DC: Smithsonian Institution Press, 2002.

———. *Rethinking the Museum and Other Meditations*. Washington, DC: Smithsonian Institution Press, 1990.

Whatmore, Sarah. *Hybrid Geographies: Natures Cultures Spaces*. Thousand Oaks, CA: Sage Publications, 2002.

———. "Rethinking the Human in Human Geography." In *Human Geography Today*, edited by Doreen Massey, John Allen, and Phil Sarre, 22–40. Oxford: Polity Press, 1999.

Wiens, John, and Maria Servedio. "Species Delimitation in Systematics: Inferring Diagnostic Differences Between Species." *Proceedings of the Royal Society of London Series B* 267, 1444 (2000): 631–36.

Williams, Raymond. *The Country and the City*. Oxford: Oxford University Press, 1973.

Willis, Susan. "Looking at the Zoo." *South Atlantic Quarterly* 98, no. 4 (1999): 669–87.

Wilson, Alexander. *The Culture of Nature: North American Landscape from Disney to the Exxon Valdez*. Toronto: Between the Lines, 1991.

Wilson, David Sloan. *Darwin's Cathedral: Evolution, Religion, and the Nature of Society*. Chicago: University of Chicago Press, 2002.

Wilson, Robert, ed. *Species: New Interdisciplinary Essays*. Cambridge, MA: MIT Press, 1999.

Index

THE CULTURAL LIVES OF LAW

Austin Sarat, Editor

The Cultural Lives of Law series brings insights and approaches from cultural studies to law and tries to secure for law a place in cultural analysis. Books in the series focus on the production, interpretation, consumption, and circulation of legal meanings. They take up the challenges posed as boundaries collapse between as well as within cultures, and as the circulation of legal meanings becomes more fluid. They also attend to the ways law's power in cultural production is renewed and resisted.

—

After Secular Law
Edited by Winnifred Fallers Sullivan, Robert A. Yelle, and Mateo Taussig-Rubbo
2011

All Judges Are Political—Except When They Are Not: Acceptable Hypocrisies and the Rule of Law
Keith J. Bybee
2010

Riding the Black Ram: Law, Literature, and Gender
Susan Sage Heinzelman
2010

Tort, Custom, and Karma: Globalization and Legal Consciousness in Thailand
David M. Engel and Jaruwan S. Engel
2010

Law in Crisis: The Ecstatic Subject of Natural Disaster
Ruth A. Miller
2009

The Affective Life of Law: Legal Modernism and the Literary Imagination
Ravit Reichman
2009

Fault Lines: Tort Law as Cultural Practice
Edited by David M. Engel and Michael McCann
2008

Lex Populi: The Jurisprudence of Popular Culture
William P. MacNeil
2007

The Cultural Lives of Capital Punishment: Comparative Perspectives
Edited by Austin Sarat and Christian Boulanger
2005